the english catholic enlightenment
JOHN LINGARD AND THE CISALPINE
MOVEMENT, 1780 – 1850

the english catholic enlightenment

JOHN LINGARD AND THE CISALPINE MOVEMENT, 1780–1850

JOSEPH P. CHINNICI, O.F.M.

THE PATMOS PRESS   SHEPHERDSTOWN

1980

Library of Congress Cataloging in Publication Data

Chinnici, Joseph P.
   The English Catholic Enlightenment.

   Bibliography
   Includes index.
1. Lingard, John, 1771–1851.   2. Catholic Church in England—History.   3. Enlightenment.
4. England—Intellectual life—18th century.
5. England—Church history—18th century.
6. England—Intellectual life—19th century.
7. England—Church history—19th century.
I. Title.
BX4705.L6334C47   282'.41   79-20250
ISBN 0-915762-10-2

© 1980 by Joseph P. Chinnici. All rights reserved. No part of this book may be reproduced, stored in a retrieval system, or transmitted, in any form or by any means, electronic, mechanical, photocopying, recording, or otherwise, without the written permission of the author and Patmos Press, Inc.

Manufactured in the United States of America

pReface

FROM THE sixteenth century until our own time three major forces have shaped the structure of the relationship between the Catholic Church and the modern world: the loss of the ideal of medieval Christendom and this ideal's subsequent relegation to the status of an archaic sociopolitical form inimical to civil and religious freedom; the development of the scientific method and the rejection of Aristotelian scholasticism; and the elaboration of a philosophy of nature that allowed for the increased secularization of social and intellectual thought patterns. The church of the post-Reformation period generally reacted to all three forces by insisting on its own preeminence while at the same time tacitly acquiescing in the basic presuppositions of the culture. Thus a state of civil and religious pluralism was accepted in practice, but the basic thesis of Christendom remained the ideal. The experimental method encouraged the development of a theology of evidences, marks, and sociological criteria. Yet in order to protect the immutable truths of faith from the inevitability of historical contingency, dogma was declared impervious to time. Furthermore, churchmen lamented the secularization of culture but accepted a theology of pure nature. This theology divorced the redemption from the creation and incarnation and limited the workings of grace to an invisible sphere. The result was a Catholic ethos or mentality riddled with ambiguity and marked by compartmentalization and cultural dislocation. *Theoreia* and *praxis* became separate. The compatibility between nature and grace, intellectual form and social reality, political institutions and ecclesiology, and culture and spirituality, which had characterized the inner and outer life of the medieval period, was shattered.

Within this context, the Second Vatican Council bore witness to a fundamental shift in the Catholic Church's elaboration of a social, philosophical, and theological anthropology. It marked the apogee of a long and often tortuous attempt on the part of Christian thinkers to break from the patterns of post-Reformation thought, to reformulate and thus refashion the church's relationship to the modern world. In the *Declaration on Religious Freedom* the church finally accepted the reality of religious pluralism and rejected the dichotomy of thesis and hypothesis. The decrees on revelation and the church consciously historicized the word of God. *Unitatis Reintegratio* spoke of continual reformation. "Christ summons the Church, as she goes her pilgrim way, to that continual reformation of which she always has need, insofar as she is an institution of men here on earth. Therefore, if the influence of events or of the times has led to deficiencies in conduct, in Church discipline, or even in the formulation of doctrine (which must be carefully distinguished from the deposit itself of faith), these should be appropriately rectified at the proper moment" (II.6). In a similar spirit the *Pastoral Constitution on the Church in the Modern World* proclaimed the intimate bond between nature and grace; it reaffirmed the fundamental openness of the modern world to God's life. Many of the theological reflections since 1965, building on these conciliar insights, have attempted to elucidate an integrated view of human beings, their world and their experience of God, and to heal the deep wound at the heart of the defensive Catholic mentality that had been shaped by the forces of the post-Reformation world.

This search for integration, the ability to theologize within a context and not out of it, to unite theory and practice, to evaluate positively one's position in history and there discover the hidden workings of God's design, is not new. Religious pluralism, political secularization, and the empirical method have been dominant realities for two centuries. They came to fruition during the eighteenth and early nineteenth centuries and are most readily associated with the historical movement of the Enlightenment. In analyzing the position of Catholics during that period scholars have recently isolated a group of individuals, both clerical and lay, who attempted to reflect upon their faith in the context of these forces and to combine the demands of Christian truth with the realities of a particular culture. The people were proponents of a "Catholic Enlightenment." Their program defined the Christian life in a way similar to Vatican II. Their goal was social and spiritual integration. This study examines the thinking of one such group of people in England from 1780 to 1850. It is hoped that it will also shed light on our present attempts to relate the church to the world.

The difficulties that confront the Catholic historian of the Enlightenment are many. First, there exist two conflicting philosophies of historical method within Roman Catholicism. The first large-scale history of the church was written by Abbè Claude Fleury (1640–1725), friend of Fénelon, confessor of Louis XV, and erudite critic of "papalism." Although Fleury wrote his *Histoire ecclésiastique* in the first quarter of the eighteenth century and often subordinated his judgment to a Gallican ideology, he presupposed and actively supported an Enlightenment understanding of critical method. Fleury argued for a uniform style of reporting, the citation of original sources, and the primacy of factual data. Unfortunately, by 1830 his understanding of historical method was no longer acceptable in ecclesiastical circles. R. F. Rohrbacher and Dom Prosper Gueranger ushered in a historiographical revolution by rejecting the ideas of the Enlightenment. Influenced by the philosophy of traditionalism, they subordinated history to orthodoxy. Both were ardent ultramontanists and interpreted the eighteenth century in the light of their ecclesiological preconceptions. Since that time, two views—whether those of Fleury or Rohrbacher, humanist or scholastic, enlightened or romantic Catholic, liberal or ultramontane, modernist or integrist—have struggled for exclusive dominance in the church. It should be noted at the outset that my sympathies are with Fleury.

Second, on a different level, two schools of interpretation

have dominated the historical evaluation of Catholic participation in the Enlightenment. As early as 1910 Sebastian Merkle debated J. B. Sugmuller on the origin and intent of the German Catholic Enlightenment. Merkle, influenced by modernism, was an irenic expositor; Sugmuller was an ardent opponent of any attempt to reconcile Catholicism with the dominant thought patterns of the eighteenth century. More recently, similar conflicting views have surfaced in two studies of the prince bishopric of Mainz. F. G. Dreyfus, in *Societes et mentalites à Mayence* (1968), argues that a negative episcopal nationalism encouraged the movement for reform of clerical education, improvement in Protestant and Catholic relations, and a participatory ecclesiology. The motivation behind the adaptation of the prince bishops was primarily state jurisdictionalism, Jansenism, anticurialism, and a schismatic ecclesiology. In effect, the Enlightenment and Catholicism were reconciled only at the expense of church teaching. On the other hand, T. C. W. Blanning sees a genuine attempt to reform the church in eighteenth-century Germany. *Reform and Revolution in Mainz* (1974) maintains that the Catholic Enlightenment was both an external and internal movement. Although influenced by Gallicanism, Jansenism, and political absolutism, some conscientious churchmen combined true structural reform with orthodox internal renewal. Almost every major movement of the eighteenth century (Gallicanism, Jansenism, Febronianism, Josephism) has its defenders and detractors. Most general, synthetic accounts have not escaped this tendency toward polarization. The present account, following the most recent European studies, tends to interpret the Catholic Enlightenment in an irenic way.

Both of these difficulties—differing views of the relation between historical method and theology, and a polarized historiography—have also been manifest in the attempts of various authors to evaluate English Catholic life from 1780 to 1850. It is well known that even so moderate a writer as Wilfrid Ward, the first major historian of the Catholic revival in England, was asked by Cardinal Rampolla, secretary of the Holy Office, to withdraw the final chapter of his work on Cardinal Wiseman. The work was suspected of modernist tendencies. Throughout his life Ward defended the freedom of scientific work within the church; still, the second edition of *Wiseman* appeared without the chapter entitled "Exclusive Church and the Zeitgeist." Ward's brother Bernard showed similar daring in his acceptance of historical method. But he, too, as his private correspondence attests, felt obliged to soften his remarks and to interpret the "old Catholic" phase of English life in conformity with the restrictive climate created by the integrist reaction to modernism. History had begun to be subordinated to orthodoxy.

The interpretation of English Catholic history during the late eighteenth and early nineteenth centuries has also been polarized. Generally, the Second Spring thesis of John Henry Newman, the suspicion of Gallicanism, the ecclesiology that developed after Vatican I, and a preoccupation with church-state issues have enforced an unfavorable interpretation of the period. Before 1829, so the traditional argument goes, English Catholics were poorly educated, "Garden of the Soul" people, dwelling in obscurity and detached from the culture around them. Those who did venture out to become politically and intellectually active—those known as "Cisalpines"—went so far as to subordinate the church to the state in an effort to achieve emancipation. Fortunately, Bishop John Milner, the vicar apostolic of the Midland District, defended orthodoxy and paved the way for the revival of the 1830s and 1840s. This view has been advanced in various ways by W. J. Amherst, Philip Hughes, David Mathew, Denis Gwynn, and others.[1] Even recent studies, while modifying this interpretation, remain within its grip.[2] Only John Bossy has thoroughly broken new ground, but he has done so at the expense of depth in his examination of the issues and personalities.[3] None of the studies interpret the period as a cultural whole, nor do they place the English Catholic experience within the broader framework of the European Catholic Enlightenment.

The following study analyzes the Cisalpine phase of English Catholic life in the late eighteenth and early nineteenth centuries. The cultural and intellectual context is stressed, with the career of John Lingard (1771–1851) providing the vantage point. This historian of England and vicar of a small town near Lancaster was the center of the group of English Catholics who labored for emancipation and generally adopted an open stance toward their society. Lingard was, without exception, the most consistent and influential member of the secular clergy during the first half of the nineteenth century. His friends and correspondents included the leaders of the Catholic Committee debates of the 1790s, Joseph Berington and Charles Butler, and a host of well-known contemporaries such as the curates John Kirk and John Fletcher, Vicar Apostolic William Poynter, and the lay leaders John Gage Rokewode and George Silvertop. Because Lingard was not actively involved in the debates of the 1790s, his thought was not excessively obscured by polemic and his position enables the historian to elucidate more accurately the philosophical principles that underlie the early arguments over Catholic emancipation. Lastly, John Lingard lived long enough to see the passing of the Enlightenment and the transformation of religious life in the romantic revival. In all of these ways Lingard serves as a mirror in which are reflected the changing patterns and moods of English Catholic life.

"Enlightenment" is defined here in its broadest terms. It refers to that movement in European thought which after 1660 sought to establish both a project of intelligibility and a social and political anthropology corresponding to the age's view of "reason" and "right." In England the Enlightenment was most readily incarnated in the thought of John Locke. In religious terms, members of the Catholic Enlightenment were those who sought "to promote a mystique of salvation in conformity with the development of secular knowledge and the perfectibility of the person in his social environment, his customs, and language."[4] The word "Cisalpine" refers to the people who followed this course in England. Among them were John Lingard, Joseph Berington, Charles Butler, John Kirk, and John Fletcher. Simply stated, this book argues that these men synthesized their Catholic faith and the thought of the Enlightenment in five areas: church-state relations, theology, ecclesiology, history, and religious practice. Their view rested on the foundations of a Lockean anthropology. They accepted political secularization, religious liberty, and a contractural theory of both civil and ecclesiastical government. They applied a critical methodology to various intellectual and theological disciplines and exhibited a culturally open approach to dogma and piety.

My analysis here is limited. I have tried to criticize the Cisalpines where necessary, but my sympathies lie with their approach and not with the more traditional interpretations of the period. The treatment of John Milner will seem simplistic to some, but after a thorough examination of the sources it is my conviction that Milner deserves little more than what is stated here. In terms of the romantic revival his views may have been prophetic; in terms of the Enlightenment they were provincial and reactionary. The Midland vicar's opinions gained ascendancy only after his death, and before 1826 the mental climate of English Catholicism belonged to the Cisalpines. The credit they deserve is long overdue. The Irish background to emancipation is important, but for the sake of clarity and unity of theme it has not been examined here; the intellectual stance of the English Catholics is comprehensible without it. There also needs to be a great deal more work on the origins of Cisalpinism, the educational background of the Cisalpines, the extent of Catholic participation in movements for religious liberty, the impact of Jansenism on eighteenth-century English Catholicism, and the relation between Cisalpinism and liberal Catholicism. My hope is that this book will furnish some insight into the significance of John Lingard in intellectual history as well as into the origins and nature of Cisalpinism, its distinctive contribution to the Catholic Enlightenment, and its relationship to the revival of the mid-nineteenth century.

It would be impossible to list all of the individuals to whom I am indebted. I would like to thank explicitly Eamon Duffy and Richard John Schiefen, who allowed me to use the fruits of their own researches on Joseph Berington and the restoration of the hierarchy. The Reverends J. D. McEvilly and Francis Edwards, S.J., Elizabeth Poyser, Rosemary Rendel, and Kevin McGinnell graciously allowed me to use the archives in their care. The basis for this work was my doctoral dissertation at the University of Oxford. The comments and patience of Dr. Peter Hinchliff, my supervisor, were a source of great encouragement. Monsignor John Tracy Ellis first introduced me to the pleasures and pains of historical scholarship. For his friendship, example, and suggestions I will always be grateful. Special thanks should be given to the president and faculty of Ushaw College, Durham. Their kindness, hospitality, and interest in the work were constant. I am indebted to the president for permission to reproduce the portrait of Lingard by Ramsay. The Reverend Bernard Payne opened the Lingard archives to me. His library work is a testament worthy of the highest scholarly standards to which Lingard himself was dedicated. To the Reverend J. Derek Holmes I would like to express my deepest thanks. He directed me to the topic, gave me his advice, and encouraged me in the various revisions of the manuscript. Lastly, and most importantly, I would like to thank the two communities without whose help, both spiritual and material, these pages would never have been written: the friars of the Province of Saint Barbara, California, and the community of the Sisters of Mercy, Abingdon, Oxfordshire, England. This study is dedicated to my Mother and Father, Nick, Peter, Rosemary, and CCC. *Quid habes quod non acciperis.*

JOSEPH P. CHINNICI, O.F.M.

Franciscan School of Theology
Berkeley, California

contents

Preface	v
Introduction. The Birth of Enlightenment	3
1. Political Foundations	15
2. The Crisis of Church Authority	41
3. A Cisalpine Rule of Faith	76
4. Enlightened History and the Romantic Revival	107
5. The End of a Movement: John Lingard and the Second Spring	134
Epilogue	188
Notes	191
Bibliography	225
Index	251

the english catholic enlightenment
JOHN LINGARD AND THE CISALPINE
MOVEMENT, 1780 – 1850

Introduction
The Birth of Enlightenment

ORIGINS are always difficult to determine. The specific social, political, and intellectual roots of a movement, much less a person, are tangled and obscure. When did Catholics first begin to respond to the crisis that broke asunder the European classical synthesis between 1680 and 1720? How did they attempt to fashion a coherent Christian faith in the midst of advancing skepticism, widespread acceptance of Newtonian science and epistemological empiricism, and the growth of civil toleration? What particular national forces governed the reflections of such diverse eighteenth-century people as Lorenzo Magalotti, Claude Fleury, Benito Feijoo, and Eusebius Amort? Such questions will continue to fascinate historians. This chapter will attempt only to isolate some of the more important cultural influences on a group of people in England who responded in their own way and within the confines of their own traditions and institutions to the questions stirred by the Age of Reason.

The fact that there was a positive Catholic response to the Enlightenment and that this response pervaded every major European country can no longer be doubted. In a monumental study of intellectual movements in eighteenth-century Catholicism, Emile Appolis identifies a group of moderate churchmen between the papal *zelanti* and the Jansenists. This "Third Party" was neither conservative nor revolutionary but stood for a moderate liberalism. Among the Italian members of the group Appolis places Prospero Lambertini

(Benedict XIV), Ludovico Antonio Muratori, Giovanni Bottari, Fortunato Tamburini, and Giovanni Lami. He argues that the French Third Party was less intellectual in orientation and marked by the support of Gallican liberties, opposition to the Curia, and an attitude of moderation toward adherence to the papal constitution condemning Jansenism, *Unigenitus*. Both the Italian and French parties possessed a desire to renew religious culture. They were loyal to the papacy and championed against the extrinicist tendencies of the Catholic Counter Reformation the interiority of the Christian message.[1] Bernard Plongeron, in a slightly more philosophical vein, comes to conclusions similar to those of Appolis. Plongeron maintains that there existed in eighteenth-century Europe a Catholic intellectual elite bound together by a common anthropology and a conscious effort to make the Christian faith intelligible to an Enlightenment person. The members of the movement were proponents of a Catholic Enlightenment.[2]

The origins of this Catholic Enlightenment lay in the seventeenth-century French reform and the inheritance of Renaissance humanism. Its members could be classified as belonging to what H. R. Trevor-Roper has called the "Erasmian strain" in Western intellectual life.[3] They were influenced by the Spanish spiritual tradition of Luis de Grenada, Luis de Leon, and Teresa of Ávila. They shared a common reliance on Jacques Bénigne Bossuet, Claude Fleury, Natalis Alexander, and Jean Mabillon. The liberal party opposed probabilism, emphasized a return to the sources, and translated this return into a drive for reform in theology, morality, and religious practice. Marked by an abhorrence of scholastic subtlety, these Catholics vindicated the rights of intelligence and criticism, related well with the *philosophes*, and promoted ecumenism. All of them made a distinction between the essentials and accidentals of faith. Some provided a theoretical justification for the reforming policies of Joseph II and the marquis de Pombal.

In the realm of religious practice the proponents of the Catholic Enlightenment protested against the excesses of baroque piety. They supported the reform of the breviary, freedom from the policies of the Inquisition, the reduction of feast days, the translation of Scripture into the vernacular, a de-emphasis on indulgences, a vernacular liturgy, the elevation of the spiritual life of the clergy, the "purification" of ecclesiastical history (of ultramontane views and legendary accounts), the reception of communion under both kinds, and the active participation of the faithful in the life of the church.

Recent studies have argued that some of these Enlightenment ideas took institutional form in the Italian Synod of Pistoia in 1786. Although the Jansenist sympathies of Scipio Ricci, the bishop of Pistoia, are well known, the purpose of the synod seems to have encompassed an attempt to bridge the gap between the church and the intellectual transformations of modernity. Its ecclesiology tried to "recreate the broken bonds of the community against a consolidated and crystallized hierarchial structure."[4] The synod emphasized the episcopal and lay elements in the church: its "ecclesiastical democracy" stemmed from a strong awareness of the importance of the individual believer. Benedetto Solari, the Dominican bishop of Noli and one of the supporters of Ricci, desired a genuine ecclesiastical reform that would be founded on Augustinian theological principles and an acceptance of republicanism.[5] The fact that many of the dogmatic decrees of the synod were definitely Jansenist in spirit and letter should not detract from its positive structural significance. In analyzing its social and intellectual roots Marina Caffiero acknowledges the importance of an empirical methodology, Newtonian philosophy, and the Enlightenment's drive against superstition.[6] This scholarship corrobrates the conclusions of those who see a link between Jansenist ecclesiology and eighteenth-century political thought.[7] The Synod of Pistoia was only one institutional example of a broad synthesis emerging between Catholicism and the Age of Reason.

The general European context cannot be forgotten in any understanding of English Catholic life from 1780 to 1829. As will be seen, the movement known in England as Cisalpinism was directly related to continental Enlightenment currents. Appolis refers to the whole phenomenon as "une internationale de la culture et de la critique." The leading English liberal Catholics of the eighteenth and early nineteenth centuries were educated on the Continent. There they were exposed to the French classical tradition, the more recent philosophical theories, and a critical scientific methodology. Almost all of them recognized their own affinities with the Synod of Pistoia. Most traveled extensively and through their travels became aware of the Enlightenment theme of cultural relativism. Many familiarized themselves with Johann Nicholas von Hontheim's *De Statu Ecclesiae* (1763) and Montesquieu's *Spirit of Laws* (1748). At least one corresponded with a leading member of the Italian Enlightenment. It is within this general European context, then, that the English Catholic Enlightenment movement was born. The participants and their educational backgrounds must now be examined.

If a generation can be defined as a period during which a certain mentality or form of life has prevailed, then the proponents of the Catholic Enlightenment in England were members of a single generation, born between 1740 and 1775. The most important members of the movement were Joseph Berington (1743-1827), Charles Butler (1750-1832), John Kirk (1760-1851), John Fletcher (1766-1845), and John Lingard (1771-1851).[8] It is known that the first three came from recusant families of the middle gentry. Lingard was the son of a carpenter. Berington (1756-70), Butler (1759-66), and Lingard (1786-93) were educated at the English College in Douai, France; Fletcher, first at Douai (1782-86) and then at St. Gregory's in Paris (1786-87) and St. Omer's in Douai; Kirk, at the English College in Rome (1773-85). Four of the five were ordained, Butler alone following a lay vocation. Later in life Butler confided to Kirk that he, too, had seriously considered becoming a priest but was dissuaded by his uncle the Reverend Alban Butler.[9] Despite their different ages and personalities, for all of these men a common educational experience provided a solid foundation for later ideas and programs.

It is difficult to ascertain the exact content of the educational scheme at Douai, St. Omer's, and the English College, Rome, after 1750. The extant material relates mostly to the English College, Douai. There the common course of studies for the priesthood took eleven years: a five-year course in the humanities (figures, grammar, syntax, poetry, and rhetoric), then two years of philosophy and four of theology. The greatest emphasis was on the classics: Cicero, Virgil, Tacitus, Livy, Homer, Thucydides, and Heroditus. The curriculum demanded a thorough knowledge of Greek and Latin and a familiarity with Hebrew. This education inculcated a passion for the study of the ancient past, a classical orientation that also marked the Renaissance and lay at the roots of modern historical consciousness.[10]

Philosophically, the English College course tended to be antischolastic and empirical with an element of critical doubt. Locke shattered René Descartes's innate ideas, and the latter's method tempered any naive naturalism that may have arisen. In 1771 Joseph Berington proposed a Douai thesis that accepted sensationalism. At the time this thesis was revolutionary. Alban Butler at St. Omer's and William Pilling, a Franciscan professor at St. Bonaventure's College, Douai, objected to the denial of innate ideas and some of Berington's other opinions.[11] By 1796 John Lingard could more easily reject Cartesianism.[12] As L. Mahieu argues, the passage from the old philosophy to the new generally took place at Douai between 1760 and 1775.[13] It should be noted that there was a growing attachment to critical logic and an aversion for metaphysics throughout the period. Education at the English College was characteristic of the Enlightenment.

The emphasis in the physical sciences department was definitely experimental. Michael Sharratt has analyzed some Douai lecture dictates from the 1757 class of William Wilkinson in cosmography. The course was thoroughly modern. Wilkinson accepted Copernicanism, at least as an hypothesis and probably as a thesis. He supported the geocentric system by citing Johannes Kepler and Isaac Newton.[14] In the general course astronomy, optics, and applied physics began to assert supremacy. Dr. Turberville Needham, a Douai priest of the period, collaborated with Buffon and was a member of the Royal Society. Lingard himself later exhibited a solid knowledge of contemporary scientific trends. The acceptance of Newtonianism was particularly significant. The researches of Appolis and Caffiero correctly note the importance of this philosophy for the Catholic Enlightenment. In Italy the method of Francis Bacon, Descartes, Galileo, and Newton was praised as freeing religion from the grasp of superstition. A letter to John Kirk from Antonio Bottieri, an enlightened professor of philosophy at Pisa, witnesses to the Italian's knowledge that several of Newton's theses had been verified by recent experiments.[15] The acceptance of Newton would later support a delimitation of the miraculous and a criticism of current piety: that which was not empirically verifiable was not acceptable.

The theology course at Douai was oriented in a similar direction. It relied heavily on a study of the sources, Scripture and the patristic tradition. The study of positive theology encouraged a critical attitude toward dogmatics and a comparative approach to church customs. In later life John Lingard remarked: "I care little for the opinions of divines. Martene has taught me that. Assuming that the customs of their times were those of all antiquity they have propagated many an unfounded notion, and one goose following another, such notions have come down to us."[16] The apologetic tenor of this course also encouraged documentary investigation. Edward Hawarden and Richard Challoner, two prominent English Catholic apologists of the eighteenth century, were particularly influential. Bossuet, cited frequently by all of the textbooks, represented an assiduous search for "pure doctrine" in Fathers, councils, and popes. He linked Berington, Butler, and Lingard with the historical and ecclesiological tradition of the Gallican jurists. In addition, since all three men exhibited a knowledge of the most recent biblical scholarship, their theological education probably included a good dose of comparative textual criticism. When combined with the experimental philosophical orientation this type of reflection supported a genuinely innovative stance, one that would look to the particular in

Christianity rather than to the universal. It was eminently suited to distinguish essentials from accidentals. Probably the most significant feature of the theological education at Douai was the treatise on Grace. There now exist at Ushaw College theses sheets from 1726 to 1796 on this subject.[17] With one significant exception, little change occurred in the content of the course from George Kendal at Douai early in the century to Thomas Eyre at Crook Hall. Generally, the treatises begin with a rejection of Martin Luther, John Calvin, Michael Baius, and Jansenius and an acceptance of the papal constitution *Unigenitus*. There follows in typical Thomistic fashion as mediated through Francisco Suárez a description of the three states of nature: integral, pure, and lapsed. Although it was admitted that the state of pure nature never existed, the teacher maintained that it was truly possible. The significant feature of the course surfaced in the discussion of man's state after the Fall (lapsed nature). George Kendal in 1728, Matthew Gibson in 1764, James Nicolas in 1772, and Thomas Eyre in 1796 presided over theses defending the proposition that "all the works of infidels are not sinful." In the state of lapsed nature the students maintained that "it is morally possible without grace to have a natural love of God over all things and to observe the law of nature; that is, for a brief time and excluding grave temptations." Throughout the period the tendency usually inclined toward moderation: "We however are convinced that no infidel can be continually without at least remotely sufficient grace." Only when Richard Southworth replaced James Nicolas as the presiding teacher sometime between 1771 and 1783 did the opinion change in any important way. In 1776 John Milner defended the following proposition: "Lapsed nature has the necessity of grace that is much greater and stronger. Nevertheless in this state it is not necessary for every work that is only morally good. But we are not able to agree with those who estimate that it is morally possible without grace to have a natural love of God above all things and to observe the law of nature."[18] Significantly, this opinion was not held by John Griffiths, William Phelan, or John Gillow when they defended their theses before Southworth in 1780. By 1784 John Daniel had begun directing the defenses on grace. He continued with a more moderate approach.[19]

The general Douai acceptance of the Thomistic views on grace indicates an approach to theological anthropology that was fundamentally conciliatory. It was possible for infidels, so the students argued, to love God above all things. A person could use his natural intelligence to discern and follow the truth. Therefore, anyone who reasonably followed the path of enlightenment (intellect) deserved respect. If this was true of the unbaptized, would it not be more true of fellow Christians? It should be noted that all those whose opinions will be discussed here as Cisalpine accepted this view. In contrast, John Milner, soon to become the most ardent opponent of the progressive faction among the English Catholics, argued that in the fallen state sin so clouded the intellect as to make a reasonable discernment and active acceptance of the truth very difficult. Consequently Milner stressed the role of external authority and institutional structure rather than inner light and spiritual relations.

John Lingard summarized the substance of the general Douai analysis of the relation between nature and grace in 1809. He argued in direct opposition to the Socinian and Methodist views of justification. For Lingard, accepting a theory of imputed righteousness and exalting a person's innate capabilities resulted in a denial of the fine balance that must exist between faith and works, grace and human cooperation. The true Catholic position steered a middle course. It recognized free will, yet acknowledged the necessity of God's initiative. Lingard supported his opinion by referring to the Council of Trent and Jacques Bénigne Bossuet, who represented the moderate approach of the Catholic Enlightenment.[20] John Fletcher acknowledged the same position when he wrote: "Amid the influence of religion, the will continues free; and along with all the energies of grace, liberty subsists entire."[21] This view was midway between Jansenism and Molinism.

It would be inaccurate to assume that the educations of

Introduction. The Birth of Enlightenment • 11

Berington, Butler, Lingard, Fletcher, and Kirk were all the same. Butler noted that when he was at Douai the "classics were well taught," but writing, arithmetic, and geography were little regarded, and "modern history was scarcely mentioned."²² The situation improved after he left. Butler renewed his classical studies and Greek when he returned to England and received an education in comparative jurisprudence at Lincoln's Inn. The philosophical opinions of Berington differed considerably from those of his contemporaries. His thinking was generally more radical, and at one stage he accepted materialism. It is next to impossible to say exactly what Fletcher's education involved. His political opinions were considerably more moderate than those of the others. The evidence that exists for Kirk indicates a singular knowledge of the *Annali Ecclesiastici*, the Florentine journal of enlightenment, and a surprisingly close contact with Italian theological circles.²³ Nevertheless, it can be safely stated that all of these men shared a common antipathy to metaphysical speculation, a love of the classics, a Thomistic theological anthropology, the use of history as an apologetic tool, a knowledge of contemporary biblical criticism, and an acceptance of the scientific method.

After their educational experiences on the Continent, the Cisalpines pursued careers in England. Butler attained a distinguished reputation as a London lawyer. The four priests, after teaching for some time, labored at various missions. Berington worked for the John Throckmorton family; he was usually at Buckland, near Oxford. Fletcher presided in Hexham, Blackburn, and Leamington. He was also chaplain to the Dowager Lady Throckmorton at Weston Underwood. Kirk spent the greater portion of his life at Lichfield. Lingard taught and administered at Crook Hall, later Ushaw College, near Durham, from 1794 to 1810. In 1811, after serving as president of the college for a year, he left for the Catholic mission in Hornby, near Lancaster. There he pursued his career as an historian.

The English Catholic world that these men entered at the close of the eighteenth century was marked by external calmness.²⁴ A superficial observer, judging from the romantic period of the 1830s, would look for signs of life and find only shadows. The church continued to be governed by four vicars apostolic in the London, Northern, Midland, and Western Districts, an arrangement that had continued since the time of James II. The decrees of Trent were not in force; attendance at the sacraments appeared lax; communication was poor. There existed no definite signs of a strong and healthy organization. The penal laws imposed certain legal restrictions. Although seldom applied, they served to remind Catholics of their second-class status.

But underneath this external calmness there were profound sociological, structural, and political transformations. John Bossy argues that between 1770 and 1850 the number of English Catholics increased from 80,000 to 750,000.[25] Geographical distribution was transformed, and an occupational and social revolution occurred. During this time Catholics migrated in large numbers to the industrial belts of Yorkshire, Lancashire, the east Midlands, South Wales, and London. As the population shifted to the towns, an increasing number of people entered nonagricultural fields. By 1770 over fifty percent of the Catholics in most parts of Lancashire were laborers, artisans, or professional workers. Lingard's congregation at Hornby consisted of farmers, farm laborers, hatters, and weavers. In 1767 the total Catholic population of Preston, Wigan, Liverpool, and Manchester was approximately 4,000. By 1810 over 22,000 lived in the four towns; by 1851, over 120,000. The same period saw the emergence of a network of rural missions independent of gentry influence. Emancipation now became a major concern of a broader range of English Catholics.

These social transformations also affected the ecclesial structure of English Catholicism. The mission in the towns experienced the rise of a type of congregationalism. The clergy, instead of relying on aristocratic largesse, came to depend on a regular subscription of the people. Trusteeism— the administration of church goods by the laity, the clergy, or both together—became common. Bossy has discovered examples of this kind of church polity at Liverpool, Wigan, Preston, Lancaster, London, Birmingham, Bath, and probably

Introduction. The Birth of Enlightenment • 13

Bristol. What lay behind it was the emergence of a "third estate," a Catholic middle class of merchants, manufacturers, and professional people, a growing convergence of Catholicism and Dissent, and the development of a system of benevolent associations. The social dynamics behind this change were to disappear by 1830.

A major outburst of political activity accompanied these demographic and structural changes. Catholics became actively involved in the life of the nation. After the First Relief Act in 1778, which removed restrictions on Catholic inheritance of property, a Catholic Committee was formed by the gentry to argue for further legal concessions. In reaction to the Gordon Riots of 1780, Joseph Berington published *State and Behaviour of English Catholics*, a work designed to appeal to and foster a liberal sentiment. Berington called for an extension of religious toleration and a recognition of civil rights for all.[26] Two years later a group of aristocrats and upper gentry of the South and Midlands formed the Second Catholic Committee. When the Dissenters applied for the repeal of the Corporation and Test Acts in 1787, the more involved members saw their chance. The committee, which now included some clergymen, entered into negotiations with William Pitt. The Second Catholic Relief Act of 1791 allowed the celebration of mass in registered chapels by priests who had taken an oath of loyalty to the government.

In 1792, after the dissolution of the Second Committee, the Cisalpine Club was formed. The name referred to the members' rejection of transalpine and ultramontane doctrines on the authority of the pope to depose princes and to dispense subjects from allegiance. As will be seen, it also implied a much more profound view of the relationship between the church and the world. From this time on members of the progressive party were referred to as Cisalpines. In succeeding years this movement for emancipation broadened. By 1808 membership in the Board of English Catholics was open to all, and from that time until 1829 there was a general trend toward cooperation with Dissenters in the struggle for full civil toleration. English Catholics slowly but definitely penetrated English society. A political awareness that had begun with the aristocracy spread to the Catholic populace.

Berington, Butler, Kirk, and, after 1800, Fletcher and Lingard were actively engaged in these political battles. They were also deeply affected by the social and structural changes in the Catholic body. They attempted to preach the Gospel message by responding to and encouraging Catholic participation in public life, the adoption of a participative ecclesiology, and the emergence of a middle-class value system. The following chapters will describe the growth and development of this program from the perspective of one of the principals, John Lingard.

1. political foundations

"THE PEOPLE of this nation are absolutely infatuated." The prospect of Catholic army officers "alarms John Bull not much less than if the Emperor Napoleon had landed on the coast of Sussex." The new men are everywhere; the ministers have been changed; the cry of "no popery" is urged against us. If it succeeds, "parliament will be dissolved."[1] These were the reflections of Joseph Berington in April 1807 when he surveyed the political and ecclesiastical chaos in England. The introduction, a month previously, of a bill to enable Catholics to hold commissions in the army and to secure for soldiers the free exercise of their religion began the crisis. Confronted with this prospect of increased concessions to the Catholics and a possible violation of his oath to protect the union of church and state, King George III once again raised the scythe of his burdensome conscience and vetoed the bill. He attempted to exact from Grenville, the prime minister, a promise never to broach the Catholic question again. Grenville refused. George dismissed the ministers and headed the government with the duke of Portland. A professedly "no popery" ministry was formed. As the cries became more shrill and popular agitation increased, Berington's analysis was further substantiated. The king dissolved Parliament. New elections were held in May 1807, and an anti-Catholic majority was returned to the House of Commons.

From the time of this election until 1829 opposition to the emancipation of Catholics was a criterion for holding ministerial office. Conversely, the campaign for full toleration grew; Catholics and Dissenters closed ranks and argued for the granting of full civil recognition to all. The writings of Joseph Berington, Charles Butler, and the Catholic Committee had supported the same issue since the Gordon Riots of 1780, but the "no popery" stance of the government, the increasing number of Irish immigrants, and the spread of the liberal political tenets of the rational Dissenters now broadened the debate.[2] Among the Catholics, a younger group of apologists, of whom John Lingard was one, assumed the leadership of the movement and continued the basic approach of the older members. Ultimately all the writings of Berington, Butler, Lingard, and others were directed to the single end of emancipation. That goal sharpened their rhetoric, forced a theological irenicism, and focused the diverse elements of their intellectual heritage into a coherent whole. In the issue of emancipation the liberal thinkers encountered the two major structural problems that confronted the Catholic Church in the post-Reformation world: the relationship between church and state and the reality of religious pluralism. Any study of their thought must begin, then, by analyzing their response to the political question of the time.

Lingard and the Separation of Church and State, 1807–13

John Lingard, professor of philosophy and church history at Ushaw College, Durham, began his long career of pamphleteering for the cause of Catholic emancipation in 1807. Early in the year Shute Barrington, the Anglican bishop of Durham, republished his *Charge Delivered to the Clergy of the Diocese of Durham*, a small pastoral broadside against the "idolatrous" and "socially destructive" principles of the Catholic religion. On May 23 of the same year, in the midst of the parliamentary crisis, a "Letter to Electors" appeared in the *Newcastle Courant*. This letter, signed "A Liege Subject," detailed the political arguments against Roman Catholicism. Lingard answered both invitations.[3]

"A Liege Subject" accepted the toleration of Roman Catholic worship, already granted by the Relief Act of 1791, and concentrated on what appeared to him to be the core objection to *political* toleration: "Where a class of people acknowledges a foreign power superior to the power of the state, under the protection of which that class lives, to admit its individuals to an equal participation of the rights of citizens with the other classes . . . would be a continual act of public injustice." To this loyal Englishman the enfranchisement of Catholics would destroy the distinction between subjects and aliens. The ultimate fidelity of Catholics, though British subjects, was to the pope, not to the constitution. Consistent with their own principles, they were incapable of holding places of public trust. The issue was one of foreign allegiance; both papal action in past centuries and the present teaching of the church confirmed this treasonable position. This was the socio-political objection to Catholic toleration.[4]

Catholic apologists had several traditional responses to this type of argument. For example, Bishop John Douglass, vicar apostolic of the London District, and fifty-eight others had signed a statement of Catholic principles. They wanted to prove that "no one [Catholic] tenet was incompatible with that true loyalty or duty Englishmen owe to king and country."[5] Their Address, dated May 20, 1807, and written by Charles Butler, was also printed in the *Courant*. Basically, they promised that a Catholic would defend to his utmost power "the settlement and arrangement of property in this country, as established by the law now in being"; that he abjured "any intention to subvert the present church establishment for the purpose of substituting a Catholic establishment in its stead"; that he solemnly swore not to exercise any privilege to disturb and weaken the Protestant religion and government. Lastly, with respect to the specific objections of "A Liege Subject" the Address offered the following answers:

1. That the Pope or cardinals, or any body of men, or any individual of the church of Rome, has not any civil authority, power, jurisdiction, or preeminence whatsoever, within the realm of England.
2. That the Pope or cardinals, or any body of men, or any individual of the church of Rome, cannot absolve or dis-

pense his majesty's subjects from their oath of allegiance, on any pretext whatever.
3. That there is no principle in the tenets of the catholic faith by which catholics are justified in not keeping faith with heretics, or other persons differing from them in religious opinions, in any transactions either of a public or private nature.⁶

John Lingard entered the controversy on June 6, 1807, by writing a letter in support of the Address. He included a statement from a standard English Catholic work, *Roman Catholic Principles*, that "it is no matter of faith to believe that the pope is himself infallible . . . nor do Catholics, as Catholics, believe that the pope hath any direct or indirect authority over the temporal power and jurisdiction of princes."⁷ Lingard, like most English Catholics, rejected the ultramontane doctrines on the direct and indirect power and confined papal action to purely spiritual jurisdiction. Charles Butler wrote in 1809: "In this country, by Ultramontane principles the assertion of the pope's right to temporal power is always understood. Now every Roman Catholic in England, Clergy as well as Laity have taken a solemn oath, in the Courts of Justice, by which they disclaim their belief of his having that right in the very strongest terms."⁸ But this acceptance of the separation of the spiritual and temporal spheres was purely negative and applied only to the ecclesiastical government. Lingard was forced to add a more significant dimension to his thought in order to answer the politico-religious objections that Shute Barrington and others offered in opposition to Catholic toleration.

As early as 1799 the bishop of Durham had acquired a reputation for anti-Catholic polemics. At that time he preached before the House of Lords and imputed the overthrow of the French monarchy and the disastrous consequences of the French Revolution to the principles of popery. He reiterated this theme and elaborated its foundation in his pastoral charges of 1801 and 1806. "The political experiment which has been made in France," he said, "has also evinced the inestimable value of religion by its temporary loss in the wide range of anarchy and desolation."⁹ Barrington argued that the followers of Christ must unite in order to diffuse the principles of a vital and spiritual religion. Romanists and Dissenters exhibited opposite errors, but both departed from the simplicity of the Gospel. Calvinists, Anabaptists, and other sects committed the sin of schism; they repudiated "Christian verity" and civil establishment. Papists, on the other hand, subverted the positive regulations of a public and social religion, divinely established, by ordinances that detracted from "the honour of God the Father," "the mediatorship of the Son," and "the sanctifying influence of the Holy Spirit." The knowledge of all this should, Barrington declared, "make us careful to prevent the contagion of erroneous and pernicious institutions: and zealous to maintain our national Church which it has cost so much learning, and so many lives, to establish."¹⁰

Other clerics defended Barrington's assertions. In general, the arguments were theological, revolving around the allegedly "idolatrous" beliefs of Catholics: image worship, transubstantiation, and the invocation of saints. The debate lasted for three years.¹¹ In 1809 the curate of Hartlepool attempted to conclude the controversy. He alluded to the core of the social-moral-theological arguments in these words: ". . . we possess in our Land, a pure and spiritual Doctrine and worship, admirably adapted to promote the cultivation, and encouragement, of genuine Christian faith, and sound morals; with the conscientious and diligent performance of all the several duties of religious, civil, social and domestic life."¹²

Lingard reacted to these basically High Church, Tory objections to Catholic claims. Given the politico-religious framework of his opponents, he made two important assertions. First, he attempted to show that popery was not "the fertile parent of religious indifference, of deism, and of atheism."¹³ Second, in response to Barrington's *Grounds on Which the Church of England Separated from the Church of Rome*, Lingard carefully distinguished between political and religious concerns. He could not see how, "to support the catholic petitions can be construed to betray an indifference to the church of England." According to the great principle of that church, everyone possessed the right of private judgment. How, then, could one be punished for dissent? An individual's religious beliefs concerned himself and God. Yet according to the bishop "our conscientious adherence to what we conceive to be the doctrine of Christ excludes us from the privileges of our birthright here, and the same will exclude us from the joys of heaven hereafter." It was astonishing that a Protestant prelate "whose creed is the offspring of private judgment, should attempt to check the freedom of religious inquiry." The mere existence of a church-state unity did not argue for the truth of a creed.[14]

Lingard's two arguments were significant because they indicated both the politico-religious context in which one English Catholic lived and the intellectual foundation from which he chose to criticize the Establishment. To show that Roman Catholicism was not the mother of infidelity argued for its social respectability—on Shute Barrington's assumption of a union of church and state. Lingard was simply meeting his opponent on his own ground. Most English Catholics did that. But to argue that freedom of religious inquiry did not militate against political enfranchisement betrayed—in Lingard's view—the acceptance of a much more radical stance. Here the polemic against "A Liege Subject" and the polemic against the Anglican Establishment joined. Lingard found himself caught between the Scylla of the pope's deposing power and the Charybdis of a national church. With respect to the Catholic tradition, he denied, along with many others, the direct and indirect temporal power of the papacy. But in terms of his own politico-religious environment, he also recognized the importance of free religious inquiry. Together, the arguments implied, even if they did not fully state, the complete separation of the spiritual and temporal spheres in both ecclesiastical and civil government. Further polemics, the Napoleonic menace, and the veto question provided an opportunity for a more explicit presentation of the philosophy behind this view.

In January 1808 the *Sun* asserted that Napoleon had written to the Catholic bishops promising to give their religion the ascendancy in Ireland.[15] In succeeding months French troops entered Rome, annexed the papal states, and transported the pope to Savona. It was in the midst of these events that Henry Grattan, on May 25, 1808, first formally proposed the subject of the veto to the House of Commons. This device, attached to the issue of Catholic emancipation, would give the king at least a negative voice in the appointment of Catholic bishops. Under it no one could be nominated to a titular bishopric without the king's approval. As a "security" the veto would counteract the possible influence of Napoleon over the pope, and through the pope on the Catholics serving in the British army and navy. The Right Honourable George Ponsonby followed Grattan's speech with supporting observations. He allegedly stated that the Catholics "will have no objection to make the King, virtually, the head of their Church; for so I think he must become."[16] In the House of Lords, Lord Grenville also proposed the veto. Eventually the Irish petition was defeated by an overwhelming majority.

This issue in 1808 paralleled those surrounding the oaths that had been imposed on Catholics in the Relief Bills of 1778 and 1791. In all three cases, the British government and the Established Church needed some positive indication of the loyalty of Irish and English Catholics, some proof of the impossibility of any exercise, direct or indirect, of the pope's temporal power. As Charles Butler explained to Dr. Moylan, bishop of Cork: "The rejection of the Veto as it is termed enters much into the subject. While some on the broad principles of general liberty and Philanthropy think the rejection immaterial, and that whether the Veto be refused or accepted, a repeal of the laws against the Catholics should take place, the general opinion seems to be that it is a pledge of political integrity which government has a right to require."[17] With this in mind, parliamentary supporters of the Catholic cause sought to furnish evidence of loyalty. These men looked to precedents like the French Concordat of 1801 for some means of assuaging government fears. Others, led by the Irish hierarchy and Dr. John Milner, the vicar apostolic of the Midland District, rejected all vetoist plans as incompatible with Catholic doctrine and discipline. On both sides there was a complex mixture of political expediency and theoretical conviction. The issue divided the Catholic bodies of England and Ireland for the next twenty years. The whole debate, helped along by the Napoleonic crisis, raised even more acutely than the debacle of 1807 the problem of social structures and the relationship of church to state. The central difficulty remained: How could religious and political toleration of a dissenting minority be accepted within a system of church-state union?

While these currents were in the air, John Lingard explicated his views on church-state relations. In 1809 he and William Talbot, a well-known Catholic apologist, published *The Protestant Apology for the Roman Catholic Church*.[18] Lingard, under the pseudonym "Irenaeus," wrote the introduction; it numbered 167 pages. The whole work addressed itself to the Catholics of Ireland. Lingard began by recalling the cries of "no popery" and "church in danger." He argued that many people seemed not to understand the difference between admitting the pope's spiritual supremacy and paying him the homage of temporal vassalage (p. cxiii). A whole bar of lawyers maintained that "the church and state are so linked and interwoven together, that any alteration in the one must affect the other, and ultimately produce the disruption of both" (p. clvii). What could be said to these difficulties?

In response Lingard wrote that to confuse the allegiance due to his majesty with the acknowledgment of the primacy of the pope jumbled principles. Every Catholic priest knew that separation from the see of Rome signified something purely spiritual; it did not mean rebellion. No king in the world owed allegiance to the pope. The sacerdotal and civil powers were distinct as to their objects and their means of enforcing jurisdiction: "The objects of the former are those connected with the purity of conscience and the attainment of eternal happiness in the next life; and its means are merely spiritual, that is, such as may act upon the soul, but not upon the body or worldly concerns of any individual; whereas the

Political Foundations • 23

objects of the latter are confined to the affairs of this world, and its means are coactive, including the right of inflicting all sorts of punishments, even that, which is called capital. These objects and means of the civil power exist independently of any religion whatsoever . . ." (p. cxiv). In support of this statement Lingard referred to the teaching of Popes Gelasius I, Anastasius II, Symmachus, and Gregory the Great. In Lingard's mind the papal claim to the right of interfering in the temporal concerns of nations had never been allowed by the Catholic Church: bishops, theologians, and canonists had always opposed it. "However," he continued, "there is a singular coincidence between the opinion of the advocates for subjecting church authority to the civil power, and the position of one of those misguided Popes, Boniface VIII, who . . . maintained that there is but one superior power . . ." (p. cxvii). The only difference concerned which power, the spiritual or the temporal, took precedence. Nevertheless, the fact was "that the two powers are each of divine institution, and that they are, within their respective spheres, both independent; a king has as little right to wear the mitre, as a bishop has to wield the scepter" (p. cxvii). Were this matter discussed even on philosophical grounds, no plan could be imagined more conducive to slavery than the uniting of the sacerdotal and regal authorities (p. cxviii).

Lingard extended this principle of church-state separation. In counterpoise to those who feared the destruction of the British constitution he asked: Are the laws of England irrevocable? Were not certain changes in the ecclesiastical system made at the time of Henry VIII? Was the civil constitution of the country overturned? Cannot one Parliament revise, amend, and modify the acts of another Parliament? Does not Blackstone teach that the king and Parliament can alter the established religion? Can any human law be opposed to the inestimable good of the Catholic communion of Christians? "Would not the state be greatly benefitted by the removal of the wranglings and bickerings caused by theological disputes . . . ?" Finally, Lingard reasoned that the king's headship of the church could mean nothing more than "that his

Majesty enjoys a supreme and independent jurisdiction in all civil and external cases over every class of his subjects, whether clergy or laity . . ." (p. clviii).

Lingard, as "Irenaeus," supported the separation of church and state and the consequent possibility of Anglican disestablishment in the midst of the veto controversy. His support of these positions indicates that he no longer accepted the social structure of Christendom as a basis of philosophical and theological reflection. As a Catholic-in-a-Protestant-state he passed beyond the jurisdictional framework of post-Reformation society, that framework which sought "to attribute to a still confessional State a predominance over the Church" or which set the church under "the control and vigilance of the State for purely political and police reasons."[19] For both practical and ideological reasons Lingard also rejected the temporal power of the papacy. His insistence on the separation of the religious and political principles denied the starting point of a *respublica Christiana*. In effect, Lingard was historicizing the medieval synthesis, something few Protestant or Catholic apologists had done since the sixteenth century. In 1813 Lingard argued that the temporal pretensions of the ecclesiastical body grew out of the political state of Europe; they both rose and fell with the prevalence of the feudal system.[20] The time of Christendom, papal or national, had passed.

In addition to necessitating this complete rejection of the medieval synthesis, the arguments of the Protestant apologists during the veto dispute also raised for Lingard the issue of true toleration. The various objections to the Catholic position followed a similar pattern: Since Catholics were detached from the "allegiance in ecclesiastical matters, which is due to their sovereign and to the laws," there was no choice but to exclude them from political power.[21] But, the Protestants argued, this was not to persecute. On the contrary, the English constitution still recognized perfect religious toleration, the "permission under the authority of Law, to every Individual to profess the religious opinions which he conceives most consonant to Scripture, and to worship God in the manner most agreeable to the dictates of his conscience."²² To go beyond this sense of toleration would be to destroy the law of the land.

The principle on which these polemicists rested their cause was the right of self-defense. To this, Lingard queried: Where lurked this mighty danger, this terrific specter, that haunted so many orthodox imaginations? Resolved into its component parts their defense meant "the constitution of the church and the constitution of the state." These were not at all the same. "Every man knows," said Lingard,

> ... that the manner in which the church is constituted, is different from that in which the state is constituted. In the church the legislative power is vested in the king and convocation: in the state it is vested in the king and the two houses of parliament. In the church the executive power resides with the king, the prelates, and other ecclesiastical officers: in the state it resides with the king and the subordinate civil magistrates, who derive their authority from him. Now the prayer of the Catholic petition concerns not the constitution of the church .... Whatever they ask regards the state only; and, in the state, they petition for nothing more than to be put on the same footing of eligibility with their Protestant countrymen.²³

The British constitution, Lingard contended, was framed to preserve the rights of freemen, and the nature of a free constitution required that it trample, as little as possible, "on the liberties and rights of the subject."²⁴ One of these rights, as valuable as property, comprised the *eligibility* to sit and vote in Parliament. This was "coeval with the constitution, given for civil not for religious purposes, and equally existing, whether the subject have any religion or none"; no government could require more than civil allegiance.²⁵ Therefore, he continued, only political danger could disqualify a person from exercising his rights of citizenship; deprivation for another reason meant persecution. Catholics, however, were subjected to civil disabilities not for political delinquency but for entertaining religious opinions. These disabilities violated the rights of conscience. Lingard asked:

Are then our temporal rights to be refused, lest the concession should be deemed an encouragement to our religious worship? For doctrines, merely religious, we are answerable to God alone. With them the state has no concern. To subject a man to civil disabilities for political delinquency, is certainly justifiable; but to perpetuate those disabilities because he entertains religious opinions, which you deem erroneous, is nothing less than persecution. Whether we are political delinquents, or not, has been discussed . . . ; but, if we are not, it is an act of justice to restore to us our political privileges. Conscience must plead, not against us, but in our behalf.[26]

The mistake of the Protestant apologists, in Lingard's mind, resolved itself into their definition of toleration. For them, toleration was a concession; for him, a right. Rejecting their approach and summarizing his opinions, he wrote:

Toleration is the true mean between establishment and persecution. To *establish*, is to select a particular creed, and to provide, at the national expense, for the support of its ministers. To *persecute*, is to select a particular creed, and to subject its professors to restraints, privations, or punishments. To *tolerate*, is to do neither. If, on the one side, the toleration of a religion does not encourage it, on the other it does not molest it. It leaves it to itself, and cautiously abstains from all legislative interference in its favour, or against it. As, when you establish a church, you do not create new civil rights in favour of its members; so, neither, when you tolerate a creed, do you impose civil disabilities on its professors. Every molestation, whether it go to the privation of life, or liberty, or property, or rights previously possessed, is persecution; differing, indeed, in degree, but essentially repugnant to the true notion of toleration.[27]

Thus, when the questions were posed for him in the debate over the veto, John Lingard openly supported separation of church and state and religious liberty based on the rights of conscience. As will be seen, this was the underlying political philosophy of the Cisalpines. The position was not just theoretical; it also occasioned a political *praxis*.

Lingard applied it with consistency in all his attempts to achieve emancipation. Only two further examples need be given here. They indicate the extent to which Lingard's political philosophy was accepted among the English Catholics and how carefully it must be distinguished from any of the continental solutions to the church-state problem.

Political Praxis, 1813–24

Toward the end of 1813 John Lingard visited George Silvertop, a prominent member of the Board of English Catholics, a friend of Berington and Butler, and a former classmate. After consultation, the two proposed what they considered to be a judicious compromise on the question of the veto. They decided that the Catholic bishops should present a petition to Parliament in which they would agree, first, not to recommend for bishop anyone of whose loyalty or morality they were not completely certain, and second, that after the death of a bishop, they would submit a list of *episcopabili* for the king's approbation, and should no objection be made, the pope would then select a bishop from this list. Lingard and Silvertop believed that this plan would be acceptable to all parties. It did not interfere with the pope's prerogative and gave the king only an indirect negative veto.

The Northern vicar apostolic, Bishop William Gibson, and his coadjutor, Thomas Smith, agreed to consider the proposal. Lingard penned a petition incorporating the plan, and Gibson, after canvassing the other vicars apostolic, was to forward it to Scotland for approval. In January 1814 Silvertop visited Bishop William Poynter in London in order to obtain his reflections. Poynter was unacquainted with the whole business. To complicate matters, it seems that Gibson had received notice from the archbishop of Dublin and Milner that the Irish bishops opposed parliamentary interference of any kind in Catholic discipline. At that point, Gibson and Smith both decided that for the sake of internal peace the plan should be abandoned. In lieu of any episcopal action, Lingard and other English Catholics resolved upon a form of petition to be presented to both houses. This was done in June 1814, but the matter was not pursued any further.²⁸

Despite its failure, Lingard's 1814 petition indicated the general belief that Catholics should seek emancipation on the ideological grounds of religious liberty and civil rights. On this issue they did not shrink from making common cause with Dissenters. Three paragraphs of the petition deserve to be quoted:

> They [the Catholics] cannot look back on the several, the partial indulgences, which have been granted to the Roman Catholics of this empire, during his majesties [sic] reign without feeling the most lively emotions of gratitude for the paternal sollicitude [sic] of their revered sovereign, and the liberal policy of an enlightened legislature: and the experience of the past induces them to cherish a well founded hope, that your honourable house will speedily concur in abrogating the remains of that penal code which has long crippled the best energies of the state; and which while it abridges the religious freedom of the subject restricts the rightful prerogative of the crown.
>
> They have been informed that one great obstacle to so desirable a measure arises from the jealousy, with which many of their protestant brethren are accustomed to view the appointment of Roman Catholic bishops in this kingdom. Whatever your petitioners may think of the grounds of this jealously, it is not for them so much to combat, as to endeavour to remove it; by submitting to your honourable house such arrangement as will in their opinion enable the government to ascertain the loyalty and devotion of its Roman Catholic prelates without at the same time inflicting any wound on the integrity of their faith or violating any essential point in the discipline of their church. In framing such arrangements it is fortunate that the object of the petitioners must be the same as that of your honourable house. For they are sensible that the redress of their grievances, to be productive of national benefit, should [be] a work of conciliation: *not the exaltation of one party of religionists by the depression of another, but the consolidation of the strength of the empire by the removal of prejudice, by mutual concession, and by an equal communication of civil interests and civil rights.* . . .

In thus presuming to lay their sentiments before your honourable house, our petitioners flatter themselves that they give a convincing proof of that spirit of conciliation with which they feel themselves actuated, and that they shall thereby contribute to *hasten the approach of that wished for day, when religious opinion shall cease to be the ground of civil incapacity, when an equal participation in the benefits, shall give to all an equal interest in the defence of the constitution; and when the sun of British liberty, shining in full splendour, shall be permitted to shed its rays, without distinction of sect or country on every class of subjects in his majesty's dominions.*[29]

Bishop Thomas Smith of the Northern District was well aware of the significance of these passages. In his letter to Bishop Poynter in February 1814 he wrote that the petition "wants amendment" particularly "in the places where I have drawn my pen" (italicized portion). Two years previously, he had complained to the same man: "I am apprehensive also of the mischief from the meetings of the Friends of Religious Liberty, in which many Catholics seem to join and to make themselves conspicuous. They are preparing a grand petition from dissenters of every description for general liberty of conscience. What do they mean by it? The principle may be certainly carried to unwarrantable lengths. Catholics should be upon their guard."[30] Clearly, at least in the mind of one vicar apostolic, Lingard's opinions could be both *too* consistent and *too* popular.

On May 28, 1816, the House approved the appointment of a Commons's select committee to study the "laws and ordinances existing in foreign States respecting the regulation of their Roman-Catholic subjects in ecclesiastical matters, and their intercourse with the see of Rome or any other foreign jurisdiction."[31] The report was evidently written with a view to the enactment in England of some of the ecclesiastical regulations in force in Russia, Austria, Tuscany, and France. It reasoned that if laws respecting the veto, *exsequatur,* and *placet* existed elsewhere, could they not be accepted by English Catholics in exchange for emancipation? Since the report was to serve as a basis for future government action on the Catholic question, the vicars apostolic felt they should respond. With this in mind, William Poynter wrote to Lingard on January 25, 1817, and on January 28 Lingard agreed to answer the report.[32]

In his work Lingard accepted as a cardinal principle the necessity of determining the extent to which jurisdictionalist ideas were applicable to England. It was a known fact that every powerful Catholic state except Bavaria had controlled the nomination of bishops and possessed the right to *placet*. Instead of contradicting the report, then, it would be better, said Lingard, "to observe that decrees of Joseph, work of Rechberger, and congress of Embs [*sic*] are of no authority among Catholics."[33] To Lingard, none of the laws were applicable to England because the bishops there possessed only spiritual jurisdiction, sovereigns could not claim nomination by right of patronage, and the king was Protestant. There had never been an instance of a prince, Protestant or Catholic, nominating to a bishopric where the bishop held no temporal privileges. On these principles Lingard divided his work into three sections: "Foreign Ordinances—Their Nature and Tendency", "On the Appointment of Bishops", and "On the Origin and Object of 'Placet.'" Basically, the *Laws and Ordinances* repeated in greater depth his ideas on the separation of church and state, the British constitution, and religious liberty.[34]

According to the principles of Catholic theology, Lingard argued, the administration of the sacraments, the office of teaching, the right of granting dispensations, and the collation or extinction of ecclesiastical jurisdiction were all spiritual matters and therefore beyond the competence of the civil power (pp. 5–6). During the first three centuries of the Christian era the church possessed no civil establishment; its chief pastors, he maintained, "enjoyed and exercised, independently of the civil power, that spiritual authority which had been transmitted to them from the apostles" (p. 13). In the fourth century the church obtained a civil establishment, and the sovereign became its protector. "Civil effects were allowed to result from religious acts"

Political Foundations • 31

(p. 14). As the Middle Ages progressed, he continued, "states belonging to each bishopric began to be considered as fees held of the crown" (p. 16). At each vacancy they reverted to the possession of the sovereign, who claimed and exercised the right of bestowing them. This practice produced enormous abuses; the freedom of canonical elections was impaired by both popes and kings. Concordats sought to remedy the abuses. At the same time, papal provisions and reservations were the subjects of angry discussions (p. 26). To balance the extensive influence of the papacy, sovereigns ordered the "seizure of all bulls and letters from Rome" (p. 26), and thus prevented the "execution of papal grants or decisions on beneficiary matters, till it should be ascertained that they contained nothing prejudicial to the customs of the kingdom" (pp. 26–27). Thus, at their origins both the right of nomination and the *placet* concerned matters of civil import or civil law. They applied only to the situation where the civil and religious principles were mixed.

This mixed situation, Lingard continued, was still the case on the national level with the church in Austria, Tuscany, Naples, Sicily, Sardinia, Piedmont, Savoy, France, Spain, Portugal, and in some parts of Germany. It was to these churches that the doctrines of Bernard Van Espen and the jurists of Combra [*sic*] applied: "They spoke of Churches which flourish under the fostering care of the state, which have the sovereign for their protector and advocate, which can enforce their laws by temporal penalties, and which derive their revenues from the munificence of the civil power" (p. 15). But when the church ceased to be established, as for example the Roman Catholic Church ceased to be established in England at the Reformation, she reverted "to the same condition in which the christian church had originally existed" (p. 14). As a current example, Lingard referred to the United States of America: "In the United States, the Catholic Clergy perform their sacred functions, and exercise their spiritual authority without molestation. The government meddles not with the appointment of their bishops, or their correspondence with foreign prelates. In the eye of the law, every creed is equal. No one is singled out as a particular object of jealousy and restriction. As long as religion interferes not with the civil power, the civil power interferes not with religion."[35] Similarly, the Roman Catholic bishops in the United Kingdom were merely spiritual ministers. They had no temporalities, "no rank in the state, no courts, no civil privileges, no civil jurisdiction" (p. 22), and so none of the laws in foreign states were applicable to them.

As a second objection to the applicability of foreign laws, Lingard noted that the cases at issue concerned the acts of enlightened despots such as Joseph II, the grand duke of Tuscany, and the marquis de Pombal in Portugal. Despotic acts were to be expected, he said, in states "where the will of the prince is the law of the land" (p. 5). No one could be surprised that arbitrary sovereigns "invaded the religious as well as the civil liberties of the subjects" (p. 5). But certainly the British Parliament would not appeal to sovereigns of this description to "learn in what matters it ought to legislate for British subjects" (p. 13). Instead, the legislators should look to the ordinances that have restored civil rights to the Protestants in Catholic kingdoms. Framers of these ordinances never thought it necessary "to make men purchase the extension of their civil liberties with additional restrictions on the exercise of their religion" (p. 39).

Lingard finished these observations and forwarded them to William Poynter by March 10, 1817.[36] They received the general approbation of most people. Their significance lies in the extent to which they repudiated any jurisdictional solution to the problem of church-state relations. Coupled with the 1814 petition they revealed the depth of Lingard's position. There could be no Febronian or Josephist solution to the veto question. In 1817 and again in 1821 Lingard seemed to support some form of government interference in Catholic episcopal elections, but a close examination of these debates shows that this stance stemmed from a temporary political pragmatism.[37] The debates did not reflect on Lingard's basic position. In 1824 he penned another petition in support of emancipation. "This plea," he wrote though elsewhere successful, has hitherto failed with your right Honourable House. They [the petitioners] rest their hopes of success on higher ground, on the acknowledged rights of conscience. They cannot believe that your Lordships will patronize intolerance, or refuse to others that freedom of judgment which you claim for yourselves; and therefore they come with confidence to ask you for the full benefit of religious toleration.

To tolerate is not merely to permit the exercise of religious worship, but to permit it unfettered with civil restrictions and disabilities. If you add these, you do not tolerate, you punish; you inflict for conscience sake the penalties, which the law inflicts for grievous offences. . . .

It has been objected by some, that they deserve not the full rights of British subjects because they prove themselves only half subjects, as long as they deny the ecclesiastical supremacy of the sovereign. But they beg your Lordships to consider, that they give to the sovereign whatever is given to him by law; and that they acknowledge him to be the legal head of that church, which it has pleased the legislature to establish in one half of the island. More than this is not expected from others; more cannot be required from them.[38]

The paragraphs summarize Lingard's continued commitment to positions that he had previously elucidated in his tracts. The foremost apologist for Catholic emancipation was intellectually committed to a religiously pluralistic society and a secularized and constitutional government. The Cisalpine tradition from which he came has often been accused of subordinating the church to the state, of advocating a Febronian solution to the veto question, and of being politically opportunistic. If Lingard's consistency is any indication, such accusations can no longer be ventured.

Intellectual Origins of Cisalpinism

The origin of John Lingard's views on the separation of church and state lay buried in the intermixture and confusion of three strands of thought. Of these the French Gallican boasted the longest history. Lingard demonstrated a familiarity with Bossuet's *Exposition of the Doctrine of* the *Catholic Church* (1671) and *Defensio Declarationis Conventus Cleri Gallicani* (1735). He also knew the ecclesiastical histories of Natalis Alexander and Claude Fleury, Pierre Nicole's *De l'unité de l'eglise* (1687), the *Regula Fidei* (1646) of Francis Veron, and the *Declaration of 1682*. All of these works and their sources (e.g., Jacques Almain, Jean Mair, Jean Gerson, Pierre Pithou, and the Parisian tradition) denied the pope's *plentitudo potestatis*. After a long evolution, the Parisian understanding of church and state was summarized negatively in the first Gallican article, which asserted the absolute independence of the king from the pope in temporal concerns. The underlying justifying principle, the divine establishment of two distinct societies—the spiritual and the temporal—then became common currency in eighteenth-century French textbooks. Lingard, coming from the strongly Gallican Douai tradition, owed much both in content and use of historical method to these French theologians.[39]

Allied with this specifically continental contribution was the influence of Redmond Caron's *Remonstrantia Hibernorum contra Lovaniensis* (1665). This work attempted to apply Gallican theological ideas to the church-state situation in Ireland in order to justify the Loyal Formulary or Irish Remonstrance of 1661. The latter had denied the legality of papal intervention in temporal affairs and had accepted the divine right of kings. Based on the Oath of 1606, it had hoped to convince Charles II of Irish political allegiance. Caron and Peter Walsh wrote detailed explications after the event. They accepted the supreme temporal power of the king, encouraged passive obedience, and confined the pope to a purely spiritual jurisdiction. Scriptural, patristic, and historical precedents were cited to prove the "usurping" and centralizing pretensions of Pope Gregory VII. The theory, as with its Gallican counterpart, tended to subordinate the church to the state. Lingard used Caron's *Remonstrantia* as a source book.[40]

Indigenous ecclesiastical traditions became the second major source for Lingard's thought. He acknowledged debts to such diverse works as Henry Holden's *Analysis of Divine*

Faith (1658), the anonymous *Roman Catholic Principles in Reference to God and King* (ca. 1680), and *Essay towards a Proposal for Catholick Communion* (1704). These catechisms were supplemented by appeals to the long tradition of *praemunire* and the numerous protestations of loyalty on the part of the English Catholics. All denied the pope's temporal power, and, at least with respect to the Catholic tradition on this point, they dissolved the medieval synthesis. In addition, Lingard's ideas reflected the current opinions of both liberal and reactionary English Catholics. The Catholic Committee articulated the view of the liberals. Its *First, Second* and *Third Blue Books* supported emancipation by confining the pope to a purely spiritual jurisdiction and separating temporal from ecclesiastical concerns.[41] John Throckmorton, one of the lay leaders of the group, appealed frequently to Fleury's *Histoire ecclésiastique* (1691–1720), Van Espen's *Jus Ecclesiasticum* (1700), Walsh's *Irish Remonstrance* (1661), and the *De Concordia* (1641) of Pierre de Marca.[42] Among the more moderate Catholics, Joseph Strickland insisted on the complete distinction between the spiritual and temporal spheres.[43] Even John Milner and Charles Plowden, considered bastions of the reactionary faction, acknowledged that the church's jurisdiction was purely spiritual and that she had acquired temporal dominion only in the eighth century.[44] Lingard's thought could hardly have been considered unique when it was also in basic agreement with Francis Plowden's *Jura Anglorum*, John Fletcher's *Church and State*, and the 1826 *Declaration* of the vicars apostolic.[45]

The third discernible influence on Lingard's church-state ideas was the most important. This was the natural law tradition of English Whiggery. The Gallican and indigenous English Catholic views were predominantly negative. Neither made a complete, positive break from the legacy of the medieval synthesis, the national principle of *cujus regio, ejus religio*. The Gallicans distinguished the spiritual and temporal spheres only to unite them in the person of the king; the English Catholics made the same distinction in order to prove their loyalty after Pius V's deposition of Elizabeth I.

Thus, both confined the papacy to sacral concerns; they did not secularize the state. In contrast, the growth of the natural rights school through Hugo Grotius, baron von Pufendorf, and especially John Locke accomplished just that aim. When Lingard spoke of "prior rights of the subject," "citizenship," and "free constitution," he placed himself within the Lockean and Enlightenment political stream. This intellectual tradition completely divorced religious belief and social allegiance.[46] It provided the political foundation for that portion of English Catholic opinion known as Cisalpine.

It was on this issue of political theory that Lingard shared a common intellectual heritage with Joseph Berington, Charles Butler, John Kirk, John Fletcher, and others. All the Cisalpines were convinced Whigs. As will be seen in chapter 2, they accepted the political settlement of 1688, argued from a position of natural rights, and defended the notion of limited government. What differentiated them from other Catholics was acutely obvious in the contrasting opinions of Joseph Berington and John Milner. Both men rejected the temporal power of the papacy. Milner admitted his acceptance of Locke's metaphysics. But, significantly, he refused to acknowledge the English philosopher's political theory. For the "angel of Castabala," as the Cisalpines later called Milner, the belief that "all power comes from the people" destroyed true authority.[47] In contrast, Joseph Berington spoke of the existence of the king for the people and always interpreted the revolution of 1688 in a favorable light.[48]

Long before Lingard penned his defense of a secularized state, his older friends had supported similar views. In 1787 Berington wrote that he was the enemy of all ecclesiastical establishments. Two years later he defended the proposition that "the establishment of national churches seems unauthorised by the spirit of Christianity; does not promote the real cause of religion; is hurtful to the general interest of the state."[49] During the debates of the 1790s, even though the polemical works of the Cisalpines did not positively encourage disestablishment, their arguments presupposed that theoretical position.⁵⁰ In 1804 John Fletcher's *Spirit of Religious Controversy* distinguished between the temporal and spiritual spheres. That early work did not support the position of Locke, but after the veto controversy arose, Fletcher, the most popular Cisalpine preacher, more clearly advocated the principle of disestablishment.⁵¹ The defensive context was probably the only reason why the other Cisalpines, John Chetwode Eustace, James Archer, and James Wheeler, did not act similarly.⁵² Most of these men were familiar with standard works written from the Whig perspective, such as the anonymous *Inquiry into the Moral and Political Tendency of the Religion Called Roman Catholic* and Charles Stanley Constable's *Review of the Question of Catholic Emancipation.* The Cisalpines borrowed their historical arguments (e.g., Bossuet's rejection of both the medieval role of the papacy and the direct and indirect theories on the temporal power) and theological justification (e.g., the divine origin of two separate societies) from the Gallican and English Catholic sources. But they took their view of the nature of government from John Locke.

It should be noted here that John Lingard was also not alone in recognizing that a Gallican or Febronian solution to the relationship between church and state could not apply to England. Joseph Berington definitely approved Lingard's *Laws and Ordinances*.⁵³ Charles Butler, the prominent Cisalpine lawyer and partial author of the blue books, never supported the veto.⁵⁴ John Fletcher's *Church and State* called the veto "an intrusion of the *civil* power, upon the right, or duty, which, in this country, in relation to the Catholic prelacy, is purely spiritual."⁵⁵ An 1810 pamphlet by James Wheeler approved a negative vote, but in a pragmatic attempt to accommodate the government.⁵⁶ It was similar to the position Lingard took in 1814.⁵⁷ All of the proposed plans carefully avoided subordinating the church to the state. Among the Cisalpines only John Throckmorton, Berington's squire, definitely advocated a jurisdictional solution. He gave the king the right of nomination to Catholic bishoprics.⁵⁸

The crucial significance of the Lockean and Enlightenment element in Cisalpine thought becomes evident when

Lingard's definition of toleration is placed in its proper context. Religious liberty was inconceivable within the Gallican political framework; it entered either as a practical necessity or as the outcome of infidelity and enlightened indifference. The theory of toleration was closely associated with the anti-Catholicism of the *philosophes*.[59] According to Bernard Plongeron the maximum opening by continental Catholics to a concept of toleration was represented by the thought of Pietro Tamburini. But his ideas were generally unacceptable and became increasingly unpopular as people reacted to the French Revolution.[60] Within the European context the typical Catholic position was very similar to that of the English Tories. It accepted the indissoluble unity of church and state. John Milner represented this view in England. He equated religious freedom with *"republicanism," "infidelity,"* and *"revolution."*[61]

In contrast, a theory of toleration that was not anti-Catholic did develop within the English political tradition. In the era of Lingard's birth the natural law approach of Locke, the Protestant emphasis on private judgment, and rationalist skepticism with respect to religious truth combined in the thought of the rational Dissenters to popularize the theory of religious liberty based on the rights of conscience. Joseph Priestley, Richard Price, and Robert Robinson were the major philosophers. Political Whiggery—separation of church and state, and constitutionalism—was the natural concomitant of this frame of mind. Charles James Fox became the embodiment of the ideal. Later Francis Jeffrey and Sydney Smith spread the message in the pages of the *Edinburgh Review*.[62] In 1811 the Protestant Society for the Protection of Religious Liberty was founded. In 1813 Parliament granted toleration to the Unitarians. That same year the Dissenters supported Catholic emancipation. The appeal to natural rights was unpopular after the French Revolution, but the Dissenters' ideas of religious toleration still became common currency in early nineteenth-century England.

This tradition of religious liberty naturally combined with the Cisalpine view of government. It made the English position unique among Roman Catholics. In 1780 Joseph

Political Foundations • 39

Berington wrote: "I chuse my own religion." "It is a concern betwixt myself and God; and it belongs to no other to arraign my conduct, or to censure my determination."[63] Similarly, John Fletcher carefully distinguished between civil liberty and private judgment and thus recognized a theory of toleration compatible with Catholic belief.[64] *Reflections on the Spirit of Religious Controversy*, and the writings of the Cisalpine apologists Archer, Eustace, and Wheeler presupposed this view.[65] Charles Butler and George Silvertop also defended religious liberty.[66] All of the Cisalpines were aware of the general movement in support of toleration. This trend was accepted because of the social pressure that came with being a member of a disenfranchised minority. Reinforcement came from the many Catholics who attended the meetings of the Friends of Religious Liberty.[67]

Thus, John Lingard's arguments in the struggle for emancipation were not unique. He exemplified the standard Cisalpine view, which was both a political *praxis* and a philosophical conviction. This branch of Catholic thought adhered to the Lockean tradition of the secularized state and supported religious liberty. It transcended the boundaries of an ideological Christendom and accepted the reality of a pluralistic society. Such ideas carried certain consequences. On June 4, 1826, John Lingard told Charles Blundell: "I would have the Catholics present an address to the King professing their attachment to him, and expressing their indignation at the charge of divided allegiance: and instead of petitions for emancipation, I would have them join with all dissenters in the Empire, to petition for the total abolition of civil restriction on account of religious opinion."[68] Later that summer the British Catholic Association penned a petition with just that idea in mind. The bishops refused to accept it. On September 29 Thomas Smith wrote to William Poynter: "Why enter into the abstruce subject of the rights of conscience? For my own part I cannot separate the *broad, indefinite assertion* of liberty of conscience now so fashionable from consequences absolutely subversive of all authority whether spiritual or temporal."[69] Poynter's theologian James Yorke Bramston agreed: "My soul desires to raise up Protestantism to Catholicism, and abhors the idea of lowering Catholick principles to meet Protestant error. I never thought it even politic to attempt to do so; but, be that as it may, and in my opinion, as your Lordship very partly hints, the broad admission of 'religious liberty' is little or nothing short of the admission of the false and foolish principles of private judgment."[70] In a joint letter issued on January 23, 1827, the vicars apostolic rejected the petition. The episode passed, but it exemplified the problem: In a social and intellectual structure of thought such as that of the Cisalpines, how did one define the role of authority? To the issues surrounding that question we must now turn.

2. the crisis of church authority

ON DECEMBER 27, 1815, the heads of almost every resident Catholic family of property in Northumberland and Durham assembled at Newcastle-upon-Tyne. The object of the meeting was to protest at the persecution of the Huguenots in Nîmes, France. Since Protestant polemicists had referred to the French incident as an example of Roman Catholic intolerance, the Newcastle group felt obliged to reaffirm the Catholic acceptance of religious liberty. After a speech by George Silvertop, the group unanimously passed ten resolutions. Of primary importance was the first, which stated: "That attached as we are to the Faith of the Catholic Church, we do maintain the right of every individual, in every age and in every country, to judge the reasonableness of his belief; and we do moreover maintain, that no man can be deprived of this sacred, inalienable right, without injustice or oppression." After the meeting some of the men dined at the Queen's Head Tavern and there joined hands for a toast to civil and religious liberty. A month later, on January 31, 1816, the General Board of British Catholics forwarded a vote of thanks to Silvertop and the others for their Newcastle Declaration.[1]

This statement of the Catholics in Northumberland and the action of the General Board became a *cause célèbre* in the pages of the *Orthodox Journal*, the most important English Catholic periodical of the time. William Eusebius Andrews, the editor and a layman of extreme views, opened the debate in the January issue. He argued that no Catholic possessed the right to judge the reasonableness of his belief. A man "has a right to examine his reason as to *which* Church possesses the promises of Christ; but having convinced himself of that, he must then submit his reason to the precepts of that Church, which can neither *add* nor *diminish* to the truths communicated to her by the Holy Spirit." Andrews asked: Whence did the Newcastle men borrow their Queen's Head ceremony? From the late Jacobin club at Paris? The editor continued the attack in the February and March issues. The Newcastle document was founded to meet the Dissenters' rule: "Search the Scriptures and judge for yourselves." The first resolution abounded with ambiguity; Protestants could infer from it that church authority was not now an article of Catholic faith. Did it not resemble the December resolution of the Dissenters at Belfast that "the exercise of *private judgment* in forming religious opinions, is *the unalienable right of every individual;* and that no Government ought to interfere between the mind of man and his God . . . ?" Clearly, the first article of the declaration of the "Northern Lights," said Andrews, implied Socinianism, not Catholicism.[2]

Several anonymous correspondents supported Andrews's contentions; just as many defended the orthodoxy of the resolution.[3] The controversy continued from January to August 1816, and filled more than fifty pages of the journal. At first glance the debate appeared isolated, only one example of the many conflicts between the General Board and its opponents. But in a broader perspective, the arguments reflected a much deeper division between the Cisalpine faction and its opponents. Submerged in the verbiage were political and theological presuppositions that contributed to a basic crisis of authority plaguing early nineteenth-century English Catholics. The issues in question revolved around three major areas: the influence of political theory on ecclesiology, the relationship between reason and faith in Catholic apologetic, and the extent of accommodation permitted in a situation of social and theological pluralism. An examination of Cisalpine thought in these areas will provide the basis for a more thorough appreciation of Lingard's understanding of the problem of authority.

Politics and Ecclesiology

In characterizing eighteenth-century views of church and state, Ursula Henriques notes that "religion and politics could not be wholly separated, since attitudes towards the problems raised in these distinct spheres of life were unified in the individual himself."[4] The truth of this insight is supported by the arguments and actions of the English Catholics. The 1816 debate over the Newcastle Declaration clearly indicated the implications of a natural rights anthropology for the exercise of ecclesial authority. The first resolution referred to a "sacred, inalienable right." In defense of this right, the author of an article in the *Orthodox Journal* who signed himself "A Catholic Priest" appealed to his Lockean heritage. He noted that the right belonged to everyone who submitted to others to judge of the reasonableness of his submission. The right of all mankind to a free and private judgment in matters of religion was not inconsistent with the exercise of an infallible guide. Clearly a Cisalpine, he wrote: "As the immediate rule of every man's actions, is his *own conscience*, and as conscience is nothing else but the *private judgment*, (or the private opinion) which he has, or ought to have of his duty, therefore it properly and necessarily belonged to the Apostles to judge of the reasonableness of their submission in the first case, and the people to judge of their's in the second." In the same context an author who signed himself "Clericus" asked: You tell us that we must submit to the Church: true, but allow me to add with the apostle, that our *obedience must be reasonable*. Now can obedience be reasonable, or can any man give a reason of the hope that is in him, without a due examination of the grounds or motives that induce him to it?" A writer who styled himself "Another Catholic Priest" carefully noted that this position did not imply a Protestant's *private judgment*—"the pretended right assumed by sectaries of judging whether this or that particular doctrine is consonant to the scriptures and of preferring their own interpretation to that of the Church."[5] The Cisalpines argued that their position was compatible with a Christian spirit of submission to all the church taught in matters of faith. They presupposed as the foundation of their thought the integrity of the individual and his right of conscience, reason, and free submission.

The opposing party was not slow to recognize the significance of this argument. One writer maintained that the Newcastle Declaration implied the right to judge of different articles of the creed. In his mind, no Catholic possessed that right. Another, who called himself "A Priest of the Old School," wrote: "The worst of all is where Clericus makes examination necessary in one who is already Catholic, in order to ascertain that the Church does not impose upon him." In the August issue of the *Orthodox Journal* "A Parish Priest" isolated the different conceptions of "right" that separated the Cisalpines from their opponents. It is clear, he said, that the Newcastle Declaration is a *declaration of rights* designed to limit and define the extent of church authority. By this statement a Catholic is given the right to decide against the church. "These liberal Catholics assert a right of uncontrolled judgment on the doctrines, and the authority itself of the Church." The writer struck at the heart of the relationship between politics and theology when he declared: "Man, supposed antecedently to entering a society, has certain natural liberties, which, after the establishment of society, he forfeits, retaining thenceforward no individual right of either resuming his former freedom, or deciding upon the obligation of the social contract itself.—He is bound to obey the laws of society without questioning its authority. The case of a Catholic, with respect to the Church, is much similar, before he entered her pale."[6]

To "A Parish Priest" there appeared to be a direct link between one's theory of natural rights and one's attitude toward ecclesiastical authority. As a political conservative, he manifested a transference of principles from the civil to the ecclesial spheres. He feared the same from the Cisalpines and realized that any acceptance of the principle of the "inalienable rights of man" forboded, at least theoretically, irreconcilable tension between the individual and the institution. To support his fears he had only to glance at the history of Cisalpine relations with episcopal authority.

As early as 1790 the different conceptions of the relationship between human rights and the established authority had begun to permeate the disagreements between the Cisalpines and their ecclesiastical superiors. The debates have been analyzed many times, and here only a brief summary of some representative episodes can be given.[7] In the spring of 1789 the Catholic Committee, the center of Cisalpine activity, composed an oath of loyalty to be attached to the Catholic Relief Bill. The bishops objected to the wording of the oath, which was as close as possible to that of the Oath of Supremacy, and agreed to condemn it. This was done in the Northern District by Vicar Apostolic Matthew Gibson's pastoral letter of January 1790. In response some of the Midland District's clergy, including Joseph Berington and John Kirk, protested against the seemingly arbitrary exercise of episcopal power and wrote in support of the oath. Their document was not antiepiscopal. It was written to defend Vicar Apostolic Thomas Talbot for not publishing the condemnation of the oath in his district.[8]

Agitation continued. In 1791 bishops William Gibson, John Douglass, and Charles Walmesley again issued an encyclical letter condemning the oath. This time the Catholic Committee itself protested. After an unsuccessful attempt at reconciliation, the committee members answered the bishops in a Manifesto and Appeal. They professed acceptance of the supremacy of the pope and acknowledged that they were bound by the decrees of the Catholic Church and her faith.

> My Lords, if Christ enjoins submission, he enjoins it when submission is reasonable; and submission must ever be unreasonable when it is not preceded by instruction and reason. Following the precept of her Divine Master, the Church of God, in tender regard to the weakness of her children, has generally condescended to conciliate, has always thought herself bound to instruct. It is a rule with her that the lowest

of her children should know of what he is accused before he is judged; and be permitted to defend himself before he is condemned. . . . But where reason is not satisfied, where conviction has not preceded, God and the collective body of his Church alone, have a right to require submission: when, under these circumstances, it is required by any other, it cannot be that rational submission which Christ authorizes his ministers to require. . . . We, the Catholic Committee, . . . do hereby before God solemnly protest and call upon God to witness our protest against your Lordships' Encyclical Letters of the 19th day of October, 1789, and the 21st day of January, last, and every clause, article, determination, matter and thing therein respectively contained; as imprudent, arbitrary and unjust; as a total misrepresentation of the nature of the Bills to which they respectively refer, and the Oaths therein respectively contained; and our conduct relating thereto respectively;—as *encroaching on our natural civil and religious rights,* inculcating principles hostile to society and government, and the constitution and laws of the British empire. . . .[9]

It was evident that an Enlightenment anthropology lay behind the protest. Because the committee refused to submit to episcopal authority and subsequently threatened to appeal to Rome, Bishop Walmesley suspended the Reverend Joseph Wilkes, considered one of the chief architects of the Cisalpine errors. The committee objected. Wilkes's congregation took his side in the dispute, and a certain section of clergy and laity also saw the act as yet another instance of episcopal tyranny. Wilkes finally retracted. He was reinstated and then issued an explanation of his retraction: "As to *renouncing* the protest, I could not justify myself to the Gentlemen of the Committee, if I made use of such a term; because it would certainly be construed to imply a renunciation of the principle of protesting against and appealing from measures and decisions, which are conscientiously believed erroneous and aggrieving. . . ."[10] Because of Wilkes's justifying statement, Walmesley denied him faculties. Still, some Cisalpine clergy and laity continued to protest. The Staffordshire priests maintained that the bishop's action was null because there had been no proper citation, no sufficient ground for suspension, no "grievous crime." Individual rights were being denied. Eventually the whole issue faded into oblivion.

It would be inaccurate to maintain that these protests against the actions of the vicars apostolic and all the protests that were to follow stemmed from the acceptance of a philosophy of natural rights. To some extent the debates of the 1790s were occasioned by the polemical preoccupations of the Catholic Committee and the missionary status of the English clergy. The former would go to almost any lengths to achieve emancipation. At times the committee was excessively antiepiscopal. In their turn, the English clergy were only expressing a justifiable grievance against the system of church government. Since 1753 the English Catholic body had been governed by Benedict XIV's *Apostolicum Ministerium*, which had reaffirmed the direct dependence of the vicars apostolic on Rome. It had not mentioned the appointment of parish priests, nor had it provided any security of tenure for the local priests. It had made no distinction between rector and curate. In short, English priests had no canonical status. In such a situation the Wilkes case was considered by many, as Ward has explained, "as an object-lesson showing the need of reformation in the method of Church government, and was used as an argument in favour of the establishment of ordinary Canon Law and parish priests, who should have all their canonical rights and privileges."[11]

Still, the argument here is that the polemics of the Catholic Committee, the protests of the Staffordshire clergy, and the Wilkes case were representative. Together with the Newcastle Declaration of 1815 they displayed a common intellectual foundation. The same men were involved in all of the debates. What was at issue was the growing awareness among English Catholics of individual liberty. The insistence on the reasonable exercise of authority, the terminology of "conscience" and "natural civil and religious rights," and the appeal to proper juridical process revealed the inner conflict between the acceptance of Lockean political principles and traditional norms governing ecclesiology. For the Cisalpines the difficulty was not the total rejection of church authority but the need to delineate where individual rights ended and ecclesial allegiance (doctrinal and jurisdictional) began. For them, any government, civil or religious, was a limited government. They did not fully state the issue, but its roots were obvious.

The use of Scripture texts also indicates that the Cisalpines were committed to an Enlightenment anthropology. In the 1816 debate "Clericus" defended the typical Cisalpine position by appealing to Romans 12:1: "I exhort you therefore, brethren, by the mercy of God, to present your bodies as a sacrifice, living, holy, pleasing to God—your spiritual service [*rationabile obsequium*]." In contrast John Milner, the leader of the reactionary party, had earlier rested his case on Romans 13:1: "Let everyone be subject to the higher authorities, for there exists no authority except from God, and those who exist have been appointed by God."[12] The difference was significant. Bernard Plongeron has shown that the former text provided the scriptural foundation for the proponents of the Catholic Enlightenment. For example, Jean-Baptise Demangeot, a liberal French priest who was accused of insubordination by his Premonstratensian superiors, explained St. Paul in this way: "Insubordination can never be the language of the *rationabile obsequium* because insubordination is not the language of reason. The *rationabile obsequium* treated with so little respect is the language of St. Paul. It is this holy apostle who, inspired by the Holy Spirit, teaches us in Romans, 12, that our dedication, our obedience, must be that of reasonable beings. The doctrine is unequivocal."[13] The Cisalpine "Clericus" would have agreed. On the other hand, those opposed to the notion of contract and any appeal to natural rights always stressed the divine origin of established authority. Charles Plowden summarized their attitude when he wrote of Joseph Berington: "The worst of Republicans are innovating priests."[14]

John Lingard inherited the Cisalpine tradition with its emphasis on individual human rights. When Lingard published *The Antiquities of the Anglo-Saxon Church* in 1806, John Milner wrote that the book would do great harm. The bishop denounced the work so continuously that Lingard considered giving up his historical investigations. When he asked for advice from Charles Butler, the latter replied in December 1809:

> Setting aside its influence upon Ushaw, I think you may venture to set at defiance the Ecclesiastical artillery. The only precaution to be taken is to forbear from writing any answer to their cavils and to avoid noticing them. This was the rule laid down by Mr. Hume. On this occasion, I have practiced what I am preaching; since the year 1791, there scarcely has passed a year without some publication from Dr. Milner, M. Plowden or some other Gent. of that school, in which my name has not been brought forward, but I have never noticed a single publication of the kind and most certainly never shall. I hope you will summon courage enough to favour us with the much desired continuation of your history. . . .
>
> Permit me to avail myself of this opportunity of requesting your sentiments on a point which, at different times, I have attentively considered particularly when cases like yours have directed my thoughts that way. I conceive that every Roman Catholic is obliged in conscience to the specific belief of every article of faith, which the church has defined, and to a general belief of all the articles of faith, which the church has not defined. But till the church defines a particular article to be of faith, can any individual or any particular description of persons require the assent of an individual to any tenet, or punish his avowed disbelief of it by ecclesiastical censures. This appears to me to be the most important question in the controversy between Catholics and protestants.[15]

In this letter Butler was stating the obvious. As Cisalpines, both he and Lingard experienced a conflict between their own philosophy and the conservative explication of church authority. Their familiarity with Grotius and Pierre Jurieu and their acceptance of the tradition of toleration from Locke to Priestley forced a reevaluation of both civil and ecclesiastical society. Since their definition of authority depended on the integrity of the individual conscience, both men struggled with the relationship between the person and the institution. If the issue was insoluble, the experience of it could hardly be denied. In January 1816 a correspondent asked Lingard if he had seen the Newcastle resolutions: "Assembled as they are for the first time in their lives," he said, "I suppose they thought it necessary to recur to first Principles and to proclaim the spiritual *Rights of Man*."[16] Lingard would have immediately known the deep significance of that first declaration.

In contrast to the uneasy submergence of the natural rights issue, the attempt to apply constitutionalism to ecclesiology caused explicit debate. It formed the second major connection between politics and theology. In *The State and Behaviour of English Catholics* Joseph Berington presented a typically Cisalpine interpretation of the reign of James II: "Bigoted, headstrong and imprudent, he had long, it seems, formed the design of new-modelling the religion of his country." Kings were made for the people, and James had broken the sacred compact. The revolution was justified. In the same pamphlet Berington also contradicted the ultramontane opinion that all jurisdictional power derived from the pope. Berington declared: ". . . each Pastor in his parish, each Bishop in his diocese, each Metropolitan in his province, and each Patriarch in his nation, is possessed of a proper and essential jurisdiction, wholly uncontroulable by, and independent of, the See of Rome."[17] Five years later the leader of the Cisalpines even more explicitly applied the contractual theory of government to the church. The bishop of Rome became the "first ecclesiastical magistrate," the "principal executive power," and "the head of the constitution." Prelates convened in general council were the representatives of the body of the church; the people were "the represented." Berington attached to this "reasoned" exposition of Catholicity *Roman Catholic Principles in Reference to God and Country*. In addition to replacing "king" by "country" in the title, he also referred to the bishops ("pastors") as "body representative," and omitted calling the pope "Vicar of Christ."[18]

In 1790 events presented the Cisalpines with an opportunity to apply practically the basic ideas in Berington's reflections. In that year both the London and Northern vicariates fell vacant. Since the method of appointing bishops had for over a century been almost exclusively resigned into the hands of the Congregation de Propaganda Fide, the London priests and laity felt that by agitating for the election of bishops they would demonstrate to their Protestant fellow countrymen their independence from a foreign power. With this in mind and further motivated by a desire to make Charles Berington vicar apostolic of London, John Throckmorton, one of the lay leaders of the Cisalpines, penned *A Letter Addressed to the Catholic Clergy of England on the Appointment of Bishops*. He argued that the current method of appointing bishops violated the rules of the Christian church and cited the councils of Carthage, Nice, Clermont, and other cases in the early church when the consent of laity and clergy was insisted upon for the proper election of a bishop. Throckmorton maintained that titular bishops had been unknown until the twelfth century; the Roman claim to name or confirm all bishops had extended itself in contradiction to the primitive disciplines. The time had now come to throw off the yoke of foreign pretensions: "Choose for your Bishops the persons who now, by a lamentable abuse, preside over you, in virtue of an authority delegated to them by a foreign Prelate, who has no pretensions to exercise such an act of power. They are Bishops of Sees where they have no faithful, you are bodies of Faithful without Bishops. . . . They are now aliens, you will make them Englishmen; they are dependent, you will make them free; they are foreign emissaries, you will transform them into English Bishops: they must rejoice in the change."[19]

John Milner, Charles Plowden, and Joseph Strickland issued immediate responses to Throckmorton, who answered with *A Second Letter*. He argued that Milner understood "church" to be "an assembly of the faithful from which the people are excluded." Plowden, in his turn, by accepting the premise that current canons determined usage and that one could not appeal to primitive discipline, implied that *"whatever is, is right."* This was absurd. Did the immediate action of the Holy Ghost account for abuses? Lastly, Dr. Strickland, Throckmorton wrote, assumed that the canons requiring the election of bishops had been abrogated. In fact, the growth of papal control had been a response to particular incidents; that abrogation of power never could acquire the status of general regulatory discipline. After countering his opponents in this way, Throckmorton then noted that church government by divine appointment was of "divine origin," but that the pope was not the fountain of ecclesiastical jurisdiction. He concluded with an appeal that the new bishops send letters of communion to Rome but not apply for confirmation.[20]

Milner responded to Throckmorton's second appeal with *The Divine Right of Episcopacy*. This pamphlet summarized most of the objections to Cisalpine aspirations. What he combated, Milner wrote, were the common prejudices of nature, country, and the times. The end of the eighteenth century had seen "unexampled frenzy for religious and political revolutions; nor have means been wanting to communicate irreligious and democratic contagion to our little fold." What Throckmorton proposed, according to Milner, was schismatical; it followed the civil constitution of the clergy, the French National Assembly, and the Church of Utrecht. Only uninformed Englishmen "being accustomed to elect their representatives in parliament, think it reasonable they should have the same right of choosing their ecclesiastical as their lay superiors." In reality, Christ had established his church as a *monarchy mixed with aristocracy:* "That Christ instituted the Church in the form of a republic, and that its visible head is no more than a point of union, without any authority out of his own immediate diocese, are heretical opinions which have been condemned in the persons of M. Ant. de Dominis, Richer, and last of all the turbulent Eybell. . . ." Milner argued that throughout history the people had exercised only a testimonial voice; proper election and appointment had depended on metropolitan and provincial prelates. "All power is from the people" did not apply to the spiritual order. Edmund Burke's *Reflections on the Revolution in France* (1790) indicated that Throckmorton's whole system would bring disaster. Lastly, Milner noted: "The body of pastors form a sort of great tree, of which the Holy See is the trunk."[21]

These twin conceptions of "political ecclesiology" continued to conflict in the years that followed. Berington's *Memoirs of Panzani* spoke of the period during which England was without a resident bishop as a time when "we always had a *church*, incomplete, it is true . . . but ever remaining a society of true believers, governed by a succession of inferior pastors, and holding communion with the centre of unity, the Roman See." Had it not been for the foreign education, Berington continued, the English Catholics would have elected their own bishops. As now conceived, church government was of a feudal nature with a *supremum dominium* in the hands of the pontiff. Four evils plagued government by the vicars apostolic: dependence on the Roman Court, an arbitrary mode of governing (e.g., Wilkes), want of subordination or a metropolitan head, and election without the consent of the clergy.[22]

Charles Plowden responded to these views by claiming that the intentions of Berington's works were always to "beat down papal and episcopal jurisdiction, to villify those who support it, to introduce a new modelled hierarchy."[23] The same line of argument can be seen in a different context, when Berington supported John Sturges's *Reflections on the Principles and Institutions of Popery*,[24] and Milner responded with *Letters to a Prebendary*. After 1800, when the veto question dominated the scene, agitation for the election of bishops ceased to be the focus of attention, but Berington still referred to the pastors as the "body representative" in *The Faith of Catholics*. Milner continued to castigate that conception of the church which intimated that pastors "like civil deputies, derive their power from the people."[25]

John Lingard's attitude to this strand of thought in the Cisalpine tradition was one of subdued approval. He thoroughly accepted political Whiggery and advocated some form of ecclesiastical constitutionalism, but he felt that ecclesiastical constitutionalism would only cause rancor and confusion in the church. This cautious approach stemmed, most likely, from Lingard's general tendency to avoid controversy. Still, when describing the ecclesiastical polity of the Anglo-Saxon period, he stated: "By Theodore the discipline of the Saxon

Church was reduced to a more perfect form. The choice of bishops was served to the national synods, in which the primate presided, and regulated the process of the election. Gradually it devolved to the clergy of each church, whose choice was corroborated by the presence and acclamations of the more respectable among the laity. But the notions of the feudal jurisprudence insensibly undermined the freedom of these elections. . . ."[26] For Lingard, "feudal jurisprudence" included incursions on the freedom of canonical election and the "possession of religious liberties" by both the civil and the ecclesiastical powers. It has already been indicated that he felt this system of law should be abandoned. After emancipation, when the agitation for the restoration of the hierarchy revived, Lingard replied to a London correspondent:

> I feel with you on the subject of your letter, and as heartily disapprove of our present ecclesiastical polity. The bishops dispose of the succession as if they held their offices in fee simple, and had a right to leave them to whom they please.
> But while I admit the abuse, I know not where to discover a remedy which may not prove a worse evil. Should the clergy quarrel with their bishops, the dispute would be carried to Rome, the advice of the jesuits would then be asked and adopted, and we should exchange our present situation for the control of a religious body, which would be more insupportable. It was on this ground that poor Dr. Smith defended the appointment of coadjutors. . . . .
> I have sometimes thought that the only feasible expedient to raising the clergy from their present degraded state would be the erection of a chapter, say of twelve members, in each vicariate, which chapter should exercise jurisdiction vacante episcopatu, and have the right of presenting three names to the choice of the pope, whenever a bishop or coadjustor is to be appointed. This would be a first step of importance: as it would not only produce the benefit for which it would be ostensibly established, but also give existence to an acknowledged authority which on proper occasions might check the irresponsible and unlimited authority of the bishops.[27]

Six years later, in a letter to Monsignor Charles Acton, the English hierarchy's agent in Rome, Lingard reiterated this reluctance to speak on the issue, although he still supported the clergy's insistence on a voice in the election of bishops.[28] The third impress of politics on theology concerned the denial of papal infallibility and the necessity of distinguishing between the essentials and accidentals of faith. Chapter 1 has already detailed the Protestant argument that by accepting the pope's temporal power—in the practical order, his power to depose kings—Catholics professed an allegiance incompatible with British citizenship. To combat this polemic, most of the Catholics separated the temporal and religious spheres and confined the pope's power to the purely spiritual order. They split, however, on the nature of his jurisdiction.

The conservatives, Plowden and Milner, distinguished between papal supremacy and the exercise of an accidental temporal power. Infallibility belonged to the former; the latter was a purely historical reality. In this fashion they met the Protestant polemic by severing their ultramontane ecclesiology from its political roots in the medieval synthesis and by dissociating themselves from some damaging assertions of continental theological conservatism.[29]

The Cisalpines, on the other hand, considered temporal power in the political order to be inseparably linked with infallibility in the theological order. By a strict adherence to the Gallican and English Catholic heritages they showed less originality but more historical consistency than their opponents. For the Cisalpines, the rejection of the temporal power included the admission that in the deposition of Elizabeth I, Pius V had overextended his jurisdiction. But to admit this was to deny what had once been the prevailing opinion that the pope possessed temporal jurisdiction by divine right. In addition, the oath condemned by Paul V in 1606 had been approved with slight variation in 1778; but this oath denounced the deposing doctrine. Therefore, the conclusion could not be avoided that both Pius V and Paul V had erred. As John Throckmorton analyzed it, Catholics were forced to reject infallibility because it had been the foundation of previous false claims.[30] All of the major Cisalpines accepted a similar reasoning.

The denial of the temporal power also raised another theological problem for both parties. Charles Plowden and Milner asserted that previous papal decrees on temporal jurisdiction were merely personal acts, but they never really grappled with the obvious difficulty: How then did one distinguish an article of faith from an opinion, a publicly binding act from a private one? Milner wrote:

> It is true, we admit the Bishop of Rome, in conformity with the opinion of antiquity, to be the head of the Episcopal Order, and his See to be the centre of Catholic union; but let these profound theologians learn, for the first time, that we do not consider the Pope as an absolute Sovereign either in faith or morality. We shall neither submit to his mandates, when they are in opposition to moral rectitude, as we acknowledge they have occasionally been in past ages, when the Spiritual Power has sometimes encroached as much on the Civil, as at others the Civil has on the Spiritual; nor shall we bow to his particular opinions, should they ever prove contrary to the acknowledged faith of the Church.

Yet in arguing with the Cisalpines on theological issues, the same individual extolled the wonder of subordination and the uniformity of doctrine and orthodoxy. To question the slightest point was to deny all.[31]

It was a further indication of the consistency of the Cisalpine position that for them the politically motivated denial of the temporal power became exceptionally vexing in its theological consequences. Charles Butler in a review of Lingard's *Antiquities of the Anglo-Saxon Church* put the matter most clearly when he stated:

> I wish Mr. Lingard would discuss what has always appeared to me the argument against Roman Catholics, which it is the most difficult to repel. When passages asserting the pope's temporal power are quoted from our divines, we answer them by saying that they are the opinions of particular divines, and not Articles of faith; but, if other opinions are advanced, which stand in no better authority than the private opinion of divines, the Authors are often censured and prescribed. This affords room for our adversaries to

say, that we have two creeds; one, which we produce to non catholics, when it serves our turn; and another upon which we act, in respect to those of our own communion.

Lingard himself confronted the same issue when he wrote his pamphlets on emancipation. His solution: If our ancestors were wrong, let them answer for their beliefs.[32]

In summary, politics and theology met in these three areas of natural rights, constitutionalism, and opinions on the temporal power. The result was an excessive concern with and reevaluation of the meaning and structure of church authority. Underlying all three areas was the basic question of the relationship of the individual to society: Where did individual rights (opinions) end and church allegiance (dogma) begin? How did one distinguish between the two spheres? What structure of ecclesiology could best handle the issue? The argument presented here is that the Cisalpines experienced these difficulties within the context of an individualistic anthropology. The major thinkers, Joseph Berington, Charles Butler, and John Lingard, were complete Whigs molded in the tradition of freedom of conscience, limited government, and separation of church and state. These political views could hardly have remained isolated from theological reflections; the opinions of Milner and Plowden testified to that. But this is not to say that the Lockean tradition was the only stream contributing to the crisis of authority. The complexity of the situation revealed itself in the theological charges hurled at the Cisalpines.

The accusation of Jansenism remained a constant element in the confrontation between the Cisalpines and their opponents. What, exactly, the term meant is difficult to determine. Each of the opponents gave his own definition. Charles Plowden compared Throckmorton's advocacy of the election of bishops to the activities of the Synod of Pistoia and the Church of Utrecht. In his mind the Cisalpines were archenemies of Catholic unity. They discredited popular piety, vilified the authority of the church, and delighted in papal scandal. Thirty years later Plowden equated Jansenism with opposition to the Jesuits.³³ His brother, Francis Plowden, gave the term an even wider significance. To him it meant any manifestation of insubordination.³⁴ On the other hand, John Milner wrote simply that "Beringtonianism" flowed from "Jansenism." Both movements denied the divine authority of the Holy See. They asserted a usurped and schismatical jurisdiction by adopting a republican system of church government. They submitted propositions subversive of lawful authority, advocated reform, and denied the sanctity and inerrancy of the church.³⁵ Lastly, William Eusebius Andrews penned a long article entitled "Jansenism in England" in an 1820 issue of the *Orthodox Journal*. He argued that the term implied semi-Protestantism. It had produced Jacobinism in France. In England, the Catholic Committee, the Cisalpine Club, and the supporters of the veto represented the same tendency. To Andrews the connections were obvious: origination in a cabal, outward show of piety, removal of the decisions of the Holy See by equivocation, alignment with ministers and Protestants, opposition to the Jesuits, and "attempts to lead the people into a disbelief of the divine existence of religion, and lessen that attachment to authority so essential to the happiness of all states."³⁶

These thinkers correctly recognized the mixture of Gallican-Jansenist ideas that permeated the mentality of the Cisalpines and contributed to their bouts with church authority. By the middle of the eighteenth century, continental religious thought had begun to combine the democratic ideas of Edmund Richer, the Gallicanism of the Parisian school, and the second phase of Jansenist reflection represented by Pasquier Quesnel. The Cisalpines mirrored this evolution by appealing to such Jansenist works as Van Espen's *Jus Ecclesiasticum*, Ludovico Muratori's *De Moderatione Ingeniorum* (1714), and the standard Gallican treatises by Fleury, Bossuet, and Alexander.³⁷ Many of the Cisalpine proposals resembled Jansenist ideas. The recognition of a *rationabile obsequium* and emphasis on conscience, reason, law, and right definitely reflected Antoine Arnauld's attempts to distinguish tyranny from the just exercise of authority.³⁸ One of the propositions in the *Third Blue Book* began: "Inasmuch as the only spiritual authority which I acknowledge is that which I conscientiously believe to have been transmitted by Jesus Christ to his church not to regulate by any outward coaction civil and temporal concerns of subjects and citizens, but to direct souls by persuasion in the concerns of eternal salvation. . . ." This proposition corresponded very closely to the Synod of Pistoia's rejection of "the exaction by force of what depends on persuasion and the heart." Such a view was condemned in Pius VI's *Auctorem Fidei*. Joseph Berington recognized the similarity between his democratic ideas of the church and those of Scipio Ricci, the Jansenist bishop of Pistoia.[39] Other parallels have already been noted.

Thus it cannot be denied that eighteenth-century Jansenism, as it has been traditionally conceived, had some impact on the Cisalpines. But it was a mistake completely to identify, as did the reactionaries, the Cisalpine reevaluation of authority with the Church of Utrecht, the reform of Scipio Ricci, or the state-oriented programs of Febronian Josephinism. Recent scholarship has tended to accentuate the differences between the continental movements. The movements united in a certain nonconformism, a combination of negative attitudes, a "para-Jansenism," but they also diverged in other areas and in emphases. Many of the reforms that were advocated had a positive basis. In relation to the Cisalpines, it should be recalled that Utrecht *was* schismatic. The vast majority of English Catholics could not contemplate such a drastic action. Joseph Berington himself abandoned it. Second, Van Espen and von Hontheim (Febronius) accorded the pope a preeminence of honour, but not a right of jurisdiction. Febronius lodged the power of the keys in all the faithful. The Cisalpines, as will be shown in Chapter 3, were dominated by the Gallican tradition of Bossuet. Their view was vastly different from that of the proponents of the *nova disciplina*. Third, and most important, Scipio Ricci's reform and Josephinism were allied with state absolutism. The Cisalpine acceptance of constitutionalism and separation of church and state definitely dissociated them from this brand of renewal.[40]

English scholarship has tended to confine the ecclesiological program of the Cisalpines to the level of pragmatic politics and to attribute their more theological reflections to schismatic tendencies.[41] The purpose here is not to dismiss this view but certainly to correct it. Bernard Plongeron has traced the influence of politics on continental ecclesiology in his *Théologie et politique au siècle des lumières*. He argues that the "Gallicanization of the Thomist tradition" (i.e., the loss of the theory of justified tyrannicide under pressure from royal absolutism) and the abhorrence of any contractual political scheme because of its associations with the *philosophes* led to the development of an ecclesiological "morale of power." In the eighteenth century basic social structures and the method of church government became hopelessly divided. The ultimate result was seen in the inability of theologians to grapple with the impact of secularization and revolutionary ideology.[42]

It is in the light of this trend that the origins of the English crisis of authority becomes even more apparent. Since the Cisalpines accepted the constitutional settlement of 1688, they had an allegiance to a contractual theory of government. Because of their Lockean political commitment, they were able to overcome the very forces that had blocked the progress of Catholic thought on the Continent. They could avoid both the problem of the morale of power and any damaging alliance with the state. Berington, Butler, and Lingard were thus in a position to accept the heritages of Gallican conciliarism and Jansenist individualism and still try to formulate a Catholic theology that was integral with their culture. In this unique way the Cisalpine movement was not the English equivalent of Utrecht, or Pistoia, or Febronianism or Gallicanism or Jansenism. It was a subtle combination of the tendencies of all of these movements *plus* the central experience of the English political tradition. The problem of authority arose, then, because of the Cisalpines' attempts to synthesize Catholicism with an Enlightenment anthropology. This cultural view of the difficulty is further supported by an examination of their opinion on the relationship between reason and faith.

Reason and Faith

In addition to the relationship between politics and ecclesiology, the debates surrounding the Newcastle Declaration indicated a second and more intellectual area of tension underlying the crisis of authority. When the Declaration proclaimed the "right of every individual, in every age and in every country, to judge of the reasonableness of his belief," it waved the specter of private judgment before the always sensitive antennae of the conservatives. John Milner wrote that no one could judge of the reasonableness of his belief but was to believe on the authority of the Catholic Church; to do otherwise meant the acceptance of the Protestant rule of faith.[43] Generally his party maintained that "reasonableness" applied only to the motives of credibility for the acceptance of the church and not to specific articles of faith. The latter were "mysteries" and so, by definition, beyond reason. Furthermore, once proposed, they should be accepted. A Catholic could not question whether or not the church taught him the truth. All those opposed to the Cisalpines concurred that the ambiguous wording of the first resolution indicated the heterodox intentions of its framers.

"Clericus" presented the typical view of the Cisalpines. He accepted the reactionary position on "mystery" and motives of credibility. There were truths above reason to which a person assented on the authority of the church. He also agreed that "the problem, above all others, was to prove the divine authority of an established institution."[44] But "Clericus" departed from his opponents in his view of the application of reason as a critical faculty of the mind to the integrity of the church's statements of belief. The Cisalpine rested his analysis on three rules: (1) One fundamental principle of faith is this truth of natural reason: *all that God has revealed is true.* (2) The discernment of faith is that act of understanding by which we judge that God has revealed this or that particular doctrine. (3) The conclusion of faith is the assent we give to this doctrine. The heart of the argument was the second rule. For "Clericus" and the Cisalpines, the difficulty was not only *if* the church spoke the truth but *how* one knew *when* the Church spoke the truth. The problem was similar to that which had arisen over the issue of infallibility: How did one distinguish an opinion from an article of faith? Once again, the impact of an Enlightenment anthropology on Cisalpine thought was evident. The breakdown of the communal tradition and the rise of individualism dictated the framework of the discussion. In its historical context, the first Newcastle resolution represented the Cisalpine response to the problems posed by the evolution of English Protestant thought from William Chillingworth to Joseph Priestley.

Lingard, in agreement with the other Cisalpines, considered private judgment, the ultimate foundation of all latitudinarianism, to be the logical consequence of the position of the Reformation. He argued that in the sixteenth century the principle had been accepted that every Bible reader formed a creed of his own. Eventually Socinians, Methodists, Evangelicals, and Deists had united in this principle. According to Lingard the Separatists had only recalled the corrupt theory of Faustus Socinus, who believed that no one was bound to accept as an article of faith any doctrine contained in Scripture which was not so clearly expressed that every man, woman, and child, with the use of reason could immediately perceive it. The Deists, in their turn, had appealed to Socinian tenets by maintaining the necessity of the greatest possible perspicacity in the mode of announcing doctrines. Therefore, Lingard concluded, although the theological opinions of the Calvinists and Methodists were directly opposed to the Socinians, yet their general creeds were the same. He wrote: "*In medio stat veritas* . . . and every deviation from it, whatever it may be at first, leads in the end to the same pernicious consequences."[45]

This analysis of the history of Protestant thought indicated to Lingard the absurdity of supposing that "any one of us (experto credite) is capable of unravelling, without any other aid than his own exertions, the great truths contained in the Scriptures, or reconciling the apparently discordant texts of that sacred volume, and of arranging all the parts of the beautiful edifice of Revelation." The authority of human reason was clearly not that great. In truth, Lingard believed, no middle position existed between church authority and private judgment:

> Either the right of private judgment must be recognized, and thus the reins be left loose to all descriptions of innovators, and full leave granted for proposing all sorts of new opinions and forming innumerable sects, when must follow the total ruin of Christianity; or if church authority in matters of faith is to upheld [sic], it must be exercised in conjunction with the great visible Catholic Church, whereas such an authority must, as I have often stated, be of divine origin, and cannot be claimed by any congregation, which has separated from the Catholic unity, and which has resisted, and continues to resist, that authority.[46]

The Cisalpines lived within the context of this history of the "Protestant idea" that Lingard outlined. They were well aware of the difficulties confronting the doctrinal position of the Church of England. They recognized the problems posed by the thorny triad of reason, Scripture, and tradition. As Catholics, they knew they could not accept the principle of private judgment. Yet they themselves were also affected by the cultural milieu that had determined the evolution of Protestant thought: the rise of the new science, the assault on Aristotle, and the philosophy of the Age of Reason. The effects of these movements were especially evident in the Cisalpines' skepticism toward the miraculous, their antischolasticism, and their nationalistic attempts to find a religious code common to all Christians.[47] The impact of the "Protestant idea" on Catholic thought could be seen in the Cisalpine appeals to Francis Veron's *Rule of Catholic Faith* (1660), Henry Holden's *Analysis of Divine Faith* (1658), and Edward Hawarden's *Rule of Faith Truly Stated* (1721). It is to these works that the historian must turn in order to understand both the intellectual reasons for the Cisalpine crisis of authority and the foundation of the attempt to distinguish between private judgment and reasonable submission.

In the preface to his catechism, the seventeenth-century

French theologian Francis Veron wrote: "What can be more sutable [sic] to reason, than onely to propose, in matters of Faith, what is necessary." To approach the problem of ecumenical relations in a "reasonable" way he thus eliminated from his *Rule of Catholic Faith* inventions, historical errors, particular practices, scholastic disputes, propositions extracted from Scripture but diversely interpreted by the Fathers, decrees not addressed to the universal church, and the constitutions of provincial councils. Veron proposed as the only content of Catholic faith "divine revelation delivered to the prophets and apostles, proposed by the Catholicque Church in her general councils, or by her universal practice, to be believed as an article of Catholicque faith."[48] By following such a method this obscure ex-Jesuit became one of the first to grasp the idea of separating the teaching of the church from the theological additions and opinions of the schools. The approach was adopted and popularized by an English recusant theologian in Paris, Henry Holden, in his *Divinae fidei analysis*. He wrote: "Yea, and that which doth much more divert some hereticks from the Catholick truth, is, that they are bound to maintain under pain of excommunication, or of being ejected out of the Catholick communion, some small abuses in things belonging to Religion, which are crept into the Church, through the carelessness of Bishops, and negligence of Pastours; or perhaps through the ignorance or interest of some inferiour Priests and Ministers."[49]

Holden's work, translated into English in 1658, became very influential in Cisalpine circles, especially in its analysis of the act of faith. This recusant theologian defined natural belief as "an assent of the understanding, which we give to anything that is told us, grounded upon the testimony or authority of him who tells it." He noted that the certainty of natural faith was taken from the testimony of the reporter and that "every assent of faith must necessarily have more or lesse certainty in it, by how-much the reporter's authority doth appear to the mind or judgment of the hearers, to be of more or lesse weight and credit." Natural certainty consisted only in the judgment of the mind. When Holden applied these same principles to divine belief, he discovered that since the assent of faith was an act of the understanding, the certainty of the assent was grounded in the reliability of the means of transmission. According to Holden, this means needed to be so evident to our external senses that it would be impossible for any Christian to be ignorant of its being or existing. It had to be able of its own nature to beget a true and most rational certainty in all men who shall come to the knowledge of it. After mentioning four types of Christian truths, Holden then followed Veron in stating the two principles necessary for a Christian truth to be an article of faith: It was necessary that "the thing it self be revealed by God Almighty, and that it be received and acknowledged for revealed, by the whole Church" and "that it have descended by universal tradition, with an undiscontinued succession from age to age, and thus delivered to the whole church, as a thing or doctrine revealed."[50]

Approximately seventy years after Holden, Edward Hawarden, the leading Catholic polemicist of his day, wrote some reflections on the nature and resolution of faith designed to meet the polemics of William Chillingworth and Edward Stillingfleet.[51] The latter had accused the Catholics of proving Scripture by the church and the church by Scripture. Hawarden attempted to break the circle by affirming that "the truth of Christianity is measured by the *Testimony* of God only, but its *Reasonableness* is built on *Rational proofs and Evidences*, by which that Testimony is applied." It was hardly accidental that Hawarden, in his preface, noted the rise of "levelling" and irreligion and the influence of mathematics on theological reflection. He stated the following propositions as acceptable: (1) No one can be obliged to act unreasonably. (2) The obligation of acting reasonably regards the first and main springs of religious worship, as owning a revealed religion, believing the Scripture, embracing Christianity, adhering to a certain rule of faith, joining in communion with a determinate society of Christians and the like. (3) No authority is to be obeyed against evidence. (4) It belongs to everyone who submits to others to judge of the reasonableness of his submission. (5) The right of all mankind to a free and private judgment in matters of religion is not inconsistent with the authority of infallible guides. (6) Every assent of divine faith is free, rational, and supernatural. (7) Every assent of divine faith relies only on the revelation or testimony of God, as on its proper and essential motive. (8) Every assent is immediately and finally resolved into the testimony of God, as into its only motive and also resolved into the proofs (inducements) as into a necessary condition of the reasonableness of it.[52]

Hawarden, Holden, and Veron became the three major sources for the Cisalpine thinking on the relationship of reason to faith. Veron's distinction between the accidental and the necessary, Holden's placing of certainty in the faculty of the mind and his subsequent emphasis on the means of transmission of doctrine, and Hawarden's prolegomenon of reason signified definite shifts from the medieval Catholic position. Each of these men reflected a growing awareness of pluralism, individualism, and rationalism. In ancient theology (medieval and classical) the relationship of reason to faith had been viewed in objective terms as the relationship between two systems of knowledge; credibility (and certainty) was the property of the object of belief. Also, this theology had not concerned itself with how a man came to faith. With the advent of the Renaissance and the Reformation this "objectivist" view began to be replaced by considerations on the psychological and epistemological problems underlying religious knowledge. The opposition of reason to faith now proceeded from the difficulty of reconciling two attitudes within individual consciousness: a spirit dominated by the principles of autonomous reason, methodic doubt, and mathematical precision, and a spirit dominated by submission and the recognition that knowledge was perhaps a function of moral disposition. The modern problem became how one could really be assured that any given mediary spoke in the name of God. This change in perspective represented the evolution from a communitarian to an individualistic point of view. When the common milieu no longer universally conveyed the most vital truths, the problem of the act of faith passed from the social to the personal plane. For the Cisalpines, Veron, Holden, and Hawarden thus represented the Catholic obverse of Luther, Socinus, and Chillingworth.[53] The shift to the psychological and epistemological analysis of faith placed a burden on the question of authority. How did one differentiate the accidental from the essential? If individual certainty depended on the reliability of the means of transmission, what were the criteria of reliability by which one judged the church's faith to be consistent? Lastly, if "no one could be obliged to act unreasonably," at which point did the individual judge it "reasonable" to submit to the church's teaching authority? Here, as in the sphere of politics and ecclesiology, the Cisalpines manifested a consistency that only heightened the excruciating difficulties of the situation. In the 1816 Newcastle debate, one party was perfectly willing to allow reason to judge the existence of the Catholic Church as the only true infallible guide, but once there, it refrained from further questioning. The Cisalpines also recognized that ultimately there was no position between private judgment and church authority, but they pushed the issue of the individual's relationship to institutional magisterium to its limit. It was significant that both sides appealed to Hawarden but differed in their interpretations of him. The difference rested on the extent to which they accepted or rejected an Enlightenment anthropology. On the one side, the result was the formulation of the highly ambiguous Newcastle Declaration; on the other, reaction to the possibility of private judgment. Throughout the debate the issue of the final rule of faith, its nature and extent, remained menacingly in the background.

Social Accommodation

There was a third major element that contributed to the Cisalpine evaluation of ecclesiastical authority. The heads of the leading families met at Newcastle for the obvious apologetic purpose of dissociating the English Catholics from the reportedly intolerant actions of their French counterparts. Their resolutions emphasized Catholic support of religious liberty and opposition to all persecution. In the *Orthodox*

Journal debate that followed, "Clericus" mentioned that the Catholic cause suffered because Protestants constantly misrepresented the Roman creed, making it stricter and more intolerant than it actually was. To correct this view, he felt that they should read John Gother's *Papist Misrepresented and Represented* (1665), Bossuet's *Exposition*, and the *Essay on Catholic Communion*. The response to the Cisalpine approach embodied itself in the simple query: Which is more important, a love of conciliation or a spirit of obedience to church authority?[54] This clash between two mentalities indicates that underneath the disagreements in politics and theology individuals differed over the attitude a Roman Catholic should take in the world of religious pluralism.

There was little doubt that most Catholics experienced the various pressures latent in demographic growth and the changing social structure. For some, the economics of religious pluralism necessitated a change in church policy. They moved freely in and out of Protestant social circles and clubs and believed firmly in the necessity of adapting certain Catholic practices. A good example of their attitude was found in a letter written in 1814 by some of the leading laymen to the vicars apostolic and through them to the prefect of Propaganda at Rome:

> It is, we are persuaded, my Lord, quite unnecessary to state the great difference which exists in the difficulties of putting into practice these Regulations between this Country & various other countries of Europe.—Living as we daily do in intercourse with our Protestant citizens, employed as the great bulk of the Catholic Manufacturers are by Protestant Capitalists, engaged as many Catholics are in the pursuits of Agriculture Mining & Commerce, where they are daily and hourly intermixed with their Protestant neighbours & from which their presence cannot without the greatest difficulties to their families & their masters be dispensed with, difficulties so great & so multiplying from the high price of labour, the increased application of machinery & the constant & daily intercourse between persons of different religions, as to render some of these regulations to be little observed, we beg leave to request your Lordship to lay before His Holiness Pope

Pius VII, in whose restoration to the Capital of the Christian World, we sincerely rejoice, our wishes that some of these regulations, rendered so difficult of observance, as in many instances not to be observ'd, may be dispensed with. . . .[55]

The letter appealed for the relaxation of the abstinence laws for the Saturdays and Wednesdays of Advent, Wednesdays in Ember Weeks, rogation days, and the vigils of Sts. Peter and Paul, the Assumption, and All Saints. "Many of the other days," it was said, "are so difficult of observance particularly the Saturdays & Wednesdays, arising from the circumstances of their being the general market days thro'out Great Britain & the custom universally prevailing of Farmers attending Markets & dining at ordinarius with their protestant fellow farmers, as to be nearly disregarded." Among others, Humphrey Weld, Hugh C. Clifford, Charles Standish, Charles Hornyold, R. Gage Rokewode, John Throckmorton, and George Silvertop signed the petition.

In addition to economic realities, other problems signified some type of Catholic opening to the Protestant world. In an 1803 report to Propaganda the vicar apostolic of the Western District, William Sharrock, noted the increase in mixed marriages, the deaths and apostasies in the noble Catholic families, the decrease of attendance at the sacraments, and the general relaxation of barriers between Catholics and Protestants. John Milner agreed and pointed to theater-going and a general tendency to rationalize certain beliefs. In 1807 Luke Concanen, O.P., informed Milner of another pressing question: Could Catholic servants attend private prayers and readings on Sunday evenings in the homes of Protestants? By reciting Anglican liturgical formulas before and after mass and in the place of vespers some priests also reflected a growing awareness of this breakdown of social barriers. John Kirk summarized a widespread mentality of the period when he told Vicar Apostolic Poynter in 1823: "I have discovered on the occasion of the opening of my organ that a general idea prevailed here, that I did not want Protestants to come to Chapel; for which reason I invited the principal families, & tradesmen, either by letter or in person."[56] John Lingard and

Joseph Berington, through their friendship with Protestants and their openness to the general movements in society, expressed similar feelings. Clearly, there was economic and social emancipation before 1829. As a result, questions about the church's role in the world and the relationships between Catholics and Protestants came to the surface.

It should be acknowledged that these instances of social mixing did not overshadow the Catholic experience of intolerance. Chapter 1 has already detailed the struggle for emancipation and the cries that accompanied it. The Protestant polemicists constantly reminded Catholics of the "pernicious social consequences" of their principles of image worship, indulgences, and confession. Joseph Berington's first attempts at theologizing occurred as a result of the Gordon Riots. The impress of social persecution manifested itself in almost all of the writings of the 1790s. John Lingard's writings, as has been noted, were penned within the context of a minority consciousness. Although the 1806 election was the last in which the electorate responded to cries of "no popery," Charles Butler could write as late as 1817: "It is certain that there has not been during these last 30 years such a Spirit of hostility to the Catholics as there is at present: It behoves us evidently to be very prudent, not to obtrude any thing unnecessarily on the public which gives offence, and to avoid all asperity of language, in our writings."[57] Thus it is evident that both positive and negative social realities contributed to a basic upheaval in English Catholic life. The central issues were the extent of accommodation and the function of authority in it.

In response to the various questions raised by religious pluralism, the Cisalpines accepted the motto: *In necessariis unitas, in dubiis libertas, in omnibus charitas.* Supported by their individualistic anthropology and reflecting the impact of rationalism on their faith, they stressed theological adaptation to the environment. Berington, Butler, and Lingard adopted catechisms framed within the context of ecumenical relations and designed to minimize the differences between Catholics and Protestants. Fasting and saints's devotions were generally deemphasized; freedom of opinion was encouraged. Joseph Berington's *Reflections Addressed to Hawkins* and *Essay on the Depravity of the Nation*, despite their excesses, betrayed the awareness of an already emancipated Catholic. In December 1809 Charles Butler summarized the basic Cisalpine attitude in a letter to John Lingard: "Perhaps no Persons now do the cause of religion more harm than those who attempt to contract the pale of orthodoxy. The general spirit of the times urges all to a great latitude of belief; every attempt to repress it entirely and to keep belief within the limits, which were supposed to be impassible at the beginning of the last century, must be fruitless. A wise man will not attempt it, but will be satisfied with confining them within the boundary that the faith of Christ has assigned."[58] It was in the context of such a view that Butler's *Confessions of Faith* and Berington's and Kirk's *Faith of Catholics* were composed.

John Lingard himself reflected well the contribution of both an awareness of ecumenical relations and a consciousness of prejudice. In his *Antiquities of the Anglo-Saxon Church* he noted with approval the lenient policy toward Saxon converts and early attempts to retain national customs. In 1809 he concluded his introduction to *The Protestant Apology* with a plea for ecclesiastical reconciliation. The epithet he wished for his tomb was: Here lies an advocate for the union of Christians. In an 1813 preface to some tracts on emancipation he expressed agreement with the bishop of Durham's hopes that the English and Roman Catholic churches would be united. Such positive motivation perdured even when the concrete reaction was caused by Protestant intolerance. Lingard summarized his general approach when he wrote to a clergyman of the diocese of Durham: "The clergyman objects to pilgrimages, and rosaries or beads. As to the first, they may be of advantage or disadvantage, according to circumstances. They form no part of the Catholic doctrine: they may be made or not, as may be judged proper. . . . Rosaries are also a matter of discretionary devotion." He appealed to a similar type of reasoning when polemicists fought Catholic emancipation on the grounds of indulgences, Latin in religious services, suppression of the second commandment, communion under one kind, the refusal to allow the laity to read the Bible, and the relationship between the invocation of saints and the mediatorship of Christ. In all cases Lingard sought to differentiate essentials from accidentals. He hoped to counteract arguments against emancipation, make the faith more enlightened, and advocate the reunion of Christians. Whatever the motive, the result was accommodation to the situation.[59]

In contrast, the opponents of the Cisalpines rejected any type of social and theological rapprochement. Milner's reports to Propaganda constantly reiterated what he considered the excesses of the Cisalpine position. In a document of 1803 the vicar apostolic argued that the Cisalpines spoke constantly of purifying religion and destroying superstition. Even the doctrines and judgments of the Holy See were opposed, he wrote, "under the pretext that they were not infallible." Milner considered opinions about the Holy See, indulgences, devotions to the Blessed Virgin and Sacred Heart, and holy water, to be dogmatic questions. He noted that certain ascetic practices—mortification and abstinence, for example—were said to be "impure, not conformed to the teachings of the Holy Fathers." In 1806 Milner published a pamphlet on a miraculous cure, which prompted one person to remark to Poynter: "Lord Hawkesbury has now a pretty document to verify his assertion that of all Christian Sects the Catholic is the most superstitious." All but a few of the Midland pastor's apologetic works possessed a strident tone. His attitude toward ecclesiastical democracy has already been noted, and his opposition to liberalization remained constant throughout his life.[60]

Francis Plowden exhibited a similar state of mind. In response to Butler's *Formularies, Confessions of Faith, or Symbolic Books* he wrote the following to Thomas Stonor's sister:

> That Mr. Butler goes too far in attempting to persuade the Protestants of the facility of an union of the Churches—that

the failure of the negotiation for that desirable purpose between Bossuet, Leibnitz, and Molinus was the most fatal precedent he could have given of its impracticability. That he is not sufficiently explicit and firm in exhibiting to the Protestants the inexorable impossibility of the Church of Christ's relaxing or waving [sic] any part of its doctrine government or essential discipline. . . . I frankly own that in my opinion he does not press enough upon the grounds of difference and generally is too much upon the accordance of the two churches. . . . It will ever be eternally true that no Union can be formed but by the Protestant becoming wholly Catholic. For the true Catholic never can become partially protestant. . . .

Robert Plowden reflected the same approach when he urged Catholic publishers to use only the Douai version of Scripture in works of piety. Thus they would avoid many errors. Among the priests, many complained about the attitude of indifference and stressed the need to emphasize that a man could *not* be saved in any religion. The Reverend J. Corbishley graphically exemplified the reactionary position in a letter to the president of the English College, Lisbon: "There is an old Hermit belongs to this Cong.on [Ormskirk] called Robert Swarbrick, who is a wise old Man. He tells me he has known this Cong.on for 70 years, and never saw a good Priest here, during the whole time!!! Women, and Wine, he says, does a great deal of harm, amongst them &c. *May we be duly aware of these rocks*!!!!! He says, moreover, that he has scarcely known a good Priest anywhere, except Dennett. The Oaths for Liberty &c has brought great Connexions about between Priests & Parsons, and Protestants in general. *Who Eat and Drink together: May we carefully avoid these Rocks also.*" For all of these men, accommodation was either anathema or too dangerous to attempt.[61]

These opinions on Catholic life in a Protestant world bore witness to the crisis of authority that necessarily accompanied social emergence. Practical emancipation forced a reevaluation of three centuries of persecuted existence, which, in turn, implied a definite stance toward the traditional "culture of Catholicism," the status quo, the symbol of authority. John Lee, a Cisalpine in the London District, described the situation very clearly:

> Catholics taken as a body are an odd set of people. I fancy I see you stare at this expression; but when we consider that "in dubiis" catholics are at liberty—& that this liberty is made use of in extolling, condemning, criticising what we please, opposing & supporting "opinions" with as much warmth as if "essentials were concerned, striving to get the last word tho' the last word bring nothing with it—when we consider the great want of that public spirit in the body which is visible among Sectaries who readily come forward to support what is represented to be beneficial to their cause—I think you will agree with me that the apathy of catholics is unaccountable & that their liberty "in dubiis" is seldom employed to a useful end.[62]

The problem was: What exactly did *in dubiis* mean? How did one distinguish a theological tradition from an article of faith? Who defined what was necessary?

In forcing the question of accommodation, social realities thus joined with political and intellectual trends to pose the central issue of the rule of faith. As a result, both the Cisalpines and their opponents lived in a state of upheaval. The latter reacted by affirming the necessity of obedience, the former by searching for an acceptable way to differentiate faith from opinion. It is my contention that the mark which distinguished the two mentalities was one of the consistency with which they tried to combine faith and culture. Thus the reactionaries could accept the reality of English constitutionalism but refrained from attempting any theoretical application of it to ecclesiology. They also advocated reason as a prolegomenon to faith in the church but denied the necessity, except in the case of the temporal power, of criteria for the exercise of that authority. Finally, they lived in the midst of pluralism but generally reacted against its leveling forces. In contrast, the Cisalpines, in all three areas, pushed the spheres of faith and culture toward integration. They presupposed the fact that such a combination was both possible

The Crisis of Church Authority

and necessary. They remained Catholic but still accepted the ideas of the English Enlightenment as represented by John Locke. Some attempts by the Cisalpines to reflect theologically within this cultural perspective, their conscious efforts to analyze the ultimate rule of faith, will constitute the substance of what is to follow.

3. a cisalpine Rule of faith

THE THEOLOGICAL reflection of Lingard, Berington, and Butler took place within the context of the development of Catholic thought since the sixteenth century. On April 8, 1546, the Council of Trent issued its decree *De Canonicis Scripturis*. In response to the Protestant declaration of *sola scriptura* the council affirmed that Jesus Christ was the one source of revelation. The word pronounced by Christ at first spread in an exclusively oral way; it was a living word, the vehicle of the power of the Holy Spirit. After the time of the Apostles, the content of this revelation was communicated by traditions deriving from apostolic teaching and by writing. Trent made no distinction between apostolic traditions and ecclesiastical usages and avoided the presentation of Scripture and tradition as two parallel and distinct sources of revelation. At the heart of the Christian religion, it affirmed, lay the Gospel "kept in the Catholic Church in a continuous succession."

During the polemics of the Counter Reformation this emphasis on the mutual inherence of Holy Writ and Holy Church bifurcated into a dualism that opposed Scripture (written word) to church (custodian of unwritten tradition). On the Roman Catholic side the writings of Melchior Cano, Peter Canisius, Robert Bellarmine, and Thomas Stapelton tended to promote a theology of *partim . . . partim*; tradition became a separate source of revelation, the direct opposite of the reformer's sole rule of Scripture. This tendency was further encouraged when the Creed of Pius IV (November 13, 1564) affirmed the existence, on a level with Scripture, of "apostolic and ecclesiastical traditions." In this fashion "tradition" came to refer to truths and practices not contained in Scripture.

With the change in the juridical theory of law from the Germanic communal viewpoint to the Roman voluntaristic one, this splitting of the organic unity of written word and oral witness had important ecclesiological parallels. If apostolic and ecclesiastical traditions were separate sources of revelation, who determined their binding force, their revelatory status? The ultramontanes, with their ecclesiological emphasis on hierarchy, tended to confine the determination of this "source of revelation" to the living magisterium, i.e., active tradition. In their synthesis the magisterium was usually equated with the pope himself. The Gallicans, on the other hand, reacted to the Roman tendency by affirming a documentary and fixed notion of tradition (i.e., objective tradition, the first five centuries of the church) and by asserting the superiority of general council to pope. In both cases, there was overreaction. The rule of faith began to be identified not with the living content of the faith received by the church but with the transmitting organism, the action, present or past, of the teaching authority.[1]

The Cisalpine crisis in authority reflected this tension involved in the dualistic approach to Scripture and tradition and in the movement from an objective magisterium (the unanimous interpretation of the content of faith received by the Church at its origin) to a magisterium of authority. The theological focal points of the evolution were the relationship of Scripture to tradition and the idea of the church.

Scripture and Tradition

It has already been noted that in response to the forces of individualism, rationalism, and pluralism, the Cisalpines searched for a rule of faith that would sharply distinguish between the accidental and essential elements in Roman Catholicism. To support their view they adopted as the rule of faith the principle of Francis Veron: All that and only that is of divine faith, which is revealed in the word of

God and proposed to all by the Catholic Church to be believed with divine faith. This principle enabled them to confine their defense and presentation of Catholic doctrine to the absolutely essential elements of the faith. For example, John Lingard could reject the personal infallibility of the pope as "no part of Catholic doctrine" and dismiss Latin in the liturgy and communion under one kind as matters of "changeable discipline and expediency." On the issue of the pope's deposing power, he could write that ". . . the books written by some madmen or knaves in favour of it have been publicly burned in Catholic countries, and the authors of them severely punished in case of their having persisted in asserting it. If some Popes, in the phrenzy of tumultuous times, and in the exercise of powers not their own, went beyond the prerogative of the see of Rome, what had their proceedings to do with the doctrine of the Catholic church?" Clearly, Veron's *regula* had its advantage. It was also supported by Berington in his edition of *The Faith of Catholics*.[2] What exactly did it mean?

As analyzed by Berington and Lingard, an article of faith first of all had to be revealed in the word of God. Revelation did not mean Scripture or unwritten tradition in the dualistic sense but more precisely "that which our Saviour taught, and his apostles delivered, before the Sacred Books of the New Testament had any existence."[3] For the Cisalpines, Jesus Christ was the fountain of every Christian truth. As Lingard put it: "Catholics, though they admit both scripture and tradition, do not consider them as independent sources of doctrine. They revere them both indeed, because both emanate from the same Holy Spirit."[4]

If Jesus was the source of revelation, the leading rule of Christianity was the commission to preach and to teach, to receive and to deliver, which Christ gave to his church, "the witness and the keeper."[5] Joseph Berington wrote to John Kirk in reference to the introduction to *The Faith of Catholics*: "[I have doubts] not that I am not sufficiently Catholic but that I am too much so. Our writers generally state, that we have two rules of faith, *Scripture* and *Tradition*, the first where the articles of belief are fully expressed, as in the *Eucharist*, the second, where the expression is not full, as in the points of *Purgatory* or the *Invocation* of the Saints. This looks like a shift, as if we shall not adopt Tradition for a rule, if we could do without it."[6] Therefore, the one rule of teaching was the basis of the authority of the church. Had the Scriptures never been written, the faith would have been the same. When the Apostles died, it was necessary to show that what they delivered, they had received. Only then did people appeal to Scripture (the written word) and tradition (the unwritten word). The former attested to the conformity of doctrine with the word of Christ; the latter provided the sense of Scripture and witnessed to the fact that the doctrine was both received and delivered. Still later, other witnesses (the Fathers, councils, canons, etc.) provided further collaboration. Most important, all of them testified to the one rule.[7]

At times, this rule of teaching was referred to as the authority of the unwritten word. This commission from Christ, safeguarded by the Holy Spirit, perdured. It accounted for the validity of the inspiration of Scripture and of those doctrines, such as infant baptism, Sunday observance, purgatory, and the invocation of saints, which found little or no support in the written word. All received justification inasmuch as they referred to the original source. In summary, the Catholic principle was that "of a teaching authority, resting on the commission given by our Saviour to his apostles, and the concomitant promise of perpetual assistance."[8]

It is important to recognize that Lingard's and Berington's approach contained an inherent ambiguity. When they spoke of "written word" and "unwritten word," they appeared to be opening themselves to the dualistic interpretation. In fact, as will be indicated, that is exactly what happened. Nevertheless, their view generally emphasized the mutual inherence of Scripture and tradition and subordinated both to a dynamic theology of preaching. Berington spoke of an "unbroken chain of living witnesses." He specifically referred to the fact that the pastors of the church—the guides appointed by Christ to judge controverted points—delivered what they received and that on ordinary occasions "no particular interference of the divine Spirit" was needed to preserve them from error. Why? Because the whole church witnessed to their integrity: " . . . the decisions of councils are witnesses; the faithful are witnesses; all liturgies and other forms of prayer are witnesses; the catechisms and books of public instruction are witnesses; and the writings of all preceding teachers, joined to the admitted testimony of the Scriptures, are witnesses. A barrier in defense of the truth once received, is thus formed, which no subtlety can undermine; no boldness surmount." The introduction to *The Faith of Catholics* approvingly quoted Joseph Priestley's statement that the books of the New Testament were the effect of the belief of thousands, "by whom the contents of the gospels were credited." In another context, many years later, John Lingard spoke of the ordinary experience of this rule of faith: "On what is the faith of Christians based? On authority. What authority? That of the church? Not in 99 cases out of 100. A boy or girl of 10 years has faith. On what is that faith founded but the authority of parents and teachers. If he or she believe in the authority of the church, it is still on the authority of parents or teachers. The same is the case with all who have not the means and abilities to make inquiry. It must be so as long as man is man. Protestants may say the same. They must believe on a similar authority. The only difference is that one is more favoured than the other. Quid habes quod non acciperis?"⁹

This theology of revelation, with its elements of communality and living witness, was not an innovation on the part of the Cisalpines. In 1826 the vicars apostolic issued a *Declaration* of Catholic beliefs that adopted a very similar stance. It pleased Berington, who wrote to Kirk: "At least the absurd words *Scripture and Tradition* are dropt, and the teaching authority established." More important, the sources for such a theology were common currency in late eighteenth-century England. Bossuet began his theology of tradition from the idea of his duty to preach the word of God. He shared with Louis Bourdaloue, Esprit Fléchier, Jean Mabillon, and Jean Baptiste Massillon—men well known to the English Catholic priests—the identification of the preached word with the word of God. The same belief supported his reflections in *An Exposition of the Doctrine of the Catholic Church* (1671) and *The History of the Variations* (1688), works that became the standard apologetic texts of the period.[10]

The English Catholics also possessed a tradition of their own that refused to bifurcate the idea of revelation and continued the classical idea of the one Gospel entrusted to the hearts of all the faithful. George H. Tavard has convincingly traced the perdurance of these concepts in the writings of Christopher Davenport, John Colville, Matthew Kellison, Laurence Anderson, Matthew Wilson, Thomas White, John Belsen, Henry Holden, Thomas Bailey, and John Gother.[11] Tavard specifically notes the influence of the common law tradition on this attitude to revelation. Coming out of such a background, a theological conservative such as Milner could write:

> . . . all *written laws* necessarily suppose the existence of *unwritten laws*, and indeed depend upon them for their force and authority. . . . in this kingdom, we have *Common* or *Unwritten Law*, and *Statute* or *Written Law*, both of them binding; . . . So absurd is the idea of binding mankind by written laws, *without laying an adequate foundation* for the authority of those laws, and without constituting *living judges* to decide upon them.
>
> Neither has the Divine Wisdom, in founding the spiritual kingdom of his Church, acted in that inconsistent manner. . . . On the contrary, the inspiration of [the Scriptures] . . . is not otherwise known than by the *viva voce* evidence of these depositaries and judges of revealed truths. This Analysis of Revealed Religion, so conformable to Reason and the Civil Constitution of our country, is proved to be true, by *The Written Word* itself—by the *Tradition and conduct of the Apostles*—and by the constant testimony and practice of the Fathers and Doctors of the Church in all ages.

Lingard himself also made a passing reference to the analogy of secular law when he refuted Chillingworth. Here was a socio-cultural source for English Catholic thought. Lastly, it was entirely possible that the Cisalpines would have been influenced by various Protestant views. Berington's reference to Priestley has already been noted. In one of his controveries Lingard quoted the classical Anglican formulation of the interrelationship of Scripture and tradition, taken from the Twentieth Article, as supporting his own view.[12]

Theoretically, such a theology should have remained open to the possibility of development. It did not. Berington referred to the growth in the precision and clarification of doctrinal language, but both he and Lingard emphasized the perpetuity and immutability of the original deposit. For example, when Berington reflected on matrimony as a sacrament he wrote: "It may, however, be granted that there is not any passage in scripture, in which any express mention is made of the institution of this sacrament." Yet he continued to treat the issue as if the sacrament itself had always been the defined article of faith that Trent understood it to be. Lingard's treatment of matrimony in *The Antiquities of the Anglo-Saxon Church* was also designed to prove its universal perpetuity as sacrament, although he privately noted some difficulties many years later. Berington's and Lingard's mutual abhorrence of any idea of development and the reasons for it were apparent in their treatment of Veron's second criterion for an article of faith.[13]

"Proposed to all by the Catholic Church to be believed with divine faith": In the thoughts of Lingard and Berington this phase represented the rock against which any dynamic and unified theology of the word shattered. Lingard in his introduction to *The Protestant Apology* noted the contempt of antiquity that had permeated the Anglican Church ever since the acceptance of the principle of private judgment. This contempt, combined with the critical investigation of the Bible, had led to the pervasive renunciation of the "old code of doctrine" in favor of modern reinterpretations. Reacting to this rise of infidelity, Lingard wrote: "But while I approve of, and commend the pursuit of biblical criticism, as tending to guard the sacred records against the unhallowed

A Cisalpine Rule of Faith • 83

attacks of infidels and fanatics, I do assert that the faith of the Christian multitude is not to be rendered dependent on it, and that the great tenets, which constitute the summary of the Church catechism, must be founded on another basis than this or that version, this or that interpretation, this or that reading of a scripture text. It must, as common sense will dictate to every impartial person, be founded on the old Christian axiom: *Quod semper, quod ubique, quod ab omnibus.*" Lingard interpreted this to mean that the Christian religion was delivered quite complete and perfect by Christ and his Apostles. "In matters of faith and essential discipline, no change whatsoever can be admitted."[14]

Second, as has been noted, Protestant justifications for separation from the Roman Church revolved around the abuses and "new doctrines and practices" that had caused that body to depart from the primitive purity of the Gospel. To counteract this strand of polemic, Berington and Lingard naturally emphasized the perpetuity and antiquity of most of the disputed points. The method of historical tracing thus began to dominate apologetic thought. Lingard used this approach in his works, and the method itself was the distinguishing characteristic of *The Faith of Catholics.*

Third, the Cisalpines inherited an exceptionally fixed and documentary notion of tradition from their Gallican and Jansenist sources. Lingard referred specifically to Nicole's *Perpétuité de la foy de l'eglise* (1664); Berington's approval of Quesnel has already been noted. Quesnel and Nicole represented the strong tendency among the French theologians to forsake the scholastic for the historical method, to absolutize history to the deteriment of providential development. The standard defense of the "Gallican liberties" in the Parisian school only supported this point of view. Bossuet in his *Defensio Declarationis Conventus Cleri Gallicani* and *History of the Variations* has long been considered by historians of dogma to be the representative of this static notion. Revelation for him tended to become a rigid block; variation meant error. A strict classicism was a characteristic he shared with his English followers.[15]

Lastly, Berington and Lingard participated in the movement throughout the Catholic world that emphasized the mode of transmission of a doctrine as opposed to the faith itself. Their dependence on Henry Holden manifested itself in their treatment of faith and reason, and this debt carried certain consequences. Holden in his *Analysis of Divine Faith* defined tradition as "nothing else but a verbal conveyance or communication of any truth, whether written or unwritten, with a continual succession of time or years from hand to hand, and from father to son, and so from age to age."[16] What such a view ultimately accomplished was the identification of church and tradition, the elevation of the magisterium to the status of the rule of faith itself. As soon as transmission became the focal point of an analysis of faith, it followed that anyone opposing the ultramontane emphasis on active magisterium should concentrate on a restrictive application of Vincent of Lerin's principle. The idea of development could only be muted by a papalist such as Milner; he foresaw the possibility of papal infallibility becoming an article of faith.[17] The Cisalpines anathematized this view, and so the destruction of a dynamic theology of the word was the unavoidable consequence of their dependence on Veron, Holden, and Bossuet and their rejection of "popish beliefs."

These forces caused the Cisalpines to be excessively rigid in their methodology and interpretation of the content of faith. A still more damaging reaction to the Protestant polemic led them at times to imply a dualistic approach to revelation. Bossuet's writings contained two conflicting notions of tradition: his theology of tradition as preached word and the theology of two sources. The same ambiguity animated the thought of the English recusants John Percy and Thomas Bailey. These men grafted onto their more unified concept a theory of the coexistence in the church of Scripture and a number of unwritten truths of revelation. They did so in order more easily to defend certain parts of Catholic doctrine against the charge of innovation. Holden's emphasis on transmission could be taken in the same direction. He spoke of divine, apostolic, and ecclesiastical traditions that became articles of faith inasmuch as they possessed antiquity, universality, and "consentment." The Cisalpines, despite their protests to the contrary, appeared to fall into the same trap. Berington defined "apostolic traditions" as "such points of Catholic belief and practice, as, not committed to writing in the holy scripture, have come down, in an unbroken series of oral delivery, from the apostolic ages." He classified prayers for the dead among them. Lingard spoke ambiguously about the whole doctrine of Christ not being recorded in the Scriptures, implying that some dogmas were just "unwritten." He referred to tradition as one "legitimate source of religious knowledge." In his introduction to *The Protestant Apology* he talked about "essential practices connected with the use of the sacraments, the form of ecclesiastical administration, the conferring of powers to preach the word of God, &c." These were unchangeable as articles of faith since they were "delivered and enjoined by Christ and the Apostles."[18] Such terminology was reconcilable with a classical concept of tradition, but in the highly charged atmosphere of polemical debate it seemed to imply a duality of sources.

Both the tendency toward a fixed notion of the faith and the ambiguous dualistic terminology indicated that the Cisalpine theology of revelation was disunified. At its center lay a contradiction between a dynamic notion of living witness to Christ and a static view of the transmission of truths. This tension between two very distinct ideas blocked any creative thinking that might have contributed to a theology of development. Here Berington and Lingard revealed themselves as men of their times, limited by dependence on Bossuet and an overreaction to Protestant polemic. This same theological heritage also led them to emphasize the issue of transmission or the conservation of the original deposit of faith. This emphasis brought with it the dominant issue in the post-Reformation debates: the question of the church. If, as Holden contended, the certainty of faith depended on the means by which it was known, where did the infallible guide reside? What was the nature of the organ of transmission? The problem was that of the *ecclesia*. In Veron's principle, what did this word mean?

Cisalpine Ecclesiology

John Lingard most fully articulated his ecclesiology in his introduction to *The Protestant Apology*. In defining "Catholic Church" Lingard specifically rejected both "that invisible sort of Church which the Calvinists have been looking for" and the Anglican apologist James Ussher's description that "the visible Church, which is Catholic and universal, and out of which there is no salvation, consists of all those throughout the world, that profess the true religion." According to Lingard, speaking within the context of Anglican–Roman Catholic relations, the Calvinist position was easily dismissed; most respectable Anglican divines rejected it. Ussher's view, on the other hand, reduced the nature of the church to a bare profession of faith and agreement in fundamental principles. Therefore, by "Catholic Church" Lingard meant: ". . . what every unbiased person of common sense must acknowledge, a great congregation of Christians united together in one close bond of faith, sacraments, public worship, and ecclesiastical administration. I mean that Church which, founded by Christ, and propagated by the Apostles and their successors, has spread itself more or less over the greatest part of the civilized world; which, although in many cases seceded from, has never withdrawn herself from the primitive Christian society; and which is as easily and openly distinguishable from other bodies or assemblages of men, as one nation is from another."[19]

This definition presented two features. First, it agreed with the presuppositions of many English divines. Given the tenor of the usual Protestant-Catholic debates, this agreement in itself indicated an ecumenical frame of reference. Lingard was probably following the example contained in such works as Bossuet's *Conference avec M. Claude* (1682), Hawarden's *True Church of Christ* (1714–15), and *An Essay towards a Proposal for Catholick Communion*: in any dispute, establish the points acceptable to both sides. Second, and in terms of the present exposition more important, Lingard's definition betrayed an important twist in Cisalpine ecclesiology. Its central elements can be understood only by comparing it with several others popular in post-Reformation Catholic circles. Robert Bellarmine and Peter Canisius defined "church" as "a congregation of men joined by profession of one and the same Christian faith, and by communion of the same sacraments, under the rule of legitimate pastors, and especially the Roman pontiff." Edmund Richer in his *Libellus de Ecclesiastica et Politica Protestate* (1611) wrote: "The church is a political monarchy, instituted for a supernatural spiritual end, under an aristocratic rule that is best of all and most convenient to nature, limited by the highest pastor of souls, Our Lord." *The Analysis of Divine Faith* put it this way: ". . . the Christian Church, Congregation or Society, is a company of men unanimously, professing to observe the beliefs and exercise of all things ordained by Christ to be believed and practiced: As also to live united to that superior Authority and Government which Christ hath instituted: And lastly, the pastors and Rectors of this Congregation be possessed of the true means whereby all these things, which are commanded by Christ to be believed and practiced, may be most certainly known without danger of error, and perfectly fulfilled." The differences among these definitions should be noted. Bellarmine, in order to combat Protestant opponents, designed his definition to support the role of the hierarchy, especially of the pope. In the development of his thought his support of hierarchy led to the overidentification of church with socio-juridic structure. It was the common failing of the ultramontanes. Richer, in contrast, made no mention of the community of faith, sacraments, and pope; to refute ultramontane opinions, he identified the government of a society with the society itself. Richer's interpretation ended in an extremely democratic view of the church. Holden's description appeared to strike a balance between the two, but he also placed the emphasis on "submission and subjection to that superior authority and Government, which Christ hath instituted."[20]

Lingard's description of the church represented an emphasis distinct from that of these three men. In view of the fact that Bellarmine's and Holden's writings were easily available, the absence of the terms "legitimate pastors," "Roman Pontiff," "monarchy," "aristocratic regime," "government," and "authority" in Lingard's analysis indicates an avoidance of certain categories. Instead, Lingard highlighted the unity of the church—the common profession of faith, sacraments, worship, and administration. In this he followed the tradition of Bossuet. The latter in his *Conference avec M. Claude* defined the church as "a society that professes to believe the doctrine of Jesus Christ, and to govern itself by his word." The bishop of Meaux adopted this definition because it was commonly accepted by all Christians. It implied the church's visibility and the offices the pope and bishops held in her. But by not mentioning these structures explicitly, it focused attention on the church as *the whole body of believers*, symbolizing the thrust of Bossuet's ecclesiology. This definition was translated by Joseph Berington in *Reflections Addressed to Hawkins*. Most of Lingard's ecclesiology was also based on Bossuet.[21]

These precedents, combined with the Cisalpine view of tradition as "communal witness," the constitutional beliefs of political Whiggery, and the Anglican environment, led Lingard to form his own definition with the same basic emphasis. A "great congregation of Christians" thus stood for more than a desire to meet Protestant opponents on common ground. It signified a basic stance toward the church, a stance that was participative and nonjuridical. Of course, the fact that his definition of "church" tended toward this communal point of view did not mean that Lingard ignored hierarchical structure. He still referred to "ecclesiastical administration" (p. lxx). It was at this point that he differed from Richer. In order to encourage union between the Roman Catholic and Anglican churches, Lingard devoted a large section of his introduction to an exposition of the Catholic faith regarding the place of the pope and the bishops in the body of Christ. To explain his own understanding, he posed and answered eight questions.

"Some wiseacres say," Lingard wrote, that the pope claims the title of Universal Bishop. This title would imply that all other bishops were his vicars and deputies, clearly, an unacceptable position. "Every bishop is an immediate vicar of Christ," yet the "bishop of Rome is the first vicar" (p. cxviii). To support this view Lingard appealed to Pope Gregory the Great, who, "while he was anxious for the rights of his colleagues, was not forgetful of his own" (p. cxxi). Lingard acknowledged that the pope "according to the institution of Christ" was the "general superintendent" of the hierarchy and the whole church, but he sought above all to defend the divine rights of the whole episcopal body (p. cxxii). In *The Antiquities of the Anglo-Saxon Church* Lingard indicated the source of his position and some practical consequences flowing from it. After discussing the role of the bishops and the place of provincial and national synods, the historian noted the following functions of the pope in the early British Church: to establish, extend, or restrict the jurisdiction of the archiepiscopal sees; to confirm the election of the metropolitans; to enforce the obedience of canonical discipline; and to revise the decisions of the national councils.[22]

A second objection many people voiced was that even some Catholics believed all spiritual power to be derived from the pope. This belief Lingard flatly rejected. He referred to Alexander's *Ecclesiastical History* (1676–86) for the proof that the bishops were always called "brethren," "co-bishops," "fratres," "coepiscopi," and "consacerdotes" (p. cxxiii). It was true that bishops applied to Rome for certain faculties, but discipline and historical precedent, not doctrine, explained this practice: ". . . as to the primitive episcopal rights of bishops, as to their power of preaching the word of God, or administering the sacraments, of superintending their clergy, of their amovibility [*sic*] from the sees to which they have been appointed, the Pope neither can, nor will interfere or disturb any bishops, except in case of delinquency, and then it is his prerogative and his duty to enforce against him the laws of the Church" (p. cxxv). Lingard then asked: Have not "some Catholic canonists and divines also taught that even the original episcopal power is derived from the Pope?" (p. cxxv). In his mind these men hardly merited a nod. They were "sycophants," "flatterers," "leaden headed dunce[s]," "silly impostors"—men serving themselves more than Rome (p. cxxv).

Moreover, Lingard argued, it was simply untrue that the pope stood above general councils or enjoyed an unlimited jurisdiction outside the control of the canons. That whole issue had been decided by the fourth session of the Council of Constance. Also, according to the third Gallican article, "the exercise of ecclesiastical power is to be regulated by the canons" (p. cxxvii). This belief was in perfect accord with the teachings of Celestine I, Gregory I, Innocent III, the Council of Florence, and Bossuet. Lingard believed that the infallibility of the church resided in the episcopal college united to the pope.[23]

Next, Lingard continued, the pope did not insist—despite the fears of many Protestants—on the right to nominate to all vacant bishoprics. The practice of nomination was disciplinary and historical in character. The first article of the Magna Carta, the Pragmatic Sanction of Louis XI, the current attitude of the sovereigns in Europe, and the French Concordat of 1801 witnessed to the claim of the ruler to nominate to vacant sees and to the reservation to the pope of only the "prerogative of conferring canonical institution" (p. cxxviii).

But several people argued against the pope's supremacy by questioning the justification for his patriarchal jurisdiction. At this point Lingard penned a twenty-page exposition on the difference between the ecclesiastical institution of patriarchal jurisdiction and the papal primacy itself. The former had been established in time to watch over the spiritual concerns of extensive dioceses, to regulate the mode of episcopal election, to hold councils, to control discipline, and for other "salutary objects" (p. cxxx). It did not touch the center of the bishop of Rome's prerogative: "to enforce the observation of the canons and to apply the authority of the church in defence of the true doctrine, against all his brethren, whether simple bishops, metropolitans, or patriarchs" (p. cxxxi). After making this distinction, Lingard refuted the men who argued that because Britain and Ireland in the early ages did not fall under the pope's patriarchal jurisdiction in the use of the Bible, the liturgy, the paschal cycle, tithes, and the conferring of the pallium, therefore they did not acknowledge the primacy. Lingard felt that to argue in this fashion was to be blind to the facts of history and to the writers of the Anglo-Saxon period, who testified to the distinction between patriarchal jurisdiction and primacy (pp. cxlv–cxlvii).

After dismissing these arguments, Lingard noted that some polemicists wished to give the pope a primacy of rank and honor but no real jurisdictional authority. This was "an unmeaning distinction, founded on a very shallow knowledge of the nature of ecclesiastical government" (p. cxlix). Christ conferred not honors but duties on the Apostles (Matt. 20; 1 Peter 5:2-3; 1 Tim. 3:1). The pope's title *Servus Servorum Dei* indicated his duty to serve (despite the later accretions of "dignities" and "honours"), and to this charge was annexed the authority needed to exercise it:

> Accordingly in the vocabulary of the Church *officium*, charge, or obligation, and *potestas*, power, or authority, are reciprocal terms; *officium sacerdotale, episcopale, pontificale*, are synonymous with *potestas sacerdotalis, episcopalis, pontificalis*. Hence it appears, that if the bishop of Rome be invested with any sort of primacy in virtue of a peculiar commission given by our Saviour to St. Peter it must consist in his being burthened with a greater charge than any other bishop, and at the same time in his possessing an authority superior to that of every one of his brethren individually considered. A primacy of mere honour would be a solecism in the code of church administration, and would suggest a notion directly contrary to the institution and intention of Christ (pp. cl–cli).

Finally, Lingard stated that the occasions on which the rights of the primacy were to be exerted, the canons that regulated them, and the mode of interference allowed in the concerns of individual churches were all *salva fide* discussed in the schools. For him, the words of Bossuet summarized the Catholic doctrine concerning the pope's supremacy:

> The Son of God, who would have his church to be one and solidly built upon unity, hath instituted the primacy of St. Peter to support and cement it. For which reason we acknowledge this primacy in the successors of the Prince of the Apostles, who, therefore, are entitled to that submission and obedience, which the Church and the Holy Fathers have always inculcated upon the faithful. As to those things, which, we know, are disputed in the schools, though the ministers are incessantly alledging [sic] them to render this primacy odious, it is not necessary to speak of them here, because they are not articles of Catholic faith. It is enough that we acknowledge a head appointed by God to conduct all his flock in his own paths, which those will readily allow who are friends to brotherly union and ecclesiastical concord.[24]

These eight points of controversy explicate what John Lingard meant by "ecclesiastical administration" in his definition of the church. They were based on Gallican and English Catholic precedents. To reject the concept of *episcopus universalis* and the ultramontane interpretation of *plentitudo potestatis,* to defend the divine institution of the episcopacy, and to rank the General Council above the pope were all maxims of the Paris school. To distinguish between patriarchal jurisdiction and the primacy betrayed a deep awareness of the Anglo-Saxon tradition and the statutes of *praemunire.* Lingard also kept his eye on the specifically Anglican dimensions of the controversy when he gave the pope more than a primacy of honor. It should be noted that in all of these points his definition of the church and his exposition of "ecclesiastical administration" were significantly integral. Together they manifested an ecumenical sensitivity and a vision of the Roman Catholic Church that was surprisingly communal and nonmagisterial. The whole analysis was directed away from power and uniformity toward service, diversity, and reconciliation. It was manifestly conciliarist and accorded well with an individualist anthropology. Yet it was not excessively democratic. Lingard both used and adapted the strengths of the ecclesial system of Jacques Bénigne Bossuet. Aimé-Georges Martimort in *Le Gallicanisme de Bossuet* has detailed the positive ecclesiological contribution of *An Exposition of the Doctrine of the Catholic Church* and *Defensio Declarationis Conventus Cleri Gallicani*. According to Martimort, Bossuet used in the *Defensio* a Pauline principle by which to understand the mystery of ecclesiastical authority: the notion of the body. The bishop wanted to avoid the projection of purely social and political categories on the society of Christ. Therefore, he emphasized, as did the early Fathers, the *congregatio fidelium* and the unity the Holy Spirit gave to it. As a result, Bossuet always began his argumentation on the authority of the pope with an appeal for and panegyric of unity. Bossuet's doctrine derived not from Jean Gerson and Pierre d'Ailly but from the African Fathers of the Church—Tertullian, Cyprian, and Augustine. Bossuet defended the Parisian tradition not so much because it denigrated the authority of Rome but because it supported the episcopacy. In this fashion the *Defensio* summarized the seventeenth- and eighteenth-century debates over *de potestate ecclesiastica* and inspired them with a deeper notion of the ecclesial body. Yves Congar has noted a similar strength in the Gallican position. Its common denominator was to oppose the absorption of the ecclesial pole by the papal pole. It always insisted on the unity of the church, the body of the faithful, and the hierarchical service to the body. Surely Bossuet's works were much more extensive, deeper, and more important than those of his English followers. But there could be little doubt that Bossuet's irenical vision lay at the base of Lingard's theological reflections on the church.[25]

John Lingard was not the only Catholic to combine this brand of the Gallican ecclesiological tradition with a self-assertive English nationalism. Joseph Berington's use of Bossuet's definition of "church" has already been noted. This man, intellectual leader of the Cisalpines and student of the growth of the papacy, emphasized the conciliar element in the body of Christ. The conciliar element was such a major part of his thought that at times he seemed to go beyond the limits of orthodoxy. In his *Reflections Addressed to Hawkins* Berington wrote: "He [the Pope] has indeed his prerogatives, but we have our privileges, and are independent on him, excepting where it has pleased the community, for the sake of unity and good order, to surrender into his hands a limited superintendence." While emphasizing the "community," a statement like this could also have been interpreted in a heterodox fashion. It was not the only time Berington expressed himself loosely.[26]

Still, it should be recognized that when he was pressed, Berington consistently granted the pope a primacy of jurisdiction. No less a figure than John Carroll, later archbishop of Baltimore, believed that the passage in *Reflections Addressed to Hawkins* could be interpreted in an orthodox fashion. Berington himself admitted that his language, at times excessive, was designed to placate Protestant ears. He penned the following creed:

> We know, as others do, what our faith is, and in that knowledge we have learned to distinguish what is human from what is divine. We believe our *Church* to be an infallible guide in all that appertains to salvation. Of this Church, we believe the Bishop of Rome to be the *head*, supreme in Spirituals by divine appointment, supreme in discipline by ecclesiastical institution; but in the concerns of state and civil life, we believe him to be no governor, no master, no guide.—We believe that the jurisdiction of bishops is of divine origin; but that jurisdiction is distinctly defined, that its limits are all known, that is, that its exercise must be circumscribed within the sphere, and be conformable to the rules of established order.—We believe that the *priesthood* is from Christ, the rights of which are as sacred as those of the pontifical and of the episcopal order, and that the forms of ancient practice, which must ever be revered, have sanctioned the exercise of those rights, and marked their limits.[27]

Berington also offered a perfectly Catholic interpretation of this document: "Under the word *spirituals* we comprise all those points, whether of faith, morality, or discipline, over which *at all times*, the Roman Bishop has been acknowledged to hold, by the institution of Christ, a primacy of jurisdiction." In 1794, at the height of the Catholic Committee's bouts with the vicars apostolic, he wrote: "I find . . . that from St. Peter to the time of Constantine there is no document to prove, that *any primacy* was *exercised* by the Roman bishop. . . . I do not say, that those bishops were not jure divino, possessed of that primacy. The right to jurisdiction and its exercise are obviously different things." In his comments on Sturges's *Reflections on the Principles and Institutions of Popery* in 1799, he did say that "much of the ecclesiastical, and all of the temporal power, at any time claimed by him [the pope] was acquired by human means, and that its exercise was lawfully resisted." Still, he referred to the Roman bishop as "the first pastor of his church" and affirmed infallibility in the "united ministers of his church." Lastly, when William Poynter questioned his use of "body representative" as applied to the bishops, Berington responded: "You think the expression *body representative*, as applied to pastors of the church, may in English be equivocal, that is, may not sufficiently express, that they are judges in matters of faith, and the *teachers* of nations, agreeably to the words of Christ addressed to the apostles.—The phrase is taken from the expression *universam repraesentans ecclesiam*, canonically applied to general councils." Berington wrote to John Kirk and asked: Are not the acts of our Parliament only forceful with the consent of a section of the executive? So also are the pope and the council related. Throughout his life, Berington held basically the same position Lingard later defended. If they disagreed it was because Berington emphasized the rights of the priesthood. Still, their differences were ones of degree and not of kind. Berington considered his opinion to be that of the Gallican school, and, inasmuch as it was, it remained orthodox.[28]

Charles Butler followed a similar pattern. In his *Formularies, Confessions of Faith, or Symbolic Books* he ranked Bossuet's *Exposition* "very near to" the symbolic books of the Catholic Church, the Creed of Pius IV, and the Roman

Catechism. Butler wrote a life of Bossuet and recommended it to several correspondents. He was pleased to find that Bossuet had disapproved the conduct of the popes with respect to England and had also defended the oath of allegiance. This leading Catholic lawyer summarized his view of "ecclesiastical administration" when he wrote:

> The Cisalpines affirm, that in spirituals, the pope is subject, in doctrine and discipline, to the church, and to a general council representing her; that he is subject to the canons of the church, and cannot, except in an extreme case, dispense with them; that, even in such a case, his dispensation is subject to the judgment of the church; that the bishops derive their jurisdiction from God himself, immediately, and not derivatively through the pope; that he has no right to confer bishoprics, or other spiritual benefices of any kind, the patronage of which, by common right, prescription, concordat or any other general rule of the Church, is vested in another. They admit, that an appeal lies in the pope from the sentence of the metropolitan; but assert, that no appeal lies to the pope, and that he can evoke no cause to blame himself, during the intermediate process. They affirm that a general council, may, without, and even against the pope's consent, reform the church—They deny his personal infallibility, and hold, that he may be deposed by the church, or a general council, for heresy or schism: and they admit, that in an extreme case, where there is a great division of opinion, an appeal lies from the pope to a future general council.

His opinion accorded remarkably well with the English idea of a "limited government."[29]

Other Cisaplines followed these three spokesmen. In 1799 John Rigby, a leader of the Lancashire clergy, published an English edition of Bossuet's *Exposition*. John Fletcher did the same in 1826. William Poynter, the vicar apostolic closest to Cisalpine opinions, relied on the *Defensio Declarationis Conventus Cleri Gallicani* in preparing his reaction to the extreme views of Charles O'Conor. Almost all the Cisalpines emphasized the "ecclesial pole" and rooted infallibility in the General Council. They also acknowledged the pope to have a primacy of jurisdiction, even though it was limited by local custom, the canons of the church, and the conciliar tradition. Lingard's views on the church, the bishops, and the papacy were not unusual.[30]

As the preceding chapter has already indicated, the papalists were not kind to these men and to their ecclesiological vision. John Milner unjustly judged them to be propagators of schismatic opinion. Others similarly dismissed the movement as "extremist." There was some justification for these opinions. At times the thrust of their notions carried the Cisalpines into the isolated backwaters of nationalism and extreme episcopalism. During the same period in which they wrote, rationalism, the policies of the enlightened despots, the Jansenist reform trend, and the secularization represented by the French Revolution threatened to destroy the church as a universal body of believers. Berington, Butler, and, later, Lingard, stood for some very similar ideas: the importance of national customs, the role of the laity, and decentralization. Any reasonable observer would not have been slow to recognize the parallels and recoil before the consequences. Yet Milner's judgment was an overreaction. It ignored the constructive elements in both the Gallican and Cisalpine approaches.

The Cisalpine program takes on a remarkable degree of coherence when viewed from the focal points of Scripture and tradition and ecclesiology. Basically, in these two areas it confronted the situation of the church in a constitutional society. The analysis of revelation as the word of God, its cultural base in the common law tradition, and its classical elements of living witness and communality accorded well with an ecclesiology of the *congregatio fidelium* and a conciliar view of ecclesiastical administration. The opinions adopted were natural concomitants of the acceptance of individual rights and the notion of contract. They met in the area of anthropology. In this sense the English Catholics, because of their peculiar mixture of Gallican and national traditions, offered a bridge across the gulf separating the church from the Enlightenment. The Cisalpines attempted to solve the issue of the rule of faith not by appealing to the magisterium of authority with its divine prerogatives but by recognizing the value of communal witness integrated with an authority of service.

Despite its positive orientation, Cisalpine theology was not without its difficulties. Its insights were fragmentary. Complete coherence shattered on the rock of the immutability of faith. The classical tradition of Bossuet, reaction to the ultramontanes, and the defense of Roman Catholicism in the Anglican controversies led to the dominance of a rather moribund theology of tradition(s) and the word of God. At this point Cisalpinism lost its dimension of a living community of believers. Furthermore, it was much too embroiled in conflicts with the vicars apostolic and over the veto question and emancipation to evolve any systematic views. What theological depth Berington, Butler, and Lingard did possess they received from their French mentors. At times political attitudes dominated positive thought: remarks against the papacy were frequent; all church authority tended to fall before an excessive consciousness of individual rights. Still, the positive elements remained and should not be disregarded.

Ecumenical Proposals

Perhaps the greatest intellectual contribution Cisalpinism offered was not the theology of revelation or the reevaluation of ecclesiastical authority but something essentially connected with the approach to these two areas: an attitude of reconciliation. In England this attitude meant an affirmative approach to ecumenical relations. The social sources of this attitude have already been detailed. The Cisalpine view of the relationship between reason and faith and the reliance of Bossuet's irenical system were other contributing factors. Paradoxically, both the greatest strengths and the greatest weaknesses of the analysis of revelation also combined to foster ecumenism. The orientation toward the Gospel itself and the tendency to freeze dogmatic truth in the first five centuries pared Catholic articles of faith to a minimum. A historical method was common to the Gallican, English Catholic, and Anglican traditions. Thus the acceptance of

A Cisalpine Rule of Faith • 99

Veron's principle by Berington, Butler, and Lingard joined with many other forces to encourage interfaith discussion. To some extent the impact of ecumenism on the Cisalpine program has already been seen, but a specific theological discussion should serve to highlight the importance of this element in their thought.

Cries of "no popery" were the immediate occasion for John Lingard's presentation of an ecumenical program. In 1807 the bishop of Durham published *The Grounds on Which the Church of England Separated from the Church of Rome*. The pamphlet was almost entirely devoted to maintaining that since Roman Catholics believed in transubstantiation and were therefore guilty of idolatry, they should be excluded from civil privileges. This kind of argument typified the polemics of the day. To counteract it, Lingard attempted to prove the similarities between the doctrines of the Church of England and the Roman Catholic Church. He did this, primarily, in four areas: the eucharist, the power of the keys, confession, and the episcopal form of ecclesiastical administration.

In the 1807 controversy Lingard argued that the creed of the Established Church was doctrinally inconsistent on the subject of the eucharist. In order to keep peace in the English Church it appeared to admit both the Lutheran and Calvinist interpretations of the real presence. The *Book of Common Prayer* said that the "body and blood of Christ are *verily and indeed* taken and received by the faithful in the Lord's supper." This act was interpreted by the Twenty-eighth Article to mean: "The body and blood of Christ, which are given to the faithful in the Lord's Supper, and are by them received, eaten, and drank, only in a heavenly and spiritual manner. . . ." Lingard argued that neither statement excluded the possibility of the real body of Christ being eaten, albeit "in a heavenly and spiritual manner." Otherwise, if only the influence of Christ's body and blood, the grace he has purchased for us, or the title to a heavenly inheritance were meant, the catechism would be wrong in stating that "the inward part of the sacrament, or the thing signified, is the body and blood of Christ." This realistic language, intended for the instruction of the unlearned, definitely implied that the body of Christ is given, taken, and eaten: "As the action of giving is prior to that of taking and eating, the body of Christ must exist in the sacrament before it is taken and eaten by the communicant. . . . It cannot be given by faith. To exercise an act of faith 'is to eat Christ,' and undoubtedly to eat, and to give to another to eat, are two very different things." On the other hand, Lingard noted, many divines interpreted "in a heavenly and spiritual manner" to imply only an act of the mind. In this view, he wondered: "What is there to distinguish the sacrament from any other religious ceremony? In any of them Christ may be the object of the belief of the mind."[31]

Lingard did not pursue the subject of the real presence in the debate with Shute Barrington; he remained content to point out the ambiguities in the Anglican interpretations. But it should be realized that this controversy presented a deep insight into his own beliefs about the eucharist. By acknowledging the fact that "in a heavenly and spiritual manner" was capable of a realistic interpretation, Lingard implied a distinction between real presence and the explanation of real presence—in Roman Catholic terms, the fact that the reality and the descriptive term of transubstantiation were not completely conjunctive. This distinction became even more apparent in his 1809 exposition.

The introduction to *The Protestant Apology* maintained without qualification that the true Church of England agreed with the Roman Catholic Church on the doctrine of the real presence. Both the *Book of Common Prayer* and the Twenty-eighth Article held this belief. Lingard wrote: "No objection can be drawn from the words, in a heavenly and spiritual manner. . . . The Catholics admit the use of such phrases in treating of the ineffable mode of Christ's presence in the eucharist." To support this opinion Lingard appealed to Veron's *Rule of Catholic Faith* and the thirteenth session of the Council of Trent. He argued that many of the English divines admitted real presence. The doctrine itself had become ambiguous only since the days when Calvinism and

A Cisalpine Rule of Faith • 101

private judgment had impinged on the English Church. It was true, Lingard acknowledged, that the Twenty-eighth Article rejected transubstantiation, but this rejection represented "a point of controversy very different from the general question concerning the reality of the presence of Christ."[32]

Ultimately John Lingard justified this interpretation of "in a heavenly and spiritual manner" by his historical investigations into Anglo-Saxon antiquities. In his 1806 edition he included a long note on the doctrine of the eucharist in the early English Church, dividing the Anglo-Saxon era into two periods. During the time before the Danish devastations, Bede and Egbert had definitely taught a real and permanent presence. After the invasions, because of the influence of Ratramnus of Corbie (Bertram), the language about real presence had become more ambiguous, especially in the work of Aelfric. Lingard explained the teachings of Ratramnus and Aelfric in this way: "After the consecration, the bread and wine have become, or have passed into, the body and blood of Christ . . . consequently they are changed. But no change has been made outwardly or corporally: therefore it has been made inwardly or spiritually: therefore the eucharist is the body and blood of Christ; not indeed corporally, but spiritually; and of consequence a mystery or figure must be admitted." Both Ratramnus and Aelfric had also maintained that the eucharist was not the same as the natural body of Christ, but by that they had meant, according to Lingard, only that the eucharistic body in its manner of existence (*spiritualiter*) was not the same as the body born of the Virgin (*naturaliter*). From this, the historian concluded that such language was not "repugnant to the Catholic doctrine."[33]

Lingard evolved two major conclusions from his studies. First, "If the body of Christ exist at all in the eucharist, it is evident that it does not exist after the manner of a natural body." Ratramnus and Aelfric employed the words *naturaliter* and *spiritualiter* to explain the difference; Trent used *naturaliter* and *sacramentaliter;* others, such as Veron and Holden, preserved the old view. "If this distinction be a test of protestantism, the Church of Rome must resign the most distinguished of her children." Second, despite the fact that Aelfric's expressions on the nonidentity of the body born of the Virgin and the eucharistic body of Christ were not usual in the Anglo-Saxon Church (Bede, Alcuin, and many manuscripts witnessed otherwise), still, they were orthodox. Lanfranc and Bossuet also differentiated between the two. "There have even been some Catholic divines who did not require so much as an identity of substance."[34]

It is important to recognize that Lingard in these reflections did not deny transubstantiation. Following Francis Veron, Henry Holden, Jacques Bénigne Bossuet, Edward Hawarden, and *An Essay towards a Proposal for Catholick Communion,* he believed that the term itself most appropriately described the change that took place in the consecrated elements. It allowed for no equivocation. The historian rejected consubstantiation as "sophistry" and held that there was an essential continuity between the doctrine of the Fathers and that of Trent. Nevertheless, he emphasized the problem of the real presence as the heart of the issue: "When once that is settled, it will be time enough to decide whether it be there by transubstantiation or by any other means."[35]

The ecumenical importance of this view was simply that it allowed Lingard to interpret the Twenty-eighth Article in its most irenical sense; it also allowed him to avoid what he considered needless acrimony over a phrase and to concentrate in the interpretation of Roman Catholic doctrine on the sacramental sign dimension of the eucharist. His position hearkened back to the controversies of the ninth century and forward to Newman's exposition in Tract 90. Interestingly enough, Ratramnus's *De corpore et sanguine Domini* (844) influenced Thomas Cranmer's and Nicolas Ridley's view of real presence. As a consequence, it was put on the Index of prohibited books from 1559 until 1900. The irenical spirit in seventeenth-century France led to a revival of Ratramnus's doctrine, which provided another source for Lingard's thinking on the subject.

Other English Catholics did not adopt Lingard's position. Joseph Berington's *Faith of Catholics* presented the standard view of post-Reformation Catholicism by speaking of Christ's presence as "real and substantial, but sacramental and ineffable." *Spiritualiter* was apparently too ambiguous. As it was, John Milner suspected Lingard of heresy. Lingard wrote to Poynter on August 12, 1822: "About 20 years ago Dr. M. accused me to Dr. Gibson on the authority of some Irish bishop of holding heretical opinions respecting the Eucharist. I insisted on seeing the original charge, which turned out to be no more than a postscript in a letter from D. Troy saying that I had attributed to Asseline the bishop of Boulogne an opinion which to him appeared new and indefensible.—Here the matter ended." Lingard's eucharistic opinions no doubt went a long way toward explaining Milner's violent opposition to *The Antiquities of the Anglo-Saxon Church*. Once again, the Midland Vicar was overreacting.[36]

The power of the keys comprised the second area that possessed ecumenical possibilities. Lingard wrote: "The real Church of England held the being a member of the great Catholic Church as necessary for salvation." For him, the Thirty-third Article contained this truth. It said that "a person 'who by open denunciation of the church be rightly cast off from the unity of the church and excommunicated, ought to be taken of the whole multitude of the faithful as an heathen and publican.' " The last phrase, according to Lingard, supposed an "amputation from the whole body of the universal Christian church." In addition, the true Church of England admitted the power of excommunication, "which had been always considered by the Christian church as the great rampart of orthodoxy, discipline, and morality." Unfortunately, the acceptance of private judgment had destroyed these elements of Christian authority in many minds.[37]

To buttress these sentiments, Lingard argued that the real Church of England rejected private judgment in the

Twentieth Article: "The Church hath power to decree rites and ceremonies, and authority in controversies of faith" (p. xiv). It was true that this clause did not appear in the 1571 edition of the articles and that it contradicted the remaining part of the same article and also the sixth one, but still "the clause . . . has been since the days of Queen Elizabeth, and is still submitted to, at least in appearance by those who subscribe the articles" (p. xiv). The Twentieth Article, Lingard believed, necessarily included the idea of a decision of the church being conformable to revelation. Otherwise it made no sense to enjoin submission. Furthermore, "the church of England, besides claiming the power of deciding in controversies of faith, means by that power the prerogative of its decrees being of an unerring nature" (p. xxxviii). For Lingard, the statute of 13 Elizabeth, the Act of Uniformity of 13 and 14 Charles II, the thirty-sixth canon passed in Convocation 1603, and other acts, by requiring an *ex animo* assent to the Thirty-nine Articles, presupposed the privilege of unerring judgment. If this was true, Lingard concluded, then the Catholic Church claimed no right that the Church of England did not assert. While the church still "requires the subscription of the articles, while the acts of uniformity are still in force, while her canons remain unrepealed, she cannot be accused of having altered, since the accession of James the first, her code of faith and practice" (pp. xl–xli).

The third major area of agreement between the two churches was the power of absolving penitent sinners. Here Lingard argued against John Tillotson's contention that "confessing sins to the priest" represented one of Rome's new doctrines and practices. Lingard simply stated that the Church of England professed the same belief, quoting from *The Order for the Visitation of the Sick* (1662) (pp. lxxx–lxxxi). Lastly, the Church of England agreed with the Roman Catholic Church on the necessity of the episcopal form of ecclesiastical administration. This argument was evident, Lingard maintained, from the fact that many English divines asserted, against the Presbyterians and other Dissenters, the preeminence of bishops over priests. The church herself defended as articles of faith the "necessity of a mission for exercising ecclesiastical functions derived from the Apostles" and the divine right of episcopacy (pp. xxvi–xxvii).

In conclusion, John Lingard believed that these interpretations of the Twenty-eighth, Thirty-third, and Twentieth Articles indicated that the reconciliation of the churches could be effected without much difficulty. For him, both Christian bodies admitted the two great maxims of the episcopal form of ecclesiastical administration and the authority of the church in matters of faith and discipline. Certainly there were differences, and many articles would have to be reconsidered in order to distinguish them from Lutheran and Calvinistic notions. But, he asked, if the seventeenth-century Anglican divines were alive, would they not exert themselves to remove whatever might separate them from the Catholic Church? Surely they would perceive that union with Rome was the only way to preserve the Anglican Church from endless schism. Lingard contended that some points of discipline—essential practices connected with the use of the sacraments, the form of government, and the conferring of the powers to preach the word of God, etc.—were unchangeable, but on many other regulations the Roman Catholic Church allowed considerable latitude.[38]

Lingard's introduction was unusual in its thorough reexamination of some of the Thirty-nine Articles, but it raised no voices in the Anglican community. Lingard did not issue an edition in England. Among the Cisalpines, only Berington was capable of deep theological discussion, and he did not enter into this specific matter. Still, Lingard's thought was not a complete anomaly. The whole purpose of William Talbot's *Protestant Apology* was to prove the similarities between the Roman Catholic doctrine and the Church of England's beliefs. *An Essay towards a Proposal for Catholick Communion*, one of the most popular treatises in the eighteenth century, was republished in 1812. A year later, Charles Butler issued an *Address to the Protestants of Great Britain and Ireland*, in which he noted the closeness of the two creeds and referred to the Bossuet-Leibniz exchange as an encouraging example of interfaith discussion. Butler also published an account of the symbolic books of the different faiths. Most of the Cisalpines attested to a knowledge of Bossuet's irenical *Conference avec M. Claude*. In 1826 John Fletcher published *A Comparative View of the Grounds of the Catholic, and Protestant, Churches*. He dedicated it to Lingard and wrote the last chapter on the reunion of the Protestant and Catholic churches. All of these men witnessed to a type of ecumenical liberality that encouraged discussion.[39]

In the theological sphere this ecumenical openness was the necessary corollary of the Cisalpine synthesis of faith and culture. In their acknowledgment of natural rights and freedom of conscience and in their support of a secularized state Berington, Butler, and Lingard accepted the reality of a pluralistic society. The necessity of theological dialogue accompanied this socio-intellectual vision. As Charles Butler described it: "The main object of *every work* I have written has been to dispose protestants to general good humour towards us, and to keep us in general good humour among ourselves."[40] Thus the correlation between social and ecclesiastical structure, the necessity of consensus both within and without the church, was the central thread running through the reflections on Scripture and tradition, ecclesiology, and interchurch relations. When viewed from the perspective of social dynamics, the standard of civility in both church and state was rational deliberation; the highest juridical end, a unity qualified by amity. Among the English Catholics the Cisalpines basically attempted to bridge the gap that separated the church from the world. This chapter has tried to detail both the positive and negative elements in their program. Theologically, their incomplete synthesis broke on the issue of development. Historically, it became submerged in the rising tide of continental reaction. The next chapter, by considering the Cisalpine historical mentality, will indicate the signs of this *dénouement*.

4. enlightened history and the romantic revival

A HISTORICAL orientation characterized most Cisalpine writings. The literary movement itself began in 1780 with Joseph Berington's *State and Behaviour of English Catholics*. This reexamination of the Catholic past from the Reformation to 1780 was followed by a seemingly endless succession of historical accounts or biographical sketches all designed to further the cause of emancipation and to shed the rays of religious enlightenment on the dogmas and practices of the Catholic Church. In 1787 Berington wrote *The History of the Lives of Abeillard and Heloisa*; in 1790, *The History of the Reign of Henry II*; and in 1793, *The Memoirs of Gregorio Panzani*, which was a partial revision of *The State and Behaviour of English Catholics* and included a document particularly favorable to the Cisalpine position. The oldest member of the movement capped his list of early productions with an unpublished "History of the Rise, the Greatness, and the Decline of the Papal Power." In 1814 he produced his most mature work, *A Literary History of the Middle Ages*. John Throckmorton followed Berington in his two *Letters Addressed to the Catholic Clergy* (1790 and 1791), which attempted to untangle the intricate strands of Catholic loyalty, Jesuit political intrigue, and papal pronouncements from the Middle Ages to the Gallican Articles of 1682. During the debates of the 1790s, the *First, Second,* and *Third Blue Books*, polemical productions by the Catholic Committee, demonstrated a similar spirit of historical inquiry. In addition, the majority of the works of Charles Butler were historical in perspective and design. This distinguished Catholic lawyer wrote *A Succinct History of the Geographical and Political Revolutions of the Empire of Germany* (1812), *Historical Memoirs of the Church of France* (1817), and *Historical Memoirs respecting the English, Irish, and Scottish Catholics* (1819–21). He published biographical accounts of Alban Butler (1800), Fénelon (1810), Bossuet (1812), de Rancé (1814), Thomas à Kempis (1814), Vincent de Paul (1819), Henri Marie de Boudon (1819), and Grotius (1826). John Kirk and John Fletcher were also devoted students of history throughout their lives. Finally, the contribution of John Lingard to English scholarship has long been noted by serious students of the past. He wrote the first thoroughly documented history of England.[1]

In the face of so many books, it might justly be claimed that the use of some type of historical investigation was the dominant characteristic of the Cisalpine movement. History, considered either as a methodological tool for promoting one's view of the world or as an intellectual form for understanding the world, became the prime conveyor of the Cisalpine outlook. It supported and reflected the same features that marked the Cisalpine approach to church and state, authority, and theological investigation: an attitude of secularization, respect for individualism and pluralism, a critical nationalism, and a certain though limited consciousness of change. It is in the origins and progress of this inchoate historical mentality that one can most easily perceive the differences among the Cisalpines, the true nature of the movement, and the reasons for its ultimate decline in influence. This chapter will present these features of Cisalpinism by analyzing the roots of John Lingard's historical consciousness, his relationship to Berington and Butler, and the Catholic reaction to his works.

Cisalpine Historical Roots

Lingard's general educational background encouraged a historical mentality. As has already been indicated, a classical interest in the sources and an empirical methodology supported the conception of history as a separate discipline. There were also other, more significant, influences. For a brief period in 1800 Lingard kept a diary of his intellectual work. Most of its pages contained observations on and comparisons between the treatment of the crusades in Claude Fleury's *Histoire ecclésiastique* and Edward Gibbon's *Decline and Fall of the Roman Empire* (1776–88). Lingard's comments were not very detailed, but they were extremely revealing since they indicated two major sources that shaped his mentality: the French tradition and English historical thought.[2]

The French scholarly tradition represented by Claude Fleury (1640–1725), the Bollandists, and the Maurists provided John Lingard with important orientations in style and critical methodology. In his "Premier discours sur l'histoire ecclésiastique" Fleury avowed his intention to recount only the facts, without preamble, affected transitions, or reflections. He attempted to use original authors, and these only after they had been examined for authenticity. Two excesses were to be avoided: credulity and too much criticism. Fleury's works were obviously partial to Gallicanism, and he used the sources selectively, but throughout his *Histoire ecclésiastique* he recognized the tools of proper scholarship: linguistics, the study of chronology, and the use of scientific criticism to judge facts, authors, and sources. He was supported in this approach by his contemporaries. Daniel van Papenbroeck (1628–1714), the Bollandist genius, scoured Europe for original manuscripts. He never considered a historical argument as more than probable. His reluctance to accept undocumented traditions led the Carmelites to denounce some of the *Acta Sanctorum* to the Spanish Inquisition. The Maurists led by Dom Jean Mabillon (1632–1707) and Jean Martène (1647–1717) collected and scrutinized manuscripts, books, and correspondence. Mabillon's *De Re Diplomatica* (1681) became the standard methodological work in the field of documentary analysis. All these men saw history as an autonomous discipline, a mode of thinking. They helped to reduce the ecclesiastical obsession with polemics and to dissolve the classical standard.[3]

The contribution of this French historical tradition to the formation of John Lingard's mentality has been generally disregarded. Yet he shared with Fleury and Mabillon his most important characteristic, a return to both the printed and documentary sources. He became the first modern historian of England to use the Simancas archives. Other common bonds also ran through their works: the scrutiny of manuscripts as to authenticity and credibility, the use of narrative technique, the importance of chronology, and the necessity of historical impartiality.[4] It was not accidental that in his first work, *The Antiquities of the Anglo-Saxon Church*, Lingard referred the reader to Fleury, Mabillon, Martène, and the Bollandists. He was merely echoing the lofty sentiments of his French forerunners when he wrote in his preface: "My object is truth: and in the pursuit of truth, I have made it a religious duty to consult the original historians. Who would draw from the troubled stream, when he may drink at the fountain head?" The methodological traits he shared with the French historians emerged even more decisively in *A History of England*. In the preface to volume 4 Lingard wrote that he was resolved "to take nothing upon credit, to distrust the statements of partial and interested writers, and to consult every authentic document within my reach. Fidelity and research are the indispensable duties of the historian."[5] Lastly, the difficulties these Frenchmen underwent provided Lingard with an impressive moral example. When he seriously contemplated ceasing his historical inquiries because of the incessant attacks of John Milner, Charles Butler wrote to him:

> I beg leave to observe to you that there scarcely is a spiritual writer whose literary life is known to us with whose works than some weak or wrong headed person has not taken offense. You know the persecutions which the very orthodox Bollandists suffered and the offense which a whole religious order took at Mabillon's discrediting the tear of Vendome. Many years elapsed before Mr. A. Butler's Lives of the Saints overcame the prejudice entertained against them from the omission of many of the Legends with which Metaphrastes and Ribadaeira are crowded. Yet all of these authors are now generally allowed to be scrupulously orthodox.[6]

Lingard's passion for objectivity and his return to the manuscript sources found slight echo in Berington or Butler. The former in his *History of the Lives of Abeillard and Heloisa* referred to the exceptional merit of Fleury's *Histoire ecclésiastique* but commended it mostly because it laid church abuses before the readers. In his *History of the Reign of Henry II*, Berington avowed some use of original documents, but this was hardly evident. *His Literary History of the Middle Ages* was a masterpiece of polemic. Butler followed Fleury in his judgments on the Inquisition and Jansenism. Throughout his works he adopted the more objective style of narration, but neither he nor Berington displayed an acute methodology. Controversy dominated their writings. They relied on the older historians more for Gallican argumentation and a critical attitude toward saints' lives. That the French scholarly tradition bore its purest fruit in Lingard and not in these two men was probably a result of Lingard's personal genius and their age differences. When the romantic historical revival began and the Gordon Riots occurred in 1780, Berington and Butler were mature men, while Lingard was only nine years old. Still, all three Catholics owed to their familiarity with French scholarship a common debt of interest in history.[7]

The impact of English historiography on John Lingard's mentality manifested itself in his apologetic intent, his relationship to the Enlightenment tradition, and his attitude toward the new school of historians. In his preface to *The Antiquities of the Anglo-Saxon Church*, Lingard noted the rise of polemical history after the Reformation. It was largely to balance this trend and to reduce controversy that he attempted, he said, to write with some degree of impartiality. The book did advance beyond earlier polemics, but it hardly broke completely from the denominational accounts. Comments on Gilbert Burnet, Peter Heylin, Joseph Bingham, Edward Stillingfleet, Tobias Smollett, Thomas Carte, David Hume, and Robert Henry pervaded its pages. These men had been historians only *per accidens* and had presupposed the bad faith of their Catholic opponents. In basing his account on documentary sources, Lingard could not resist an occasional sideswipe. The comment on Paul Rapin's and Thomas Carte's interpretation of St. Dunstan was typical: "To have been praised by the monastic historians is, in the estimation of modern writers, the infallible criterion of demerit: and their superior discernment has politely divided the whole body of our Catholic ancestors into two classes; of knaves, who under the mask of sanctity sought to satisfy their avarice, and of fools, who credulously condescended to be the dupes of this hypocrisy. Among the former they have allotted a distinguished place to the celebrated St. Dunstan." Catholic historians were not exempt from similar strictures, but the book was still obviously biased in both purpose and content. It displayed the same minority consciousness and apologetic tone that marked the works of Butler and Berington.[8]

In contrast, *A History of England*, although written from the same stance, avoided the enthusiastic judgments of youth. In it Lingard carefully concealed his bias underneath a dispassionate narrative and a mass of documentary evidence. He refused to read the earlier historians lest they unduly influence his judgment. He wrote to John Kirk in December 1819: "Through the work I made it a rule to tell the truth, whether it made for or against us, to avoid all appearance of controversy, that I might not repel protestant readers, and yet to furnish every necessary proof in our favour in the notes. . . . Had it been like the Anglo-Saxon Church, it would have been read only by Catholics." Two years later he again manifested this very calm but calculated effort to "serve religion." He proposed to show that Cranmer, had Edward continued to reign, intended to "burn the believers in transubstantiation. He got no more than he meant to inflict." Lingard also consciously softened his treatment of Elizabeth and proposed the following paragraph in review of his accomplishments: "The author has treated the persecution of the reformers under Mary, and of the puritans and the catholics under Elizabeth, with a candour and impartiality which though it may displease the bigots of different communions, will, we are confident, be rewarded with the approbation of those readers, who are aware of that intolerant spirit which prevailed among all religious parties, in the sixteenth century, and who lament that traces of it are still suffered to disgrace the statute book after the lapse of more than two hundred years." Finally, the reason for writing *A History of England* in the first place had stemmed from the desire to avoid a particularly offensive ecclesiastical scandal that had occurred in the Norman period. Rather than relate it, Lingard had turned to writing secular history so that he could adopt an objective position without doing harm to Catholicism.[9]

Lingard's relationship to the Enlightenment tradition was ambiguous. With Butler and Berington he inherited a general attitude of disparagement toward the Middle Ages. In addition, he obviously reacted to the religious sentiments of Hume and Gibbon. The former furnished him with the negative example of an uncritical methodology and a tendency to subordinate facts to philosophical beliefs. Charles Butler unfavorably compared Lingard's style with Gibbon's, and there may have been some unconscious borrowings in this area. *The Antiquities of the Anglo-Saxon Church* more than *A History of England* betrayed the adverse influences of these two major eighteenth-century English historians. The earlier work abounded with "philosophical tirades" and, as Butler analyzed it, "frequent use of antithesis." In contrast, a simplicity of style and neutrality of judgment marked *A History of England*.[10] In a letter to his publisher, Lingard compared this work with Hume's and discovered that he came off victorious in his treatment of Alfred the Great, the life of Harold, the establishment of feudal law, the Magna Carta, Richard II, and Edward IV.[11]

A History of England also indicates the most important positive characteristic the Enlightenment bequeathed to Lingard. Hume, William Robertson, and Gibbon had brought the ideas of Montesquieu and Voltaire to England. In their hands history writing had become secular and nonpartisan; a sardonic tone of superiority had encouraged a critical attitude toward religion and human nature. When Lingard defined history as "little more than a record of the miseries inflicted on the many by the passions of the few," he exhibited a similar type of skepticism. The influence of rationalism on his view of faith has already been treated. When applied to the history of religion it furthered a nonpolemical viewpoint. His emphasis on political narrative, while it departed from the wider view of Voltaire and Gibbon, mirrored the impact of secularization. This important element enabled Lingard to balance his apologetic intentions with a critical objectivity. As a result, modern studies have evaluated his history favorably, and on many issues contemporary scholarship has supported his conclusions.[12]

The Enlightenment's inability to sympathize with the Middle Ages and its tendency to see history as "philosophy teaching by examples" would perhaps have influenced Lingard more detrimentally than they did had he not been raised in the midst of a deeper intellectual revival. After 1770 some important discoveries of primary materials, a new view of the power of tradition, and a shift from skepticism to a more providential attitude radically altered the approach to history. Sharon Turner and Robert Southey represented the strengths and weaknesses of this movement. They shared with the Enlightenment a confidence in the power of the intellect and a belief in the supremacy of modernity. But they added to these characteristics some important touches of enthusiasm, recognition of the originality of any given period of history, and national pride. Turner's *History of the Anglo-Saxons* (1799) preceded Lingard's by several years. The Catholic historian reacted to its religious views and rewrote much of his *Antiquities of the Anglo-Saxon Church* to disprove it. Still, he recognized Turner's importance and shared his zeal for English origins. In Southey, this religious romanticism tended to submerge critical sense. He intended his *Book of the Church* (1824) to be a reply to Lingard's *History of England*. In a letter to his publisher Lingard easily dismissed the attempts: "In his reigns of Henry, Edward, and Mary he has done little more than make a compendium of Fox, and has related without the least semblance of a doubt as to their accuracy the hearsay stories collected by that writer."[13]

In the midst of the general romantic movement the man closest to Lingard was Henry Hallam. This constitutional historian avoided any idealization of the past but joined Southey and Turner in imaginatively identifying with a subject. Lingard, while disagreeing with Hallam in some ways, noted that he had read "The State of Europe during the Middle Ages" (1818) with "profit and delight." He also manifested a Whig interpretation (more moderate than Hallam's) and strains of a belief in progress. The common ideology behind the two men could be seen in Lingard's advertisement to the first volume of his *History of England.* It is the historian's duty, he said, "to trace the silent progress of nations from barbarism to refinement: and to mark the successive improvements in the arts of legislation and government. But in the performance of this duty he must keep a steady rein on the imagination; or he will mistake fiction for truth, and write a romance in the place of a history."[14] In short, Lingard may have kept a "steady rein" on this imagination, but he joined Southey, Turner, and Hallam in recognizing its existence. That important trait, however slight, connected him with the romantic revival and helped balance a predominantly Enlightenment attitude. Its full significance emerged very clearly, for example, in the differences between Lingard's dispassionate comments on the crusades and Berington's overt denunciations.

In addition to these influences of the English historiographical tradition, one other broad influence on John Lingard's mentality should not be disregarded. John Miller in *Popery and Politics in England, 1660–1688* has noted that Protestant historians, in their desire to protect the Elizabethan settlement, were slow to concede that sixteenth-century conditions ever changed. Their view of history and Catholicism was static. Conversely, in our analysis, the Catholic was forced to argue for historical mutability. As chapter 1 indicated, he could not deny the fact of Pius V's deposition of Elizabeth. He could only maintain that the times had changed; that Catholics no longer accepted certain principles; that the medieval synthesis had shattered; that England was not Italy or France. The same environment that formed the fixed approach to dogma thus encouraged an understanding of relativity in the political and social orders. The Cisalpines shared this consciousness of change with their Gallican supporters.¹⁵

In summary, the roots of John Lingard's historical mentality were buried deep in his educational background, familiarity with the tradition of French scholarship, exposure to the trends of English historiography, and recognition of political and social relativity. All these currents converged to form a distinctive and paradoxical amalgam of apologetic intent/objectivity, philosophical judgment/empirical observation, and cynical detachment/romantic sympathy. At times one trait dominated another; most often the technique of dry classical narrative submerged any spark of romantic insight. Despite recognition of historical relativity, Lingard could not conceal his dislike for the Middle Ages. His greatest characteristic—strict adherence to documentary sources—was also in some respects his great limitation. *A History of England* relied almost exclusively on political records, so much so that Joseph Berington, a man with a broader, more cultural orientation, wrote: "The reign of Elizabeth to me deserves less praise, on account of its omissions. He says nothing of the manners of the people, which must have been modified by the changes in religion; nothing of the literature, though many able men, as we know, existed during the long period of her reign (Shakespeare); nothing of the (usual) progresses she made in the country, when she showed herself & familiarly conversed with the people, & from which circumstance was her popularity, and fame which is come down to us of the glorious days of the great Queen Bess."¹⁶

Despite these limitations, Lingard's historical mentality would have been impossible without the mixture of all four elements. They combined with the growth of social toleration from 1780 to 1819 and his personal genius to differentiate him from the other Cisalpines. Charles Butler possessed some romantic appreciation for the past; Joseph Berington, very little. On the other hand, Butler lacked a strong touch of Enlightenment skepticism; Berington had more than his share. In the writings of both men apologetic motive blocked complete openness to objectivity. They lacked Lingard's strong predilection for original sources. The writer of *A History of*

England was also an apologist and exhibited a rationalist strain, but he managed to transcend these characteristics. M. A. Tierney summarized Lingard's distinctive position when he wrote:

> Berington and Potts, Milner, and many others, had in vain employed the arms supplied by history for the defence of their own Church, and in opposition to the favourite prejudices of Protestantism. Lingard, therefore, came to pursue a different course from that of his predecessors. *They* had appeared as advocates—*he* was an unimpassioned narrator: *they* had avowedly argued for a victory—*he* simply stated the case that was before him: *they* had drawn their own conclusions, and exhibited their own views—*he* allowed the narrative to tell its own tale, and to make its own impression, and to suggest the inferences that would naturally arise from it.[17]

These "inferences" that the Cisalpines wanted their readers to assume must now be considered. Despite their differences, history has testified to the friendship of Berington, Butler, and Lingard; their opponents have judged them to be similar in outlook. What, then, was the positive intellectual core of their historical view? The following will examine the Catholic reaction, both domestic and foreign, to Lingard's historical writings. This historian, as the youngest, most objective, and least polemical of the men, probably best provides an indication of the essential structure of Cisalpine thought.

The Core of Cisalpine History

The Antiquities of the Anglo-Saxon Church, Lingard's first major work, appeared in 1806. Four years later a second edition was printed. The author intended it to be an apologetic work. In his preface Lingard noted that he was dissatisfied with the results. Still the book generally impressed the reader with its documentation and knowledge of Saxon customs. Its enthusiastic spirit has already been noted. Despite some criticisms, Butler judged *The Antiquities of the Anglo-Saxon Church* a success and hoped Lingard would continue his account with the Anglo-Norman Church.[18]

Significantly, not all the Catholics agreed with Butler, and the type of criticism they leveled plagued Lingard for the rest of his life. John Milner accused the author of heresy because of his eucharistic opinions. Richard Thompson, a priest friend with an *esprit ardent*, concentrated on the tone of the work. While giving his "unequivocal approbation," he objected to the use of the word "presbyter" instead of "priest"; the description of St. Augustine as marked by the "anguish of disappointed zeal"; the references to the "credulity" of the monks and the "curiosity" of pilgrims; and the phrases "imposing solemnity" and "imposing pomp." Thompson complained in particular about Lingard's analysis of the Saxon proselytes' motives for conversion. According to Lingard they had been "disgusted with the pleasures or troubles of the world." His critical friend also felt that Lingard approved the Saxon apostles' deference toward the state. With respect to deference to the state, *The Antiquities of the Anglo-Saxon Church* said that the success of the Saxons disproved those who think that "no church can be firmly established, the foundations of which are not cemented with the blood of martyrs." For someone like Thompson, this "savoured too much of the Church of England."[19]

A third respondent wrote in a fashion similar to Thompson. Did not Lingard convey a very false meaning of religious obedience when he wrote: "When the commands of the superior are contrary to the law of God, the monk is exhorted to throw off the *shackles* of obedience, and *boldly to hazard the frowns and vengeance of his Abbot*, rather than incur the displeasure of the Almighty." There were remarks from other quarters that Lingard used the word "brotherhood," substituted "pontiff" for "pope," and did not belong to the "old school" (i.e., did not defend the papal supremacy or monastic institutions). Richard Southworth struck at the heart of all the criticism: "In short, I consider our Anglo-Saxon Church in the light of an *ancient venerable Matron*, the parent of many glorious Saints, and models of Christian wisdom, and perfection. Wherefore, if she is to be brought to public view, I would have her clothed in a dress suitable to her character, adapted to inspire in those who behold her, sentiments of respect and veneration."[20]

Lingard hardly knew what to respond to complaints like these. Having set out to write an apology, he found both his orthodoxy and piety suspect. For the most part he staunchly defended his approach, but he seriously wondered if he should continue working. After encouragement from Charles Butler, he did. Yet if he thought he could avoid these reproaches by writing a secular history, he was seriously mistaken. The reactions to *A History of England* made the earlier criticisms seem mild.

Lingard published the first three volumes of his monumental work on May 10, 1819. Within eight days over five hundred copies were sold. The historian wrote to his friend Robert Gradwell in early June: "As yet I have heard nothing against it. But I am told it was secretly whispered, before it was published, that I had sold my principles together with my ms. These persons will not fail to assert that their predictions are verified. For I have written in a different manner from that observed in the Anglo-Saxon Church. I have been careful to defend the Catholics, but not so as to hurt the feelings of Protestants."[21] He did not have long to wait for the expected reaction. On June 19, 1819, John Milner wrote to the *Orthodox Journal*, beginning a nine-month controversy between the vicar apostolic and the historian over the various "Catholic" merits of the work.[22] Milner wrote under several pseudonyms. He was supported by "No Unbeliever," "Minimus," T. (William Talbot), and the editor, William Eusebius Andrews. "Candidus" jumped to the defense of Lingard. Who he was remained a mystery to all. Some thought John Fletcher; others, John Kirk. Internal evidence indicated that he was Lingard himself, who also pleaded his cause as "Amicus Justitiae," and "Philorthodoxos."[23] The debate centered around two major issues: the historian's un-Catholic and almost latitudinarian spirit and his derogation of authority.

After complaining that Lingard allowed the errors of Hume, Smollett, and Oliver Goldsmith to stand, Milner wrote: "Nor has he displayed the beauty of holiness, irradiating the doctrines and heroes of catholicity, in the manner that he might have done." The author "seems to have as great a horror of miracles as any protestant can possibly wish to find in him." William Talbot agreed. He asked: What is *A History of England?* "A flowing *jejune*, a naked narrative of facts, already known to the readers, the protestant part of which he appears to court in a very undisguised manner. . . ." Both men cited as their prime example Lingard's treatment of St. Thomas of Canterbury: The historian did not call him "saint," described him as "tinged with enthusiasm," and related that he died for "what he *thought to be his duty*." Milner especially castigated the omission of several miraculous events testifying to the divine approbation of celibacy. He described Lingard's work only after censuring Berington, Alexander Geddes, Butler, and John Chetwode Eustace. The vicar apostolic assumed that all these men breathed the same general atmosphere of latitudinarian spirit. "No Unbeliever" put it this way: Lingard's momentary lapses differed from the consistent betrayals of the others, but in all cases "let the voice of piety prevail."[24]

In response to these accusations Lingard recalled all the times he employed the title "saint," defended his use of "enthusiasm," and said that he omitted the miracles because they were not reported in the most authentic histories of the period. It was evident to him that the objectors understood neither the purpose of the work nor the laws of criticism. Was it not true that Bede himself called St. Gregory only "Gregory"? Did not Milner omit some miracles from his *History of Winchester?* Had not John of Salisbury said that Becket's mind was adversely influenced by too much study of canon law, the histories of the martyrs, and the Holy Scriptures? "Candidus" also defended Berington and Butler. His whole attitude was best summarized in his comments on Eustace: "There is a liberal spirit, which is the genuine spirit of pure Christianity, which is admirably expressed in that well-known adage, *in necessariis unitas, in dubiis libertas, in omnibus caritas*, which is equally removed from the opposite extremes of latitudinarianism on the one hand, and of intolerance on the other, and which we should all do well to cherish and to cultivate."[25]

The second major objection leveled at *A History of England* was much weightier in its implications. Lingard wrote that in order to combat Pelagianism Germanus of Auxerre had twice visited Britain, "with the concurrence of Pope Celestine." Milner violently rejected the use of "concurrence." He felt that Germanus had been sent as a papal delegate and that he had suppressed Pelagius's doctrine not by his own authority but by that of the pope. "Candidus" considered the objection to "concurrence" too trivial to merit attention. Milner pursued the issue. "Concurrence" was not verbal quibbling; the use of the word represented the pontiff as a "coequal bishop." In reality, he argued, Germanus as the pope's *vice sua* with legatine powers furnished proof that as early as 429 British churches had acknowledged the papal supremacy. "Amicus Justitiae" replied that no record testified that Germanus had exercised powers derived from the pope. Instead, the documents said that he had been sent by the bishops of Gaul and that he and Lupus had consecrated Dubricius after the latter had "been elected by the king and clergy and people, metropolitan of Wales."[26]

This last assertion by Lingard appeared to be too much for the editor of the *Orthodox Journal*. Andrews, referring to Bede, wrote that Germanus had acted at the "command of the Holy Church." "Command" meant more than "concurrence," and "as this is stated to be a command of the *holy church*, it must come from the pope, because the church cannot speak but by her head." "Amicus Justitiae," Andrews charged, destroyed the divine right of the see of Rome and attempted to establish an ecclesiastical democracy in the fifth century. Lingard attempted to respond to these damaging assertions, but Andrews rejected his letters as "the most worthless and self-refutable that have been submitted to his [the editor's] judgment since the commencement of his literary labours."[27]

If Lingard's opponents in the *Orthodox Journal* felt that his use of "concurrence" was bad enough, they also noted that he deserved further censure for even attempting to respond to a vicar apostolic. "No Unbeliever" wrote that "Candidus" actually dared to summon to the bar of the Inquisition "the divine authority of the unshaken pillar, the Midland prelate." He supposed that "in a time of similar arrogance Candid would, in consistency, have made the authority of St. Cyprian, St. Austin, in a word, of all the successors of the apostles individually, the subject of inquiry, and, with Jansenius, come to the conclusion of sapping the infallibility of the church dispersed, by appealing for the necessity of a general council." To Andrews the attitude of "Candidus" was subversive. Did he not know that bishops were appointed by the Holy Ghost as guardians of the faith and that "it is *their right* and *duty* not only as bishops but also as doctors of the catholic church, to denounce works of an innovating or erroneous tendency. . . ."?[28]

At this point, after lasting almost half a year and consuming nearly fifty pages of the journal, the controversy abruptly concluded. Andrews proclaimed Milner the victor in the January 1820 issue. In the next number "Candidus" responded that he retracted nothing. Compromise was impossible. The correspondents remained unsatisfied. Milner only hoped that the next volume of *A History of England* would refute the errors in Berington's *State and Behaviour of English Catholics* and Butler's *Historical Memoirs of the English, Irish, and Scottish Catholics*. Lingard felt that the vicar apostolic owed him a public apology. The battle was only beginning.[29]

When John Talbot had first read his father-in-law's strictures on Lingard's *History*, he had disagreed with the criticisms. On February 21, 1820, he had written to John Kirk: " . . . no man is well received if he is violent and blustering . . . in that case he is generally excluded from Society as one who knows not how to behave himself in it. & such would have been the fate of Mr. Lingard's book if he had acted as some wish, & had introduced [sic] the miracles of St. Dunstan & S. Thomas of Canterbury etc etc to our acquaintance. It would have been too strong a food for Protestant stomachs. . . ." These opinions changed greatly when Lingard's version of the English Reformation appeared. In November 1820 Talbot wrote twice to Kirk and focused on the historian's faults of language and omission. To him *A History of England* seemed to concede too much to Protestant prejudice. He complained that the book implied the decadence of monastic institutions, admitted the abuse of image worship, approved a married clergy, attributed too many actions to "policy" and not "principles," treated religion in a flippant manner, questioned the faith of the illiterate poor, and failed to explain the Roman doctrine on indulgences, private judgment, and the supremacy of the pope. These issues plus a whole host of other facts led to the conclusion that "perhaps the only testimony in favour of Catholicity throughout the whole work is to be found in the last lines of the last page, where it is said that the Catholic religion possesses more restraints upon vice than the new one." Talbot judged Lingard in relationship to Milner and found him wanting: "There is a strain of pious feeling and religious sentiment in the works of this able writer which I should have been glad to have observed more largely in Mr. L."[30]

Lingard replied to these objections. Most of them he could not understand, and he wondered if the critic wrote with a prepossession against him. The historian denied that his work approved a married clergy or favored the cause of the reformers. Many issues seemed trivial. He summarized his feelings in this way:

> But where one has laboured earnestly for the sole service of religion (I am not conscious to myself of any other object whatever) it is a mortification to find a brother pronouncing that the work will never prove of any service. Yet I had no cause to complain. When a book is published, every reader has a right to form and express his opinion of it, its plan, and its execution—Laugh at me for these limitations—"*it, its plan, its execution*"—In writing then I meant to abstain from saying anything in justification of the critics in Andrews, whose infallibility reaches even to the motives of the writer.[31]

The letter did not compromise. It only tried to emphasize the fact that both men were motivated by the same end but differed in approach. With such an attitude, Lingard hoped that he and Talbot could serve the same cause. In retrospect, it was evident that no matter how hard Lingard tried, he could not satisfy his critics. They objected to his very cast of mind.

For his part, after the appearance of volume 4 John Milner determined to end all debate on *A History of England*. He appealed for an authoritative judgment. In 1823, when Lingard was mentioned as a possible coadjutor to the Northern vicar, Thomas Smith, the ever-vigilant "Angel of Castabala" wrote to Propaganda. After recounting his role in Lingard's vocation, Milner noted that the young man, although orthodox, had not fulfilled his expectations in piety or zeal for religion. It was true, he said, that the historian had defended Catholicism in many tracts and treated the Anglo-Saxon Church with gravity, but he had also excessively favored the cause and opinions of Protestants, not without scandal to the pious Catholics. To prove this, Milner then related his objections to *A History of England*. He recalled the earlier debate over Thomas of Canterbury's "enthusiasm," and, in addition, said that Lingard both praised Thomas Cranmer's courage in arguing against the sacrifice of the mass and implied Nicholas Ridley's Protestant sincerity. This letter was followed by a continuous stream of requests to have Lingard's work condemned.[32]

The reactions to Milner's charges varied. Rome by this time had been accustomed to his frequent attacks on anyone who disagreed with him. Therefore the matter never came before the official tribunal. Robert Gradwell, rector of the English College, wrote to Poynter: "Dr. M has been writing another tirade against Dr. Lingard's history, which only excites laughter at Propaganda." Still, it was no laughing issue in England. The denunciation at Rome represented the depth of division between the two sides and the extent to which the Cisalpine view threatened a man of Milner's persuasion. The debate filled the pages of private correspondence.[33] It was true that after volume 6 on James I and

Charles I appeared in 1825, the issues tended to fade. The debate ended partly because when Milner died in 1826, there was no one of equal stature who could argue with Lingard. As late as 1828, Thomas White, a priest confidante of both Lingard and Milner, could still summarize the emotional atmosphere of the affair:

> What you relate respecting Dr. M & yr history quite astonishes me. Admitting ye mode of expression with regard to Bp Ridley to have an appearance of *condescension* towards his Brethren & Descendants, I shd not have supposed any Person wd. make a serious representation, almost equivalent to an accusation, in the Court of the Propaganda. *Here*, in Engd. it might be spoken of in conversation & discussed as a matter of opinion but neither here, nor anywhere, ought it (me thinks) be produced to criminate you, unless you were known or suspected to lean towards the side of Protestancy. As to the dispute about St. Tho. Cant. I shd indeed have thought yt. the respected cramming wh. all must have had 3 or 4 years ago, when the dish was so often served up, wd have satisfied any stomach & have produced ad satietatem at least, if not to a more powerful effect.[34]

Looking back between 1819 and 1825 on the controversy, Thomas White may have justly wondered how the participants could have gorged themselves on a diet of details. To some extent the reason was obvious. A similar conflict had plagued the Catholic body in England for the last forty years. In the course of the long debate Milner purposely linked his attack on Lingard to his former disagreements with the Cisalpines. "Candidus" had no other choice than to respond by defending not only Lingard but also Berington and Butler. Nor was it completely accidental that the vicar apostolic denounced *A History of England* at the same time that he waged constant war on Charles Butler and penned a Lenten pastoral against *Roman Catholic Principles*.[35] As far as he and certain other English Catholics were concerned, the conflict clearly did not stop at the use of the words "concurrence" or "virtue," or the description of Thomas Cranmer, or the number of miracles reported, or the failure to defend the strictest Catholic teaching. The rough polemics of the 1790s may have disappeared; so, too, the excessively antipapal and anti-Jesuit tone of Berington's works. But the same problem remained. *A History of England* manifested a distinctive mentality, the roots of which could not be destroyed. Lingard's books had to be denounced because they reflected the two poles of Cisalpine thought that had always troubled the English Catholic world: the consultive approach to ecclesiastical authority and the attitude of openness toward an English Protestant world. These elements appeared to the controversialists as the hard core of Cisalpine history. They were the troublesome strains linking *The State and Behaviour of English Catholics, Memoirs of Panzani, Historical Memoirs of the English, Irish, and Scottish Catholics*, and *A History of England*.

It should also be noted here that although the 1806–23 controversies focused on the issues of authority and openness, even as they have been outlined in chapter 2, there was a subtle change in emphasis. Milner and the two Talbots shifted the center of the debate from the field of dogmatic and institutional accommodation to that of "spirit," "tone," "Catholic attitude." To some extent this shift was dictated by the fact that Lingard's main work was a political and not an ecclesiastical history. But the complaints against *The Antiquities of the Anglo-Saxon Church* and the "Candidus" argument also mirrored the beginning of the general romantic reaction to a "cool" spirituality. Spirituality had been of secondary importance in the 1790s; it was to dominate the last portion of Lingard's life and was one current that indicated the passage from the eighteenth century to the nineteenth. Thus, in an indirect fashion, the objections to Lingard's books unveiled part of the core of Cisalpinism. Here, as in other areas, the real issue under debate was acceptance or rejection of the Enlightenment's climate of opinion. What, exactly, this acceptance or rejection entailed was even more starkly revealed in the French and Italian reactions to *A History of England*.

The French edition of Lingard's *History of England*, published between 1825 and 1831, experienced a mixed reception. In his advertisement the liberal translator, Le Chevalier de Roujoux, gave a very favorable judgment. He found the work to be clear and factual, needing mostly unimportant explanatory notes.[36] In contrast, the ultramontane and royalist *Le mémorial catholique* found it more difficult to assess the true merit of the work. That journal issued five review articles between November 1826 and April 1827. Its comments were extremely indicative; they defined Lingard's place within the continental tradition and summarized his major fault in foreign eyes. First of all, the reviewer credited Lingard with having rejected the approach of the philosophical historians. He noted that *A History of England* differed so much from previous works that Lingard had been reproached for hiding his Catholic feelings. Even so, the Englishman's method appeared to be much better than that of Augustin Thierry's. The latter sold history into the slavery of sentiment; he decided *a priori* that all the actions of the Holy See were oppressive and imperial and so judged everything in that light. Fortunately, the writer concluded, one easily recognized the superficiality of Thierry's approach when Lingard was put before his eyes.[37]

Despite judging Lingard to be Catholic in comparison with Thierry, *Le mémorial catholique* did not feel that *A History of England* totally escaped damaging bias. The second article considered Lingard's approach to the Middle Ages and significantly placed his views in the same spectrum with those of Hume, Voltaire, and other *philosophes*. All seemed to describe the "ages of faith" as times of ignorance, superstition, and barbarism. They misrepresented the action of the church on Christian society. The reviewer could hardly pass over these false judgments. It was "with pain" that he singled out several of Lingard's reprehensible interpretations, especially his views of the actions of Innocent III. In the opinion of the reviewer, *A History of England* described the activities of that pontiff as encroachments on the civil power; Lingard seemed afraid of contradicting the dominant ideas of his country. Was this not to furnish arms to the enemy? (pp. 21-36).

The third and fourth articles considered Lingard's interpretations of Henry VIII and Elizabeth to be very Catholic. (pp. 106–24, 169–90). The last review was more critical. It singled out the historian's treatment of Charles I. Here, it seemed, *A History of England* erred by excessive impartiality. The writer in *Le mémorial catholique* argued that the political revolution under Charles I had been the necessary consequence of the religious revolution which had made Henry VIII absolute monarch. Since this principle was so evident, the reviewer believed that Lingard's dispassionate narration of the history of Charles I disregarded the obligations of the historian. Did he not realize that "in history doctrines must be considered and not events; those [doctrines] which the *cavaliers* defended were false and anti-social. . ." (p. 271). Still, despite these criticisms, the reviewer could not dismiss *A History of England* as completely worthless. In his final remarks he tried to be just and gave Lingard the benefit of the doubt. The last article considered the work to be an indispensable guide to English history and concluded with a recommendation (pp. 260–72).

In summary, the very ambiguity of the articles in *Le mémorial catholique* was important. In contrast to the English polemicists, the French reviewer could approve Lingard's defense of Catholicism. On the other hand, ultramontane and royalist presuppositions forced him to concentrate on those parts of the history which Milner and others had ignored. In a world racked by the French Revolution, Lingard's political views were clearly unacceptable. The reviewer judged shrewdly when he classified the English historian with the eighteenth-century *philosophes*. He astutely recognized that even in spite of its factual basis, a history written from Enlightenment principles had no ideological support in restoration Europe. In a certain sense, his remarks prophesied the future for Cisalpinism. The end of Cisalpinism was even more graphically indicated when the editor of *Le mémorial catholique* printed a devastating attack on Lingard's work by another anonymous correspondent. This appeared in September 1828, and was expanded and translated into Italian almost immediately.[38]

Osservazioni sulla storia d'Inghilterra, printed clandestinely and published anonymously, was "furtively distributed in Rome, being put under doors in the night, left on staircases or in halls, etc. so that every person of any consequence was furnished with one." Giacoma Ventura, a Theatine of strong opinions, was probably the author. Robert Gradwell, in a passage that deserves full quotation, described Ventura's background in this way:

> There is at Rome, as well as in France, a faction of Catholic Zealots, ultras in everything, in divinity, in ethics, metaphysics, history & law. They lay down abstract principles, & then draw from them the most extravagant conclusions. As Hutchinsonians lay it down that all wisdom is in the Bible & hence expatiate into wild conclusions; so these lay it down as a maxim, that church authority and Catholic truth are everything in science. All the rest is infidelity or atheism. The head of these at Rome is a Theatine from Palermo, Padre Ventura. He is a great metaphysician & a prolific writer. About 1825, the Pope, who had heard that Ventura was a great man in his way, invited him to Rome, & gave him a professor's chair at the Sapienza. I do not recollect whether it was called the chair of metaphysics, or ethics, or political principles; it was such a jumble of all three. He dictated his course. One volume was printed. I believe the Imprimatur was refused the second. The book was that of a mountebank; & his lectures were laughed at by the young as buffoonry [sic]. Men of reflection thought he was not only revolutionizing philosophy; but, and this was my own opinion, undermining religion. I am sorry that I had such a contempt for his system & extravagances, that I cannot now trust myself to report them. I think he defined man to be intellectus organizatus, or substantia spiritualis corpore induta. He represents the British Government as a perfect monster & the worst of all governments. The Church is the fountain of power; then Kings follow who derive their power from the Church. Less perfect and further from religion are limited monarchies because part of the authority which the monarch derives from the church is withheld by others. Less perfect still are republics which have less of the principle of original authority & more consequently of infidelity in their construction. But the English constitution is a rebellion against ecclesiastical principle and consequently atheistical.[39]

Knowing this, the rector of the English College could hardly have been surprised at the vehemence with which "Bastia" attacked *A History of England*.

According to "Bastia," Lingard's work contained principles that conformed very little to the Catholic doctrine on society. First of all, the book disregarded the true nature of history; it substituted chronology for the historian's obligation to "guide us to an understanding of the facts" (p. 7). For example, Lingard wrote from a poor perspective. By establishing England as the center of his observations and denying the view of the larger Christian Republic, he failed to treat the Middle Ages as "a great day of Catholic action, which put under Divine Law (that is) under truth and justice, the material and brutal forces that ravaged society" (p. 7). Second, *A History of England* reflected the prejudices of the *philosophes*, the eighteenth-century heirs of Protestant principles. Instead of recognizing that the actions of the popes in the Middle Ages had been favorable to the establishment of order and liberty, the book always criticized the actions of the spiritual power in its rapport with political society.

> Sharing firmly this idea, that political society, long a being subordinate to spiritual society, should be fundamentally separated, which, as the historical order of things show, is in fact contrary to that established by the church over several centuries, the author then finds himself forced to consider the facts that are a consequence of this order violations of the legitimate constitutions of society. Now all aspects are transformed. The popes who fought to maintain this order of things are nothing more than fanatics, although all in good faith; if not this, then they were nothing more than contemptible plotters, bold kings responsible for all the confusion which has arisen from all their unjust pretenses. The councils, particular or general, that sanctioned this same order, were dominated by absurd prejudice. . . . In a word, spiritual power, of the type exercised by the church, is nothing less than a permanent usurpation of the most sacred rights. . . . (pp. 10–11).

"Bastia" believed that the absurdity of such a view hardly needed to be proved: Was it not strange that Dr. Lingard stopped at the ideas of the eighteenth-century Encyclopedists, when present-day deists and atheists rushed to defend the papacy? As if this were not enough, *A History of England* even supported the principles of the social contract. Lingard wandered further from the truth than had the actual heads of that party which confessed the doctrine of the sovereignty of the people: "The fanatical hate against Christianity by the philosophers of the last century, the violence of their assertions, forewarned the readers to guard well against these assertions, while in the work of Dr. Lingard, the honorable character of the author, his priesthood by which he is covered, his erudition in details, his decent and measured language, all work together to produce an illusion around these anti-catholic and anti-social errors. . ." (p. 14). In short, Lingard's work supported the disposition of Gallicanism, adopted by the English Catholics to placate the Protestants. It was obvious that "this history in its spirit is much more noxious than many of the works that have been put on the index of forbidden books in Rome" (p. 18).

The "Bastia" pamphlet caused quite a flurry of activity. English Catholics in Rome expressed their deep concern in letters to Lingard. They feared a condemnation and wanted him to respond; a friend met with the pope. Fortunately Pius VIII told them that he disregarded the accusations; his ear "though attempted, has not been poisoned."[40] Domenico Gregori, the Italian translator of *A History of England*, also felt he should defend the historian. In order to secure an imprimatur for the book, he wrote "correcting" footnotes to many of Lingard's interpretations.[41] Ironically, as a friend, he turned out to be the Englishman's worst enemy. The notes "became most diffuse, dissertations every now and then for pages together in the ultramontane style."[42] Gregori objected to Lingard's reflections on Gregory VII, his criticisms of the crusades, the use of the words "temporal pretensions" when speaking of the spiritual power, the denial of the authenticity of the Isidorian decretals, the interpretation of the effects of the Western Schism, and the description of Julius II. He cautioned his readers against applying the principles of the Magna Carta to other political systems.

Lingard later discovered this wolf in lamb's clothing and

wrote marginal comments for his Italian edition. One "correction" that captured the tenor of Gregori's additions seemed particularly offensive to the historian. Where *A History of England* had disparagingly attributed Innocent III's deposition of King John to the mistaken notions of feudal jurisprudence, Gregori had defended the medieval approach. Lingard commented: "This note is full of the most miserable sophisms. The pope has the power of inflicting spiritual punishments—true—but to deprive a prince of his crown is a temporal punishment. It is for him to decide whether the oath of obedience any longer obliges. But did the people call upon them to give such decision—did their censures make any such decision. Instead of saying the oath no longer obliges they said *we absolve* you from the obligation.—They did not make themselves sovereigns—yet they gave the crown to other princes. Was not that something like making themselves sovereigns?"[43] This marginal response indicates the intellectual chasm that separated Lingard's world from that of Gregori's. In a certain sense, as a comment on a note to a note, it symbolized the futility of any reconciliation. Here all argument had to cease. The Italian translator had appealed to Joseph de Maistre, Chateaubriand, and German ultramontanes in support of his opinions. The same climate of opinion had divided Lingard from *Le mémorial catholique* and Padre Ventura. To a man of Cisalpine persuasions the warm winds of ecclesiastical romanticism must have appeared very ill indeed.

Taken together, the English, French, and Italian reactions to *A History of England*, precisely because they proceeded from this romantic milieu, touched the central nerve endings of the Cisalpine mentality. They indicated the primary issues on which the movement foundered in the nineteenth-century church: acceptance of political secularization, an individualistic anthropology, a more democratic structure of ecclesiology, and a culturally open approach to dogma and piety. After the debacle of 1789, men had awakened from the slumber of what they considered to be Protestant and latitudinarian principles to find a stark choice between total anarchy or a centralized, organic conception of social, ecclesial, and intellectual order.

Authority and unity became the watchwords of a new age. Socially, the union of throne and altar and the principle of hierarchy once again dominated. Just three years after the "Bastia" pamphlet, *Mirari Vos* (1832), the charter of nineteenth-century political Catholicism, condemned rationalism, Gallicanism, and liberalism. As the church fully attached itself to the conservative political system, Lingard wryly asked Nicholas Wiseman to tell Pope Gregory that as long as the pope adhered to Robert Peel and the duke of Wellington, he would receive no more veneration from Lingard than that owed to the head of the church. In the realm of ecclesiology, monarchical sovereignty and infallibility became inseparable. Joseph de Maistre wrote: "Christianity rests entirely on the Sovereign Pontiff." Nothing could have symbolized the difference between the Cisalpines and *Du Pape* more than the latter's reinterpretation of Bossuet's "Sermon on Unity" to exalt the authority of the papacy. In addition, the new philosophy of traditionalism, which Gradwell had referred to in his description of Ventura, struck at the sensationalist psychology of Locke and the general rationalistic attitude of the eighteenth century. Traditionalism combined with the upsurge in religious sentiment to emphasize another approach to church history, one closer to that of Milner and John Talbot. Eventually, Prosper Gúeranger replaced Mabillon, and Claude Fleury gave way to René-François Rohrbacher. John Lingard's *A History of England* had nothing in common with this world.[44]

Here is not the place to trace the growth and progress of this nineteenth-century mentality. To some extent it will be revealed in the analysis of Lingard's relationship to the Second Spring. For the moment the point is simply that in the light of the romantic reaction the nature of Cisalpine history and Cisalpinism itself becomes clear. All the major problems that have been studied in the first three chapters of this presentation emerged again in *A History of England*. Berington, Butler, and Lingard did indeed have a common, principled approach to the world. It could only be described, whether in politics, ecclesiology, theology, or history, as the English phase of the Catholic Enlightenment.

5. the end of a movement: john lingard and the second spring

THE PUBLICATION of *A History of England* and the full emergence of the romantic critique marked the end of the influential period of Cisalpinism. By the 1820s the social and intellectual forces that had nurtured the outlook had passed away. At that time, the impact of the Irish immigration became increasingly manifest; the emerging life of the Catholic "third estate" began to retreat before the needs of the urban poor. The conversions of Ambrose Phillipps and Kenelm Digby represented the beginnings of a Catholic revival in the universities. In 1828 Nicholas Wiseman replaced Robert Gradwell as the rector of the English College, Rome; the change symbolized the influx of religious romanticism into the capital of the Catholic world. In 1829 political emancipation was achieved, and a year later the Cisalpine Club formally dissolved itself. The years between 1819 and 1832 also saw the deaths of most of the major protagonists of the now-stale debates over toleration, authority, theology, and history: among the Cisalpines, John Throckmorton, Joseph Berington, and Charles Butler; in the party of reaction, William Gibson, Charles Plowden, and John Milner. As John Bew wrote to John Kirk in 1819: "Look around and see how few scattered stragglers remain. . . . [They] have each in their [turn] sunk into the stream; & we are hastening on to the same fate—a few years more & not one will be left of the whole number." After 1832 only John Fletcher, John Kirk, and John Lingard were

The End of a Movement • 135

left from the intellectual generation born between 1740 and 1775.[1] The inheritors of the Cisalpine mentality lived in the shadow of the French Revolution and mirrored the growing impact of continental ultramontanism. This new group, born between 1790 and 1800, included Frederick Charles Husenbeth (1796–1872), Thomas Michael McDonnell (1792–1869), Edward Price (d. 1858), Daniel Rock (1799–1871), Mark Aloysius Tierney (1795–1862), and John Walker (1799–1873). It achieved definite literary ascendancy after 1825. Although their Cisalpine roots were evident, these men possessed no single issue around which to coalesce opinions. Political emancipation had destroyed the common goal. During the next two decades Tierney and Rock fought for the restoration of the hierarchy; McDonnel preached the message to the poor in Birmingham; Husenbeth, the man most indebted to John Milner, carried on the tradition of Cisalpine piety; Walker and Price were intellectual dabblers. Cisalpinism as a single, coherent movement had ended. Eighteen-thirty in England, as on the Continent, truly marked the end of an era.[2]

Thus when John Lingard was fifty-nine years old, he found himself the sole systematic proponent of the Catholic Enlightenment in England. The next twenty years saw not so much a development in his thought as an attempt to respond to changing conditions with Enlightenment principles. The response came primarily in the area of pastoral reform, the sphere in which the tenor of the English Catholic revival was most evident. Looking back on this last period of his life, Lingard summarized the course of events and his own anguish at the romantic shift in opinion:

> Why; in consequence of the catholic emancipation, I trusted that the catholic church in England would throw open its portals to draw within it men of influence and education, which I thought could never take place, if we insisted on practices calculated to enforce on the minds of protestants that much of our religion consisted in superstitious or fanatical practices. But of the then bishops there was not one who could be persuaded to see the matter in this light ex-

cepting Dr. Baines. My hopes rested therefore on him and by his death were disappointed. For as you know since that time every strange practice every kind of fanaticism has been imported from France, Italy and Ireland and every effort made by ourselves to strengthen on that head the prejudices of Protestants. And what good has it done? 22 years have elapsed since the act of emancipation: and during that time has a single peer joined us? or with two or three exceptions, has any gentleman of birth and consideration. I wish the preachers and I may say the fanatics of other climes had remained in their own countries: for here, if they have done some good, I fear they have done more evil. So good bye to them.[3]

It is the purpose of this final chapter to trace in detail the causes of this view of the Second Spring of English Catholicism. The triumph of religious romanticism has been treated many times. Here, John Lingard's approach will be studied only so that a complete picture of Cisalpinism can be given, especially its spirituality, and insight gained into the alternatives confronting English Catholics from 1830 to 1850.

The Idea of Reform

In February 1831 a group of priests in the Midland District began publication of the *Catholic Magazine*. The editors, among whom were John Kirk and Thomas Michael McDonnell, noted that the new political and religious existence of Catholics demanded a change in their attitude toward civil life. The editors pleaded for public support and promised to conduct the magazine on a "liberal and enlarged plan." Although they would avoid political questions, the editors hoped that the periodical would become a powerful medium for the propagation of Catholic truth in all areas of life. The front page carried the motto of St. Augustine: *In necessariis unitas, in dubiis libertas, in omnibus charitas.*[4] Within five months such optimistic hopes were shattered on the rocks of Catholic divisiveness, and the gulf that had separated Cisalpine from reactionary for so long was found to be wider than ever. Even emancipation, the editors discovered, could not unite two different conceptions of Catholic life in the modern world. In the pages of the *Catholic Magazine* between 1831 and 1835 debates over miracles, the Litany of Loreto, religious instruction, and devotional forms exemplified this cleavage.

The argument over miracles lasted from July 1831 to March 1832.[5] Dr. Henry Weedall sparked the conflict when he wrote a long and favorable description of the liquefaction of the blood of St. Januarius. For him, it was easier to believe the miracle than many of the scientific theories offered to explain it. Lingard, who had been requested to write for the periodical, immediately responded. He felt that before any miraculous intervention could be affirmed, it must be proven that no known laws of nature were operative. If there was any doubt, the miracle remained only "probable." For example, many substances liquefied with a change in temperature; the miracle of St. Januarius could best be affirmed by the use of a thermometer. R. S. Y. and the editor agreed. They wanted experimental evidence. Y. even raised the possibility of mass psychology explaining the phenomenon. He argued for chemical analysis, names, dates, facts, controlled conditions, verified human testimony. If these certain procedures were not followed, a Catholic might be exposed "to egregious evagations and fanatical delusions," pushed into the necessity of "incurring irreparable loss of his reputation as a man of science or of prudence."[6]

Two writers came forward to defend the miracle. Frederick Charles Husenbeth, whom some believed the inheritor of John Milner's zeal, accused H. Y. [Lingard] of "vapid effusions" and a "hazarded conjecture." Contrasting Weedall's "pious and fervent mind" with the "cold, sceptical composition" and "frigid self-conceit" of H. Y., Husenbeth lamented these days of "incredulity and liberality." H. Y., he suggested, belonged with the Middletons, Addisons, and Eustaces of this world. Another priest, "Philalethes," filled his letters with similar accusations against the proponents of the liberal outlook. Neither he nor Husenbeth acknowledged the force or ultimate validity of the scientific approach. For both, the witness of popular tradition required presumption of belief.[7]

In February 1832 Lingard tried to end the debate by establishing common ground for discussion. He described what he believed to be the "Christian zeal" that could reconcile the two sides. Lingard's letter took the form of a dialogue between two Italians—Antonio, whose piety was "controlled by the wariness and severity of his judgment," and Ippolito, a man "distinguished by a peculiar warmth of feeling and singleness of purpose." Antonio supported H. Y. Most significant, he noted that the only real argument which Husenbeth and "Philalethes" possessed was the one from authority. But why believe them? "The question is not one of doctrine, but of fact; which cannot be determined correctly without a clear knowledge of the phenomena, and a comparison of them with the established laws of nature." Antonio asked with disquieting urgency: Why could not English Catholics discuss with temper and decorum? "It is, that we have, among us, individuals, who, fancying themselves the standards and guardians of orthodoxy, visit, as if it were the sin of heresy, every deviation from any of their favourite, though ill-gounded and contracted notions." To Lingard it was evident that the "bastard zeal" and "offspring of passion" which had plagued the relations among Berington, Butler, and Milner had not yet disappeared. Under the guise of Ippolito he pleaded instead for that true zeal whose offspring was charity.[8] Lingard's plea fell on deaf ears. The reason was significant. He had seemingly juxtaposed the mentalities of Antonio and Ippolito and then built the bridge of true zeal between the two. In fact, he had made a distinction without a difference. Both Italians, like Lingard, presupposed that reasonable scientific criteria were needed to delineate the area of the miraculous. Both were Enlightenment Catholics, one just a bit more enthusiastic than the other. But as Lingard himself hinted, what was really under discussion here was the old issue between the rights of criticism and the prerogatives of authority. The grounds of the conflict had only shifted from dogma and history to popular devotion. The conversation between Antonio and Ippolito showed that Lingard could accept Henry Weedall's defense of the miraculous—on scientific grounds. Unfortunately he could not even consider that spirit which castigated him as a "theological Guy Fawkes" merely because he demanded evidence before belief. As a result, he ended up talking to himself, and the debate, like so many others before it, reached no definite conclusion.

During the following year a second major issue—that of the religious forms best suited to the "spirit of the age"— deepened the gulf that divided the Cisalpines from the men of the Catholic revival.[9] Once again Lingard began the debate. He had been permitted by John Fletcher to "feel the public mind" on the suitability of the Litany of Loreto in an English prayer book. Fletcher wanted to publish a new edition of *The Catholic's Prayer Book* without the litany. Lingard came forth under the guise of a Catholic newly converted from Protestantism. He signed his letters to the *Catholic Magazine* as "Proselytos." To Robert Tate he wrote: "Aware I should have opponents, I sought to mollify the indignation by the long account of P's unavailing efforts to carve his religion out of the Scriptures. It was my intention then to promenade P through a variety of Catholic chapels, praising this thing and condemning that, for the purpose of affording me occasion to point out such improvements as I thought might be made in our public service, etc. and at the same time such defects as I think exist in the manner of reading, preaching, and discharging the different duties of the ministry."[10]

In the course of his narration "Proselytos" made many observations on the insufficiency of the Bible as the sole rule of faith, the importance of national antiquities, and the plethora of vituperative controversial writings on both the Protestant and Catholic sides. With respect to Protestants, he felt that "if they are in error, it is their misfortune rather than their fault," since they have generally, like Catholics, received their faith on trust. When he entered Catholic chapels the convert appreciated the simplicity of the ornaments, the silence, and the impressiveness of the clergyman. Unfortunately, he noted, the voice of the priest was too often harsh and unmusical, his enunciation quick and indistinct. The priest began the services with a prayer to the Blessed Virgin followed by short and rapid invocations: "It seemed a race between priest and people. I had heard of Protestant dancers, jumpers, and ranters; I now thought myself admist a set of Catholic gallopers." Furthermore, Catholics even called the Virgin "Morning Star," "Gate of Heaven," "Tower of Ivory," "Ark of the Covenant," and "House of Gold." These phrases were incomprehensible, offended the more correct taste of the present age, and offered little rational meaning. They were new accretions. "Christianity," Lingard concluded, "is not an art or a science, in which new discoveries may be made. It must come in perfect shape from the hands of its divine author, and have been delivered in that shape by the apostles to their disciples."[11]

The inheritors of Milner's mentality, newly injected with romanticism, could hardly have ignored such a direct attack on Catholic practices. Husenbeth, Joseph Curr, and a Spanish refugee priest, Mariano Gil de Tejada, objected to the attitude of "Proselytos" toward Protestants and his "disedifying sentiments" concerning the litany. "Lauretanus" [Curr] wrote: "Proselytos is no proselyte, but a Catholic 'bred and born,' and of superior talents and acquirements too, and consequently not to be tolerated in his advocacy of principles and opinions, which would be censurable even in a real neophyte." For all of them, Protestants were at least indirectly culpable for their errors. "Proselytos," according to Husenbeth, may be orthodox "in all matters of faith; but very accommodating, or if it please better, very liberal, in those matters which wonderfully shew the degree of true Catholic spirit, which animates the faithful." The criticisms of the pseudoconvert only indicated the extent to which Catholics released from penal restrictions had mixed with their neighbors, abandoned religious practices, and learned to pay tribute to modern refinement. The Litany of Loreto had been a practice of centuries; it required "less ingenuity than devout feeling" to give the virginal epithets a "rational meaning." "Pastor" lamented: "Now-a-days men love to question and dispute, where their forefathers would have respectfully believed and obeyed."[12]

Even more than the debate over miracles, this argument about the Litany of Loreto indicated to Lingard the impossibility of Catholic agreement on a single approach to religious practice. The *Catholic Magazine* followed the conflicting viewpoints for a year. Lingard was not without his defenders, but he was outnumbered. His letters became more and more direct. The historian talked about the distinction between doctrines and usages essential to Catholicity and the practices that were the result of human reasoning. He called his opponents "monopolizers of orthodoxy," men who "by the injudicious introduction of the litany" shocked the religious feelings of Protestants, scared them from the altar, opposed the designs of God in their favor, and shut the door of salvation in their faces. Lingard considered himself the better interpreter of the "spirit of the age." He asked: Have they shown that the litany is understood by the people? "I conceive that every rational man will deem it preferable to put up his petitions in language which he can understand, than to employ for that purpose a jargon of mysterious, unintelligible, aye, even 'portentous sounds.' "[13]

Eventually Lingard's contentions offended the influential Nicholas Wiseman, rector of the English College. In 1834 this future leader of the Catholic revival withdrew his contributions to the *Catholic Magazine* because he considered the attitude of "Proselytos" offensive. In writing to a friend, Wiseman captured the core of the difference in spirit between Lingard and his opponents:

> I have not as yet written to Mr Kirk about the Magazine. I hardly have courage to do so, from fear of some pettish or secondary motive being attributed to me for an act proceeding from pure conscience. A propos of the controversy on the Loreto Litany some man said that its beautiful mystic terms were not "suited to the taste of the present age." Who so wrote thus knew but little of the taste of the age, but moreover must have a soul devoid of poetry, and be ignorant that there is such a thing as poesy in prayer. I read the other

day the *Iambes* of Auguste Barbier a young poet now rising in France to the first eminence. . . . Only note the words underlined, compare them with the Litany, then remember that they were written and published in wicked, infidel Paris in 1833, that so you may compare the taste of the age and time *there* and among *some catholics* in England.

Clearly, the argument was that between a man born during the Age of Reason and one born after 1800. Lingard had already sensed the true roots of the problem when he had written that the *Catholic Magazine* was a disgrace to the clergy and he wished it discontinued. "We must keep pace with the age. To judge from the Magazine we do not." By 1834, then, the historian's difficulty was evident: he had outlived his time.[14]

There were two other issues on which the Cisalpine spirit encountered difficulties.[15] From February to April 1834 Lingard wrote several letters on religious instruction. As "Catechistes" he believed that "agitation is the way to reform in religious as well as political matters." The historian objected to the children's catechisms then in use. He considered the Douai version a "confused and methodless work." "Catechistes Junior" continued the plea for change. In true classical style he called for an end to ambiguous terminology and vague phrases. A catechism ought to combine "brevity with perspicuity; correctness of doctrine with accuracy of language; and to admit nothing, either redundant or contradictory; nothing complex or intricate." During the same period Lingard also presented his reflections on the prayer books in use among Catholics. "Sacerdos" called *The Garden of the Soul* "obscure, and sometimes, unintelligible to the ordinary reader." "Angla" defended Fletcher's attempt to update devotional forms. "Anglus" agreed. Lingard summarized the thrust of this whole Cisalpine pastoral program when he noted that he wrote as much for Protestants and Dissenters as he did for Catholics. Prayer books, catechisms, and litanies seemed tedious to many, but "in my opinion, it is of vital importance to religion, that our Prayer books and Catechisms be made so strictly correct as to defy the most rigid criticism. They are the most powerful engines for the propagation of Truth, that we possess."[16]

It should be noted that the objections to these last suggestions reflected a mixture of a conservative appeal to an older tradition and an increasingly popular romantic rejection of the "classical temper." "Missionarius" argued that "Sacerdos" was too hypercritical and his ontology poor. This correspondent rejected Fletcher's *Prayer Book* because it mutilated the venerable edition of Richard Challoner. Lingard had stated that "devotion, though substantially the same in all ages, has in all ages, like 'the devout sex,' sought to dress herself in new fashions." To this statement "Missionarius" replied: "Devotion is an old-fashioned thing, which goes on unmoved by meretricious novelty."[17] In a similar vein William Eusebius Andrews upbraided "Proselytos" and "Catechistes" for a vain display of "classic taste" in an attempt to weaken respect for traditional devotional works. To "Paulinus" "Angla" represented the encroachment of a "forward female" on the teaching prerogatives of the pastors; prayers were better for being old, not new. John Woods also attempted to defend the romantic attitude by an appeal to tradition:

> But we must attend to the prejudices of Protestants—that is, we must speculatively argue with them, that their prejudices are founded upon error, and, at the same time, practically confirm them in these same prejudices, by sacrificing that which we maintain to be proper and laudable. But what sacrifices will content them? Not those which *can* be made by Catholics, the most ambitious of pleasing them. Remove holy water and the crucifix; silence the little bell; extinguish the candles; burn the vestments; discard the Litany of Loretto [sic], and the veneration of the Cross; administer the sacraments, and say Mass in English, etc.—will they, then, join with us in adoring Jesus Christ, truly present in the blessed Eucharist? Will they submit to the confession of their sins etc. Unless they will, the chasm, which separates them from us, can never be filled up; but, if they will, their minor objections will disappear, like a thin mist before the sun of truth and light.[18]

These arguments indicated that a situation was fast emerging in which the Cisalpine ecumenical orientation would be rejected by appealing to an older piety. The men of the Catholic revival would soon possess both the argument from tradition and the argument from reform.

The debates over miracles, the Litany of Loreto, religious instruction, and devotional forms were exceptionally important. First of all, they obviously mirrored the growing acceptance of the romantic outlook and documented the overwhelming shift in Catholic opinion after 1829. The attitude of John Milner had ceased to be that of one among many and was now the acknowledged norm of orthodox opinion. This shift is well known and has been adequately treated many times. But second, and for the purposes of this study more central, the arguments indicate that between 1831 and 1835 there still existed a vocal reformist group among the older clergy. It included John Fletcher, John Kirk, John Walker, and Mark Aloysius Tierney. These men naturally grouped themselves around Lingard and supported his plans. Eventually, Lingard's influence accomplished the conversion of Frederick Charles Husenbeth.[19]

The *Catholic Magazine* itself was obviously an organ of "enlightened opinion." In addition to supporting Lingard's position in the controversies, the periodical carried articles on biblical criticism, called for an improvement in seminary education, and pushed for the restoration of the hierarchy.[20] In each of the areas it discussed, the *Catholic Magazine* made no significant departure from the attitude of Berington, Butler, and other Cisalpines. For example, as early as 1795 Joseph Berington, Bishop Douglass, and John Milner had exchanged a series of letters discussing miracles in a controversy that continued for two years.[21] Milner had felt that Berington questioned miraculous events because "you are sensible that your projected reform of alleged superstition with respect to images, relicks, etc. can never take place, whilst Catholics are persuaded that God has sanctioned the opinions and practices in question by acknowledged miracles." According to Milner, Berington's criteria for judging supernatural intervention (e.g., nothing undefined can introduce suspension in the laws of nature) were false; they cultivated Protestant opinion and relied too heavily on a wrong conception of "evidence." Needless to say, Butler and Lingard had labored under similar preconceptions and "faulty assumptions."[22]

During the period before emancipation the Cisalpines had also criticized Challoner's *Garden of the Soul* (1740) and advocated a change in the forms of prayer. In 1813 Berington had written a *Prayer Book for the Use of the London District*, which had become one of the sources for Fletcher's *Catholic's Prayer Book*. The latter had catered to the "enlightened portion of our community" and was "more accommodated to the spirit, and circumstances of the present time." Joseph Berington, moreover, had criticized the catechism of Roman Catholics: ". . . the same bad arrangement and confusion of ideas, in speculative and in practical, in mystery and in moral truths, pervade the whole. A mind thus tutored, can see nothing distinctly: the whole system of ideas must be confused, answering to the catechistical process whereby they were introduced. It will be well, if instability in belief be not the consequence of a method so incoherent and undefined."[23] Lastly, even though emancipation had destroyed much of the stimulus for Catholic political involvement, the editors of the *Catholic Magazine* still followed Cisalpine principles. In July 1831 they recalled that the connection between church and state was one "which may be dissolved with perfect safety." A year later they indirectly rejected the teaching of Gregory XVI's *Mirari Vos*. The *Catholic Magazine* consistently justified its "radical" reputation by supporting the cause of democratic principles and civil and religious liberty for all.[24]

All of this meant that while the Catholic Church in England shifted most of its attention to internal issues, Lingard and those associated with him tried to inaugurate long-cherished ideals of reform based on a Cisalpine anthropology. Bernard Plongeron has written that one of the marks of the Catholic Enlightenment was the attempt to apply the "principle of intelligibility" to the field of popular religious culture.[25] In England, as has been argued, the men committed to this approach accepted, as axiomatic, state secularization, religious pluralism, a constitutional government, an empirical methodology, and a definition of man that centered his dignity in the reasonable use of his freedom. The consequences of these principles in ecclesiology, theology, and history have already been detailed. When the Cisalpines (consciously and consistently) and the inheritors of their mentality (unconsciously and much more sporadically) applied this type of "intelligibility" to the pastoral life and popular religious attitudes, they advocated an ecumenical sensitivity; a rational clarification of the area of the miraculous, the language of prayer, and the formulas of catechetics; and a purification of the devotional imagination. These issues naturally emerged into open debate after the question of church and state had ceased to control discussion.

Historians have tended to ignore the early debates in the *Catholic Magazine*. In analyzing the impact of the Second Spring, they have usually begun with the ideals of Nicholas Wiseman, the foundation of the *Dublin Review*, the devotional revolution exemplified by Luigi Gentili, and the importance of the convert movement and Irish immigration in reshaping the Catholic body. As a result, Catholic life "before" and "after" emancipation has been contrasted. The notion of reform has been identified with those who supported such signs of the romantic renewal as clerical dress, frequent communion, retreats, Gothic architecture, improvement in seminary education, *les petites devotions*, indulgences, prayers for the conversion of England, and increased Roman influence and episcopal supervision. Those opposed to these programs have been described as inheritors of the "old Catholic" mentality: Gallicans, a *gens lucifuga*, poorly educated men whose devotional spirit was less than satisfactory. As Wiseman wrote to the Earl of Shrewsbury: "I fear that the public feeling amongst us is too corrupt, and our catholicity, as cold as our politics are hot; and that consequently it will be difficult to draw forth any sympathy from our public, for anything purely religious, without some exciting ingredient." That exciting ingredient for him was the spirit of Novalis, Joseph von Görres, F. X. Baader,

Alessandro Manzoni, Félicité de Lamennais, and Alphonse de Lamartine. It showed the "longing after the revival of a christian principle as the soul and centre of thought, and taste, and feeling."[26]

From the perspective of 1850 such a view of the progress of the Second Spring was surely legitimate. The *Catholic Magazine* had ceased publication in 1836. By the 1840s Cisalpine thought had lost its original orientation and become more and more defensive. Therefore Wiseman's became the dominant current of opinion, and the signs of revival he advocated definitely injected a new and vital element into Catholic life. However, the point here is simply that in the light of the early debates in the *Catholic Magazine*, it is evident that at least part of the roots of the conflict between one group of "old Catholics" (the Cisalpines) and the proponents of the Second Spring lay not so much in disagreement over the idea of reform as in the presuppositions supporting it and the ways and means of effecting it. John Lingard himself expressed the crux of the interpretative difficulty very well. He wrote to John Walker:

> That there may be need of reform among us in many points I concede: but that reform should be based, not upon *national* customs among the Romans or Italians; but on those among Englishmen. Lights and serenading &c are to foreigners in Italy the most natural manner of showing respect: not so with us. Our great object should be to extend the Catholic religion among us, and for that purpose I hold it necessary to make converts among the higher classes or at all events among the higher of the middle class of society. If you do not get any of them, men will seldom be persuaded to join a society of religionists, who do not number among them a single person of any respectability in the whole district. That I have often found to my regret. If this be the case we are bound in consequence to eliminate every thing unnecessary that is calculated to indispose such persons from joining us, or to augment their antipathy to us. . . . if our bishops a few years ago had thrown wide open the portals of the catholic church to receive without unnecessary parade, and with as much condescension as possible all who

offered themselves, we should have a great addition not I mean of men deeply imbued with the true spirit of religion, but of men whose example might countenance others, and whose families might propagate and perpetuate the catholic faith.[27]

This letter witnesses to the social and pastoral limitations of Cisalpinism. It also reveals positive ideals buried deep in the culture of the Enlightenment. It should become clear in the following reflections that the Cisalpines consistently applied their principles to every area of church reform.

Scripture and Reform

The Cisalpines had always supported the popular diffusion of the Scriptures. The interest was dictated by an apologetic response to the charge that Catholics were forbidden to read the Bible, a genuine interest in biblical scholarship, and a desire to form an educated laity. As early as 1786 Alexander Geddes, the Scottish biblical scholar associated with Berington and Butler, had published a *Prospectus of a New Translation of the Holy Bible*. He had attacked the Douai-Rheims edition, "a literal and barbarous translation from the Vulgate . . . accompanied with acrimonious and injurious annotations." Seven years later Geddes defended the first volume of his new translation as a tolerable and credible version for the use of British Catholics. It displayed obvious Cisalpine preoccupations since it was consciously conciliatory (omitting most of the "odious" notes in previous editions) and designed to refute the system of "transalpine Popery." During the same period Joseph Berington and Charles Butler had also been interested in the scholarly study of the New Testament. Later, in 1813, the Catholic Board had founded a Bible Society and printed a stereotyped edition of the New Testament with the approbation of Vicar Apostolic William Poynter. Thomas Rigby, a priest with well-known Cisalpine inclinations, had edited the notes, which consistently omitted Challoner's harsh phrases and betrayed definite apologetic intentions. Finally, throughout the preemancipation period John Milner had attacked what he called the "Bibliomanists,"

Cisalpines who encouraged the circulation of the Scriptures among the uninstructed Catholics and who capitulated to Protestant prejudices.[28]

Coming out of this tradition and encouraged by his own educational background, Lingard naturally considered the Scriptures to be a powerful force for the diffusion of Catholic truth. It was not unexpected, then, that in 1836 he should have published *A New Version of the Four Gospels*. This book was his first scholarly theological attempt to respond to the open climate of postemancipation society. As such, it represented a concrete example of the Cisalpine approach to preaching the message in the environment of the Second Spring. Lingard definitely wanted the book to get into the hands of Protestants. In a letter to George Silvertop he noted that his version was made in order to induce some readers to consider the biblical questions seriously and, without prejudice, to agree with the author.[29]

Lingard knew that the most significant feature of *A New Version of the Four Gospels* was its introduction. This short work, probably the most perspicacious of all of Lingard's writings, displayed a typical Cisalpine preoccupation with historicity. The writer used it in this context to exalt the authority of the church and to prove the impossibility of the Protestant principle of *sola Scriptura*. Lingard stressed that the Gospels were written in particular social, political, and religious situations. He argued that to understand them one had to know the meaning of idiomatic expressions, literary forms, and Jewish customs. Those who compared the four texts would discover that they abounded with inaccurate quotations, omissions, repetitions, and geographical confusions. The fourth Gospel contained nothing about the law, the renunciation of property, the punishment of the Pharisees, the destruction of Jerusalem, and the dispersion of the nations. Even Our Lord's discourses, the most important part of the New Testament, were clearly not verbal translations. Each writer had selected, arranged, and condensed according to his own judgment. "The inspiration of the writers secured them from doctrinal error; but it did not invest them with those literary acquirements which are the results of education and study (p. xii). Further, Lingard continued, no writer hinted that he had in mind the instruction of future generations, men of different habits, climates, or descent. These facts implied that the Gospels were "only occasional narratives, suggested by circumstances, and intended for the immediate use of particular persons" (p. xvi). They had never been meant as "historical records to convey to all future generations a faithful account of the actions and doctrines of our blessed Lord" (p. xvi). After applying this critical literary sense to the Gospels, Lingard then asked the fatal question: If these narratives are so defective, were they composed to form the historical part of a religious code from which alone, without oral testimony or tradition, people must draw knowledge of Christian faith and practice? (p. xix). The intelligent reader could form only one conclusion.

In his notes Lingard went even further in applying his type of critical method to the Gospels. He inverted Mark 9:12 and 13 because he believed that their present order was "the mistake of some copyist" (p. 172). On John, he commented that the Resurrection narratives contained several discrepancies because of "want of skill in historical composition" (p. 415). Chapter 21 may have been added by the Evangelist after the Gospel was finished. It was also obvious that there was no more scriptural warrant for baptism and the eucharist being sacraments than for the washing of the feet. Surely the lack of scriptural evidence for sacraments showed that the church interpreted the writings in the light of other instructions. For the historian, Matthew also required a proper interpreter. The "sin against the Holy Spirit" in 12:31 applied only to eye witnesses; it did not impugn the church's teaching that all sins could be forgiven (p. 49). Similarly, Mark 10:21 was meant only for Jewish converts (p. 178). Here Lingard revealed his middle-class roots when he argued that this instruction to the rich young man to sell to the poor, rely on providence, and own all things in common could not be applied to Christians of all times. Finally, the historian displayed the sharpness of his critical needle when he hazarded two Christological reflections. On Matthew 16:20

The End of a Movement • 151

he wrote: "It would appear that our Saviour never gave himself out *publicly* as the Messiah, nor suffered his disciples to do so. He contented himself with sowing the good seed, and waited till his resurrection for it bearing fruit. This, indeed, was the first time that he acknowledged the fact to his apostles" (p. 73). As if this were not enough to raise eyebrows, Lingard commented on Matthew 24:36: "This must be understood of the son as to his human nature. In quality of man, his knowledge during his mortal life was limited, like his power, to the object of his mission. He had not the power of granting the petition of the sons of Zebedee, but after his resurrection he possessed all power in heaven and on earth. He had not now the knowledge of the day or hour; after his resurrection undoubtedly he possessed it" (p. 113).

These reflections showed once again the deep connection between the Cisalpine mentality and the acceptance of a critical methodology. In the introduction and notes Lingard's genius systematically applied to the Gospels the common analytical principles of Berington and Butler. In the process, the historian's ideas coalesced well with the Cisalpine emphasis on oral tradition and teaching authority. Within the context of the Second Spring, *A New Version of the Four Gospels* embodied the most far-reaching effort of the English Catholic Enlightenment both to preach and to defend the church with modern techniques. The project was not without its difficulties. The extent to which it was a departure from the traditional apologetic and the fact that it had no future in the climate of religious romanticism were illustrated in Nicholas Wiseman's reaction.

The April 1837 issue of the *Dublin Review* carried Wiseman's public reflections on *A New Version of the Four Gospels*. The author spent most of his time noting the deficiencies in the Douai-Rheims version. In the last two paragraphs he took issue with Lingard's change of "Christ" to "messiah" and "gospel" into "good tidings," but he generally commended the drift of the notes and introduction. Wiseman accepted the fact that the Gospels were "occasional pieces" that could hardly have been intended as a rule of faith. He concluded: "Considering the work in this light, we have an additional pleasure in bearing witness to the learning, diligence, and acuteness of its author."[30]

If Lingard was pleased with these approving comments from a well-known biblical scholar, he sadly misinterpreted Wiseman's meaning. In fact, the most significant feature of the article was that out of seventeen closely printed pages only twenty-five lines referred to *A New Version of the Four Gospels*. Wiseman avoided detailed comment because he considered parts of the work "unsound and dangerous." Among his private papers the leader of the Catholic revival left a twenty-five-page manuscript noting the errors in Lingard's work. In it he took particular issue with the historian's interpretation of some of the Gospel texts (e.g., Mark 10:21) and his contention that the writers had not intended their work for the instruction of future generations. Wiseman wondered what the author of *A New Version of the Four Gospels* thought about biblical inspiration:

> . . . though we willingly admit that the Gospels were suggested by particular circumstances, and directed immediately to particular persons, yet, as the sacred penmen were under the action of the Holy Ghost when they wrote them, it cannot be doubted but that they intended to benefit the Church in general, & future generations. This is certainly the view the Christian Church has always taken of the four Gospels, & accordingly she has always looked on them as a rich treasure delivered to her by the Holy Ghost. . . .
> The translator's surmise that the Evangelists show want of *skill* in historical composition is, I suppose, a piece of wisdom, which he has not in common with any other Catholic commentator, & which is not very respectful to the sacred penmen. Will he deny that the Spirit of God guided them while they wrote? If they composed their narratives under his direction, they put down such circumstances only & in such order as He suggested and ordained in His infinite wisdom.[31]

The leader of the Catholic revival also disagreed with many of the translator's interpretations of certain words. *A New Version of the Four Gospels* read "trust" instead of

The End of a Movement • 153

"faith," "perverseness" instead of "hardness of heart," "Hail, thou favoured (of God)," instead of "full of grace." Other translations and notes were "rash," "contrary to every Catholic interpretation," "wrong," "malicious," "vicious," "contemptuous," "*temerarious*, or probably erroneous," "absurd," and "theologically incorrect." The author's inversion of two verses "would alone suffice, I should imagine, to put the book on the Roman Index." His Christological comments were "false, & even heretical": "The doctrine . . . respecting the limited knowledge & power of Christ as man before his resurrection tho' it be that of the Protestant Grotius, cannot without temerity be held by any Catholic, as it is opposed to the universal doctrine of Catholic Divines, and to the universal feeling of the Faithful. Petavius . . . is of the opinion that to deny that Christ, from the moment of his conception, enjoyed the beatific vision, tho' not strictly heretical is however erroneous, and haeresi proximum."[32] In short, according to Wiseman, the author of *A New Version of the Four Gospels* had completely failed in his task.

Wiseman's reaction to *A New Version of the Four Gospels* pointed to two important realities descriptive of the middle years of the Catholic revival. The fact that a scholar of international reputation and a man well abreast of the scientific approach to Scripture rejected Lingard's interpretations reveals the extreme difference in attitude between a Cisalpine and even an intellectual of the mid-nineteenth-century revival. At first glance, they shared a common method. But Lingard's work obviously proceeded from the critical and skeptical mentality of the Enlightenment. *A New Version of the Four Gospels* contained tremendous insights, but its interpretation of certain Gospel texts seemed arbitrary. The failure to refer to the witness of traditional authorities to support a particular judgment betrayed a deeply individualistic cast of mind. The Christological reflections raised dogmatic issues that could not be resolved by a strict historical methodology. Here the Cisalpine aversion for speculative thought was a real limitation. On the other hand, Wiseman's comments revealed a strong tendency to guide individual opinion, even *in dubiis*, by the witness of tradition. His commendation of the Vulgate, constant referrals to the "Church," castigation of certain views as "erroneous" and "temerious," and appeal to "the universal feeling of the faithful" indicated that his acceptance of the critical method was controlled by the moral and dogmatic considerations that formed the true foundation for his thought. For Wiseman, method was valuable only as a support for the central issue of speculative truth. As the years of the Second Spring progressed, these fundamental divergencies between the two mentalities clashed more and more.

Second, Wiseman's refusal to criticize publicly *A New Version of the Four Gospels* stemmed from the recognition that he could not openly disagree with the representative of the older view. Lingard's influence was still too strong, his prestige too great, and his opinions too accepted. This was to be the case until the historian died. Although *A New Version of the Four Gospels* was disliked at Ushaw, John Walker, George Silvertop, and M. A. Tierney probably agreed with its approach. Lingard himself heard reports that the Oxford theologians had favorably accepted his introduction.[33] Clearly, from 1837 until 1850 the strong appeal of Cisalpine thinking could not be ignored.

Catechetical Reform

John Lingard's *Catechetical Instructions* was his second major theological attempt to present Catholicism in the atmosphere of post emancipation England. The book had a long history. In 1830 the historian wrote to Frederick Charles Husenbeth to express his dissatisfaction with Francis Martyn's version of the traditional Turberville-Challoner *Abridgment of Christian Doctrine*. Husenbeth had wanted to return to the older, more simple catechism. Lingard remarked: "I certainly dislike several of the answers as difficult for children, and in some cases, if not incorrect, as teaching at least opinions of divines for doctrines of the church. . . . I mention the subject, because in a country like this, where we are constantly engaged with protestant controvertists, it is folly to add to other difficulties that of defending opinions, which are not necessary parts of our creed. And that is done, if into elementary but authorized treatises of doctrine we admit more than has been defined." In his own parish the historian became so disgusted with the *Abridgment of Christian Doctrine* that he took a pen and scored out "all long and unnecessary questions," and "all long and unnecessary clauses" to make the work intelligible to children.[34] His complaints to the *Catholic Magazine* have already been noted. Dr. Thomas Penswick, vicar apostolic of the Northern District, then asked Lingard to compose two catechisms for general use. One, for beginners, was published as "A First or Shorter Catechism" in the 1834 *Catholic Magazine*. Because of Penswick's death, the one for adults remained unpublished from 1836 to 1840.[35] With advice from vicars apostolic James Yorke Bramston and Thomas Griffiths and the more theologically minded priests, Lingard amended and revised this longer work.[36] In his private correspondence he emphasized his desire to furnish educated Protestants with a concise explanation of Catholic doctrine. Robert Tate urged him to notice the Oxford divines; John Walker wanted a book for converts.[37] Lingard himself wished "our bishops would endeavour to meet the prejudices of the Puseyites, as far as faith will agree."[38] He explicitly tried, as he had done in *A New Version of the Four Gospels*, to exalt the authority of the church. The complete work was finally published in 1840. It was a remarkable example of the Cisalpine mind: its social limitations, its mixture of Gallican theological background with an Enlightenment search for intelligibility, and its ecumenical sensitivity.

Compared with the four dominant editions of the Douay catechism, Lingard's *Catechetical Instructions* reveals a strong consciousness of changing social patterns.[39] The book was particularly novel in its approach to certain moral issues. For example, to the question "What then are the works forbidden on Sunday?," Lingard's catechism answered: "Every sort of handicraft and servile work, unless it may be excused on the ground of its moral necessity." A footnote added that the Sunday work prohibition, since it was church law, was always tempered "with a due regard to the wants and habits of men, and therefore with the allowance of those works which custom and civilization has rendered morally indispensable." In a letter to John Walker, Lingard noted that one reason for this mitigating answer was the fact that the railway was about to be opened.[40] He appealed to the French theologian Louis Bailly in support of his interpretation. *Catechetical Instructions* similarly qualified the obligation of Sunday mass attendance, took a moderate stance on the question of temperance, and omitted any reference to the harmful effects of plays and comedies.[41]

In addition to these changes, Lingard's work considered several questions that the earlier manuals had ignored. It included statements on suicide (forbidden) and dueling (forbidden). Among the spiritual works of mercy, the author listed the procuring of the "benefits of education, of religious instruction, and of divine worship for the poor and destitute." Lingard was well aware of the number of poor in his own parish. The most significant additions were made in reference to the seventh commandment. The 1812 and 1832 editions of *Abridgment of Christian Doctrine* had only mentioned "stealing" and the moral principles involved in "buying and selling." Lingard was more expansive. He enumerated six different ways a person could take or keep "without the actual or implied consent of the owner": theft, robbery, "false and fraudulent representations," "breach of contract," "incurring debt without means or intention of discharging it," and "refusing to pay a just debt." In a footnote the historian included these reflections on "breach of contract":

> In contracts between master and man the employer and the employed, a breach of contract on either part is almost always a breach of this commandment. If the workman take his stipulated wages, though he has spent part of his time in idleness: if he receive the price for which he covenanted, though he has not performed his work in a workmanlike manner, or in place of sound, has employed unsound materials, he becomes possessed of that to which, by the terms of his contract, he has no right: and in like manner, the employer,

if he refuse without just cause to pay according to agreement, becomes possessed, without giving an equivalent, of the property of the employed. For the property of the poor man is his labour.[42]

The combination of all of these changes with Lingard's attempt to mitigate Christ's teaching on the renunciation of property in *A New Version of the Four Gospels* indicates both the social strengths and weaknesses of the Cisalpine mentality. The *Catechetical Instructions* were obviously written within the context of a growing capitalist and middle-class value system. Lingard addressed himself not only to educated Protestants but also to the Silvertops (coal mine owners), Coulstons (bankers), and Butlers of the Catholic world, the self-reliant, reasonable men so well described for France by Bernard Groethuysen.[43] Inasmuch as he attacked certain problems that the earlier catechisms had avoided, Lingard was genuinely attempting to elucidate a Christian response to the growing emergence of Catholics into positions of economic respectability. Earlier, the sermons of James Archer and John Fletcher had mirrored similar concerns.[44] Lingard's concern for the moral force of contracts pointed to the social origins of Cisalpinism. There was a close link between "enlightenment," the breakdown of the Catholic squire system, and involvement in industrialization. Ironically, when the *Catechetical Instructions* attempted to preach the message in this way to its own contemporary world, it manifested its own irrelevance. For how exactly did Lingard's social presuppositions respond to the needs of the hordes of immigrants, those masses of the economically and educationally deprived who were transforming the face of English Catholicism?

Lingard's *Catechetical Instructions* also reflected the curious Cisalpine mixture of a Gallican theological background with the Enlightenment's search for intelligibility. First of all, the author studiously avoided the use of what he considered metaphysical, incomprehensible, or inaccurate terms. For example, the 1812 and 1832 editions of *Abridgment of Christian Doctrine* had compared the reality of the

Trinity to the existence of three powers in the soul.[45] Lingard wondered what knowledge a learner could have of the philosophy of the human mind. He therefore omitted any analogies and simply referred to Scripture. In his definition of a "sacrament," the historian carefully described "grace" as a "spiritual benefit."[46] He refused to use the term in his explanation of the Lord's Prayer and privately confided to Charles Newsham that Grace was a thing he never could make ignorant people understand.[47] "When I looked into Cat. Con. Trid. and found that grace was a divine quality or light infused into the soul &c. I was scared. To this, I said, I can affix no distinct meaning, how can the poor people possibly understand it? If you can devise for me any definition that is intelligible to them, I will thank you—otherwise I must leave *Grace* out."[48]

This abhorrence for abstraction and search for rational clarification extended to a refusal to give the word "daily bread" a metaphorical meaning: "When the poor man prays daily for his bread, he understands what he prays for: tell him that he prays also for *supernatural helps,* and you bamboozle him." In contrast to the *Abridgments of Christian Doctrine,* Lingard made no mention of "supernatural quality" when he defined "faith."[49] The discussion of Christ avoided excessive emphasis on the word "nature," and the explanation of "Catholicity" excluded the phrase "*subsists* in all ages."[50] Lingard used "deadly sin" instead of "mortal sin" and omitted the word "limbo."[51] In his desire for precise terminology, he spoke of the "regulations of the Church," not the "commandments."[52] Other answers betrayed the author's concern for historical accuracy and his knowledge of current scientific problems.[53] In all of these minor ways the *Catechetical Instructions* witnessed to a Cisalpine search for intelligibility.

Second, the Gallican and Enlightenment strains combined to determine what the *Catechetical Instructions* included and how certain doctrinal issues were discussed. Both traditions, either historically or philosophically, had distinguished between the essentials and accidentals of faith. Lingard, then, mixed reasonable criteria, historical methodology, and antischolasticism. He rejected the "ends of sacrifice" and the usual form of the spiritual and temporal works of mercy.[54] He made no mention of the traditional theological virtues and vices, gifts of the Holy Spirit, two precepts of charity, eight beatitudes, evangelical counsels, angels, relics, or sacramental characters.[55] In his private correspondence Lingard indicated the intellectual foundations of this approach when he discussed the communion of saints, the sacraments, and indulgences.

In January, 1836 Lingard wrote to Vicar Apostolic Bramston: "There is one subject to which I beg to call the attention of your Lordship, 'The communion of saints.' In our late catechism this is made to extend to the saints in heaven, & the souls in purgatory, an interpretation which I have long thought unknown to the ancients, and a refinement of more modern divines. In the catechism of the Council of Trent, though much care is taken in the explanation of the article, & equal care is recommended to the clergy in explaining it, there is no mention either of the saints or the souls in purgatory: the whole is confined to the christians upon earth." Lingard queried: Which opinion should I follow? Eventually, he equivocated. In order to avoid trouble with the hyper-orthodox, he defined "communion of saints" as "that union of charity and brotherhood, which binds in one body all true members of the Catholic Church."[56] This was wide enough to include any interpretation.

In the section on the sacraments Lingard followed a similar line of approach. He significantly avoided the dominant scholastic and Counter Reformation theological heritages. The *Catechetical Instructions* refrained from describing sacraments in terms of "matter" and "form" and emphasized the subjective dimension, the disposition of the believer.[57] Lingard wrote to Newsham: "I like not the phrase that the sacraments efficiunt quod significant. Till the 12th century almost everything that could be called sacred was called also sacrament. Then the schoolmen resolved to confine the word to those sacred rites to which Christ had by his promise annexed certain graces, and hence that which was the consequence of the performance of those rites, was said to be given or effected by them, though God was the real author of the grace." Lastly, the section on indulgences harkened back to earlier disputes. Lingard confessed to Robert Tate: "As to indulgences, they are mysteries which I do not understand. I know not how to explain them so as to satisfy the disciples of Dr. Milner who had ultra notions on the subject formed from the condemnation of the synod of Pistoia. We have enough to do to defend the doctrines of the church, why should we put in catechisms doctrines of divines, and impose on ourselves the onus of defending them? Veron says that nothing more is of faith, than that indulgences are serviceable or salutory."[58] To John Milner, this would have been "enlightened piety" at its most dangerous. Lingard obviated the difficulty by taking an ambiguous stance and including a historical footnote on the evolution of indulgences.[59]

The *Catechetical Instructions* was marked by one other dominant characteristic. Lingard combined all his talents to fashion an exposition of Catholic doctrine explicitly directed to Protestants. Although the advertisement addressed itself to "the young" and the "more aged," a sharp eye would have easily discerned the author's true intention. For example, earlier catechisms had presupposed a situation of infant baptism. Lingard took the "catechumen" and the "convert" as his norm; almost as an aside he asked the question: "Is infant baptism valid?"[60] In other sections he noted the distinction between the importance of belief and the open profession of it. The latter was not always necessary. The historian slyly referred to the offer the fourth-century Christians had made to Victorinus to profess his faith before a small and select audience.[61] He wrote to John Walker:

> I know not what G. Errington thinks, but I think that Dr. Wiseman goes the wrong way to work. The prospect is promising. There are many who yearn to join us. What then should we do? Why certainly make the way to such junction as easy as possible. Is that done? I think not. I observe that on many occasions public recantations are made. If made spontaneously I have no objection. If required, I say it is wrong. Of a man who has deserted us, and returns, it should be required perhaps as reparation of scandal. But

these men have never left us. Remember your friend Victorinus in St. Augustine. Was it required that he should make profession of faith publicly? No; the Roman clergy offered to him that he should do it privately. He would not—but they wished to spare his feelings and considered his appearing among the faithful and acting as one a sufficient proof to the congregation that he was become a christian.[62]

Lingard also indirectly noticed the Oxford divines. He often quoted the Protestant version of Scripture. The *Catechetical Instructions* was thus a somewhat poorly disguised attempt to show that Catholic doctrines were "not such a mass of folly as they suppose."[63]

Structural changes were equally significant. In listing the marks of the church, Lingard included a single question on "How is the Church one?" He placed this question *after* explaining "holy" and "catholic." The order contrasted sharply with earlier, more polemical approaches. Second, only at the conclusion of the creed did he reflect on the *church's* inability to err, thereby giving a strikingly communal orientation to the notion of infallibility. Traditional catechisms had placed infallibility within the creed after the question on apostolic succession. Third, the *Catechetical Instructions* did not mention "prayers to the saints" under the article on "communion of saints." Lingard transferred the issue to the penultimate chapter of the book. Fourth, Lingard considered the "Our Father" under the rubric "Prayer." He separated it from the "Hail Mary" and placed the latter under "Prayers to the Saints." These were dramatic innovations with definite theological overtones.[64]

If these changes had not been enough to convince the reader of Lingard's irenical intentions, his specifically doctrinal innuendos would definitely have caused a stir. His section on Article X of the creed carefully included the fact that God's forgiveness of sins, offered through the church, depended on the sinner's sincere repentance. Holy orders was described as a "sacrament by which the bishops, priests, and others are ordained to the ministry of the altar and receive grace to perform their respective duties." Did Lingard not know that in the traditional definition priests received "grace and power"? The definition of the sacrament of penance emphasized the subjective dimension. It made no mention of priestly absolution. When Lingard did refer to this reality, he used the word "Minister." The section on the eucharist introduced the notion of remembrance: "Why did he leave us his body and blood in this sacrament? That we might receive it in memory of his death for our redemption." Compared with the usual Catholic approaches, these ideas seemed Protestant.[65]

Lingard's ecumenicity extended even to the deepest issues of faith. In order both to defend the Catholics against the charges of idolatry when they worshipped the sacrament and also to appeal to Protestants, Lingard consciously employed what seemed to be Nestorian terminology: "When the apostle saw before him that body in possession of life, which a few days before had been taken down dead from the cross, he exclaimed, My Lord and My God. (John XX.28) To whom or to what did his worship then apply? Was it confined to the body then before his eyes? No: it was directed to the Divine Being, whom he believed to *dwell in that body*. The presence of the body was the occasion, the presence of the Godhead the object of his worship. So it is with the Catholic. . . . The sacrament is the occasion, the Godhead the object of the worship."[66] After the *Catechetical Instructions* appeared, Lingard realized that perhaps this went too far. He wrote to Husenbeth: ". . . the other day looking at it again, and considering that I am not in the odour of sanctity with a certain party, who are fond of making charges in Rome, I thought it best to score out the whole passage. . . ."[67] Finally, in referring to the mass, Lingard defined "sacrifice" as "oblation to God." The rationale was presented in a letter to Newsham:

> Suppose I say—oblation of a victim to God—yet is [not] that too much? Have we not sacrificium laudis? I purposely confined myself to *oblatum*, because it must be of *something*, and thought the next words *oblation of the body and blood* sufficient for the purpose to which I referred it. There is, I think, too much refinement among [divines] with respect to the necessity of change in sacrifice. For in fact the dis-

pute between us and protestants is a dispute about words. The prot: defines, that is, says that by sacrifice he means so and so, and thence concludes that the mass is no sacrifice; the catholic defines, that is, says that by sacrifice he means something else and thence concludes that it is a sacrifice. If both agreed that it [was] an oblation of the body and blood of our saviour, there would be an end to the dispute, as far as religion is concerned.[68]

Such views could only provide grist for the ultramontane mill.

Lingard's catechism had a mixed reception. The book was well received by the second generation of Cisalpines: Robert Tate, John Walker, F. C. Husenbeth, and M. A. Tierney. Lingard reported to a friend that even many Puseyites had purchased it. In the small town of Stamford seven copies were bought by clergymen. At Stonyhurst the book was used by the more learned divines. The *Catechetical Instructions* went through three editions in four years. However, the dominant party of the Catholic revival was disgruntled. The letters in the *Catholic Magazine* certainly indicated that many priests would object to such a wholesale wooing of Protestant prejudices. Richard Thompson, usually a good barometer of the more enthusiastic older clergy, wrote to Vicar Apostolic Bramston in 1836: "The form & manner etc. [of Lingard's work] may be the best that could be devised; but, I am rather of the old School, and . . . prefer the old one before its modern corrections, only a little modified."[69]

After the publication of the catechism the atmosphere became so tense that Lingard wondered if Charles Dolman had been asked by Wiseman not to reissue a third edition. Lingard heard reports that the Jesuits branded his views on the eucharist as "heretical."[70] Nicholas Wiseman's opinions may be imagined. His ecumenism, like that of the early Lamennais, was uncompromisingly ultramontane. A year before Lingard published the *Catechetical Instructions*, Wiseman had written his article against the Donatists in the *Dublin Review*. It had stressed the unity of Catholic polity, the need for one great spiritual organization, and the importance of authority.[71] This vision was far removed from

Lingard's decentralized, representative, and nationalist conception of the church. Also in 1839 Wiseman had written to Propaganda a memorial that had included a section on "The development of the Catholic spirit among Protestants." The author had reported with delight the increasing interest of Newman, John Keble, and Edward Pusey in Catholic life: the liturgy, the breviary, monastic institutions, real presence, the necessity of tradition and authority, prayers for the dead, use of images, the absolving power of the priest, the sacrifice of the eucharist, and devotion to the Blessed Virgin.⁷² Paradoxically, Wiseman and some of the more learned Protestants were combining essentials and accidentals precisely when Lingard was seeking to divide them.

Ultimately, then, the *Catechetical Instructions*, like *A New Version of the Four Gospels*, could play only a small role in the drama of the Second Spring. At its best the book represented the doctrinal synthesis of a declining Catholic vision. Its economic views presupposed a middle-class culture; its reductionistic method was generally unacceptable; its rationalist emphasis, antiromantic; its ecumenism, as Lingard himself had indicated, suspect. After Lingard's death the *Tablet's* obituary dismissed the work in one sentence. It was simply "Gallican."⁷³ Lingard published the book when he was sixty-nine years of age. Although he was to reedit his *History of England* and *History and Antiquities of the Anglo-Saxon Church* during the next ten years, his creative work was now complete. From 1840 onwards, Lingard—and the mentality he represented—became increasingly removed from the mainstream of church life. His reactions to the changes in English Catholicism became progressively more defensive. In order to place them in proper perspective one additional element in the Cisalpine reform must be examined.

The Reform of Religious Practice

John Lingard knew that any effective church reform had to extend beyond theology into areas of religious practice. Therefore, during the years of the Second Spring he applied the Cisalpine principle of intelligibility to the liturgical and devotional life of the Catholic. Throughout the period he presupposed a situation of religious pluralism and aimed for reasonable expression. Lingard summarized much of his more concrete approach in a letter to Robert Tate: "You wish to have my notions respecting a reform in our service in great towns. My notions are that the English Prayers should be such as would at least instruct and edify protestants: that they should be read slowly, distinctly, devoutly, and that the sermon should be well composed, and well delivered. For of the Mass Prots. understand nothing, it is only by the prayers and sermon that you can induce them to repeat their visits and think of the doctrines of our religion. On both those subjects I endeavoured to awaken the apathy of Dr. Smith and alarm the piety of Dr. Penswick; but all in vain."[74]

His ideas of liturgical reform were first publicly enunciated in *A Manual of Prayers on Sundays and during Mass*. The book was the direct result of the social revolution wrought by emancipation and the passage of the 1832 Reform Bill. In 1833 Lingard wrote to John Jones: "Judging from appearances that the very foundations of the established church are crumbling beneath it, I inferred that we ought to throw wide open the portals of our own church, to receive such Protestants as may be willing to seek refuge within its walls. . . ." With this idea in mind, Lingard composed a manual designed to reconcile the "taste of men of education" to "our peculiar form of worship."[75] He presented a new arrangement and translation of the psalms, and, most importantly, assimilated the prayers of the people with those of the priest.

Lingard's Sunday service began with "prayers," which included the recitation of psalms, orations, and invocations. Usually the priest spoke first, and the people responded in their turn by an antiphonal "Come let us sing to the Lord," or "Amen," or "Praise and glory be to thee, O God." In an effort to make the psalms comprehensible Lingard combined some, shortened others, and omitted offensive and unintelligible verses. He included the "Miserere" to show well-educated Protestants that Catholics in their public services "pray for the forgiveness of sins." Compared with Challoner's *Garden of the Soul*, Lingard's book showed a marked avoidance of specifically Catholic forms—for example, he omitted litanies. *A Manual of Prayers* also further emphasized congregational participation.[76]

The most dramatic innovations came in the section "Prayers at Mass." Here a careful comparison of Lingard's work with Challoner's *Garden of the Soul* reveals the extent to which a Cisalpine could assimilate priest and people. Where Challoner's book had given only prayers, Lingard's manual included several English collects, provided epistles and Gospels, translated the preface of the Trinity, and followed the canon very closely. Lingard allowed the people to recite with the priest the form of absolution: "May the almighty and merciful Lord, grant to us the forgiveness, absolution, and remission of all our sins." At the consecration Lingard encouraged the people to read St. Paul's words of institution. As he explained to John Jones: "I made the experiment as to the mass, at the same time assimilating the prayers of the people, as much as might be, to those of the priest, since both are officers in their respective stations. Meum ac vestrum sacrificium."[77]

In addition to *A Manual of Prayers*, other, more disparate evidence indicates that Lingard had a coherent Cisalpine vision of liturgical reform. He complained about the operatic excesses of some church services, "the sacrifice exhibited as a sight to all who would pay money to behold it; the bishop performing as the first dancer in the ballet."[78] He lamented that many Catholic chaplains began their Sunday services with a prayer to the Blessed Virgin instead of to God the Father. He believed that the common practice of saying the rosary during mass was suited only for illiterate people and not for those who could follow a prayer book.[79] Lingard always encouraged intelligible communication between priest and people. He castigated Augustus Pugin's Gothic Revival precisely because it did not suit the needs of nineteenth-century people. It screened from sight the high altar and the ceremonies. When someone in London suggested an English liturgy, Lingard wrote: "Why, I thought that we were reverting to the medieval ages, when the rule was to let the people know nothing of the service—that was *all* in Latin—but to catch their ears with the sound of music, and to catch their eyes with the glare of lamps, gold, silver, etc. & to trust to these two things for the impression made on their minds."[80] In an effort to encourage communication, Lingard wanted the services read in a solemn and impressive manner; too many priests mumbled. Sermons were to be prepared and read.[81] He furnished new translations of the "Pater de Coelis," the psalms, "Te Deum," "Benedictus," and "Doxology" in order to present a "faithful and intelligible" version to English readers. Lingard definitely preferred John Gother's sober, precise, and classical style of collect prayers; they avoided incomprehensible flights of fancy.[82]

There are indications that Lingard also supported a vernacular liturgy. He wrote to John Walker on the Catholic burial services: "Now all this [the solemnity and affectivity of the Latin] tells against us. We recommend all this on that account to the laity, and yet take care that it should not affect them by performing this affecting service in a language which they cannot understand. Is not this furnishing our adversaries with a strong argument against us?"[83] It is difficult to say exactly what Lingard did in his own chapel, but he has left one striking description of his Cisalpine approach to Holy Week services:

> After I have distributed the palms in imagination to the imaginary tenants of stalls in the choir, I give the remainder to the man, who acts as my acolyte, who walks up and down the alley, standing at the end of each bench, and giving a palm to every one who holds out his hand for one. This I like because it prevents all the noise & turmoil of people leaving their seats to come for them. For the passion I have a man seated at the bottom of the chapel, and facing the altar, who when I begin the passion, reads it in English in a loud voice, so that every one may hear it, a great advantage to the people: for I believe that many pass from year to year without troubling themselves one jott [*sic*] about the particulars of our

saviours [*sic*] sufferings—and moreover it is listened to with great interest by those who cannot read. When I have done, I sit down in an arm chair, till the reader has finished. It is a great help to me reading in a very subdued voice, and sitting— and is much liked by the people, as several who have come from Lancaster for the day have assured me.[84]

Lingard's liturgical views were unique because of their completeness. He had the advantage of living into the post-emancipation world. But it is important to realize that most of his ideas had Cisalpine precedents. Joseph Berington definitely supported the vernacular. He believed that the Latin liturgy still existed only because the sixteenth-century reformers had so strongly reacted against it.[85] Nor was it accidental that *The Garden of the Soul* had acquired a new addition by 1800 in which, instead of Challoner's mass prayers, the ordinary of the mass was translated and printed in a column parallel with the Latin. The English translation disappeared by 1842.[86] Also in 1800 John Kirk and another Cisalpine edited Berington's version of Gother's *Prayers for Sundays & Festivals*. The book went through four editions before 1829. It was known for its emphasis on congregational participation. In the preface Kirk noted that group answers to the prayers were added because the method created interest and raised attention.[87] John Fletcher continued the practice in *The Catholic's Prayer Book*. He admitted in private that this work was designed with an "eye to Protestants."[88] Further, the 1826 edition of *Prayers before and after Mass* included a selection of readings so the people could follow the epistles and Gospels. All these ideas were related to the ecumenical and constitutional notions that were so much a part of the Cisalpine mentality. They coalesced well with their participative ecclesiology. Thus, John Lingard emerged from an intellectual atmosphere familiar with liturgical renewal.[89]

The devotional life of the Catholic was the second major area in which Lingard witnessed to the Cisalpine vision of pastoral reform. The *Catechetical Instructions* contained the key principles of his approach. In contrast to the earlier editions of *Abridgment of Christian Doctrine*, his work included the "affections" in its definition of prayer, "the raising up of the mind and heart to God." The book continued:

> In what manner ought we to pray?
> With attention and devotion.
> What is meant by praying with attention?
> To attend to the meaning of the prayers which we utter.
> What by praying with devotion?
> To excite in our hearts the feelings expressed by our words.

In a footnote Lingard wrote that prayer essentially consisted of "religious feelings."[90] By this he meant a *"wish to do what reason & religion suggest."*[91] He carefully distinguished between feelings and the forms designed to awaken them; he believed that the latter changed, the former remained.[92]

In order properly to assess the Cisalpine devotional mentality this short analysis of prayer must be placed in the forefront. By stressing the role of an individual's affective life, Lingard avoided the Enlightenment's tendency toward excessive rationalization. His was not the "high and dry" moralism of the eighteenth century. On the other hand, he recognized the importance of understanding: a person had to pray with attention; his feelings had to conform to reason and religion. In this view, the *lex orandi* did not dictate the *lex credendi*, but neither did the latter dominate. They existed together in a creative tension. Thus Lingard could write that if feelings and forms did not correspond, prayer became a mockery. All the demands of mind and heart had to be met. His attitude toward the Second Spring was largely dictated by the meaning he attached to these words.

In Lingard's view, "reason" and "religion" meant that whole complex of forces which characterized Cisalpinism. When these convictions were applied to the devotional life they once again dictated an approach that was both reasonably critical and ecumenical. For example, Lingard's view of the Litany of Loreto graphically exemplified his insistence on intelligibility. Instead of "Tower of Ivory," and "House of Gold," he preferred the following:

> Holy Mary, who didst lead a simple, and laborious life, in poverty and obscurity,—Pray for us.

> Holy Mary, who didst make it the great business of thy life to increase, each day, in the love of God; and in the desire to be united again to Jesus,—Pray for us.
> Holy Mary, who, now reigning in heaven, lookest down upon the earth with the feelings of compassion towards us . . .
> That, in imitation of thy example, we may labour with earnestness to acquire some share of thy virtues . . .
> That, like thee, we may, in all things, consult the will of God, and on all occasions, follow it,—Pray for us.[93]

Here was a litany, in his mind, that was both comprehensible and theologically accurate, one that combined spirit and form. Berington, Butler, Kirk, and Fletcher would have agreed.

The strong desire to "attend to the meaning of the words which we utter" accounted for Lingard's hope to purify devotional literature of unsuitable or legendary stories. At one time the vicars apostolic, through Bishop Milner, requested Lingard to compose breviary lessons for the English saints. Unfortunately, the "Angel of Castabala" gave such restricting instructions that Lingard felt he could only abridge original accounts. When he exercised his critical sense, Milner accused him of heresy. Eventually Lingard's lessons were published and furnished F. C. Husenbeth with some material for his 1830 edition of the *Breviarum Romanum*.[94] Husenbeth's version, however, did not meet Lingard's standards of accuracy. During the years of the Second Spring, Lingard was constantly complaining about the Roman lessons. He wondered why the breviary narrated Gregory VII's deposition of the German emperor. Was this not nonsense to an educated Englishman? On another occasion Lingard asked John Walker: "Am I obliged *sub mortali* to read as truths, & where the office is publicly performed, to read to bystanders, as truths, what I know to be falsehoods." When one of the prayers said that Sts. Patrick and Cuthbert had been carried by angels to Mount Sinai, Walker noted his agreement with Lingard, remarking caustically: "We all think a little from Pio Nono to me—yet on we go from age to age." Lingard's reactions to the *Lives of the English Saints*, which the Tractarians published in 1844 and 1845, mirrored similar preoccupations with critical standards. "I have been reading," he wrote, the life of St. Augustine by the Puseyite—very pretty, very imaginary, and very fabulous. He gives us every fable about St. Peter, St. Paul, Aristobulus &c &c in Britain. His canon is not you are to prove the facts, but to believe them, if they are not disproved. It is written as you would delight to write. Ex. gratia. . . . Newman prefaces it [the life of St. Richard] by telling us that miracles are the facts proper for church history, as feats of prowess are for profane history. You may perhaps be occasionally deceived by the accounts of miracles, but so you may by accounts of courage &c in profane history. They are going too far. They will injure their own character and influence by their credulity.[95]

Rationalism played a definite part in all these reflections. But in his desire for reform Lingard was also showing himself to be the descendant of the Bollandists. Their more critical approach to devotional literature had been well represented in eighteenth-century England by Charles Fell and Alban Butler. Charles Butler had continued the tradition.[96] Emerging from this climate of opinion, the writer of *The Antiquities of the Anglo-Saxon Church* did not oppose devotional literature; he wanted only to unite his piety with his criticism.

Lingard's Cisalpine definition of "reason" and "religion" also led him, predictably, to stress the ecumenical dimension of Catholic devotional life. After emancipation, Lady Stourton prophesied to Lingard that there would be a great accession of Protestants to the Catholic Church. Lingard agreed but noted that his hopes rested on a foundation different from that of many people. He wrote to Robert Tate:

> I was amused at Allerton with Lady Stourton's prophecies. She is as good a prophet as those on whom she relies. The present crisis will bind to mother damnable many of her children who before cared not for her. Yet there will be stragglers who might enter our fold, if any invitation were held out to them. But of that our ecclesiastical rulers seem not to think. In fact we have too many bigots among us, who look upon any alteration for that purpose as an unworthy concession to Protestant prejudice, and who probably, had they lived when Our Saviour appeared on earth, would have thought his assumption of human nature unworthy of the dignity of the Almighty.

Throughout the years of the Second Spring Lingard supported what he considered to be a *realistic devotional ecumenism*: "To make any number of converts we should give milk to the babes, be content with essentials, and not mind anything else . . . being convinced that once admitted they would practice as other Christians did."[97]

It was partly because of his ecumenism that Lingard opposed many of the external signs of the Catholic revival. He castigated the Yorkshire clergy for sprinkling the congregation with holy water and advocating public processions: "Is it not making religion ridiculous in the eyes of protestants? We wish to catholicise England: and the wise men among us do it by means, which must necessarily have a contrary effect." The idea of burning a sanctuary lamp before the Blessed Sacrament was silly. What purpose would it serve? "To light robbers to break open the tabernacle etc." Did not these foreign customs "by making religion *ridiculous* in the eyes of protestants *prevent it from spreading here*"? The introduction of jubilees *a la Romaine* and the attachment of indulgences to confraternities of "the Sacred Heart, of the Scapular, of the Rosary, of the Bona Mors and of others id genus" were even worse. "But nonsense apart, there are in my mind many mysteries in these same jubilees and indulgences, which had better not be thrust on the notice of the public." The emphasis on the extraordinary mortifications and fastings of the saints only furnished "Protestants with a strong argument against us." The system of retreats introduced by Luigi Gentili contained a great deal of humbug, "much to set the imagination to work, and prompt sensible men to act contrary to common, aye to evangelical sense."[98]

Lingard especially objected to what he called *les petites devotions*, which included prayers to the Sacred Heart of Jesus, May devotions, forty hours, solemn renewal of baptismal vows, public processions of the Blessed Sacrament, and use of scapulars, relics, and medals. Lingard's letters during the Second Spring abounded with references to these practices. On Sacred Heart devotions he commented: "They might as well have a festum occulorum or lateris, as cordis. Besides where would they stop? They would soon have a festum cordis Mariae." When that did occur, Lingard's advice to someone in Preston was to "insist on a direct answer to the question, in what the heart of the B.V. differed from the hearts of other women." In June 1849 he remarked to John Walker: "The month of May is expired and with it, I hope, some follies to which the month of May has given birth." In another letter Lingard summarized the core of his attitude:

> What do you mean by Dr. Wiseman and his maryanne or something like that? Is he preaching up some new fangled devotion in honour of the virgin, some month of May? In truth I begin to dispute all my former convictions, and to believe that I ought not to have the least reliance on my own judgment. Here is he preaching in favour of a new petite devotion, you restoring the antiquated custom of the aspersion of holy water, others setting up processions with the cross or the crucifix, all of them practices in themselves certainly unnecessary, in their consequences, as far as I can see, calculated to confirm the prejudices of well educated protestants and to prevent them from considering the essentials of our holy religion: and yet all advocated by men, whose judgment I respect and of whose zeal and sincerity I can have no doubt. What then am I to think of myself, to whom, what they judge at least useful, appears pernicious.[99]

This opposition to external practices was an essential part of Lingard's intellectual heritage. The earlier Cisalpines had always rejected ostentatious display as injurious to the Catholic cause and abusive of true religion. Joseph Berington railed against scapulars, medals, and beads. When John Bew became president of Oscott Seminary in 1794, he promised "to instill into the minds of his Pupils the purest Principles, and the most enlightened piety." Among other things, he meant the avoidance of the external practices associated with Sacred Heart devotions, relics, holy water, and numerous indulgenced prayers. John Kirk joined those who opposed external practices when he criticized "extravagant expressions" applied to the Blessed Mother. The sermons of James Archer warned against errors in the devotional life, and John Fletcher emphasized the sanctification of ordinary actions, a sentiment shared by Charles Butler.[100]

In summary, what should be made of Lingard's attitude? This analysis has stressed the positive connection between the historian's Cisalpine vision and his approach to religious practices. But it cannot be denied that many negative elements also contributed to the mentality. These have been excessively detailed by historians of the Second Spring. First of all, the Cisalpines were overcritical of foreign enthusiasms. Berington sprinkled the pages of his writings with attacks on the "cumbrous weight of ceremonies and unmeaning pageantry" that stemmed from the "warmer imaginations of some nations." To Charles Butler many devotional practices served as a cover for alien and papal encroachments. In 1823 he wrote to Kirk: "All persons who come from france [sic] agree that ultramontanism and devotions and practices of the ultramontanes are spread with great activity." Ultimately such an approach was inextricably allied with Bossuet's Gallicanism. Inasmuch as Lingard's Cisalpinism was dependent on this Gallican theological heritage and on distinctively English political beliefs, his piety reflected a strong current of nationalism.[101]

Second, the fixed approach to tradition caused most Cisalpines to reject summarily any new practice. Lingard was only following Berington when he castigated devotions to the Sacred Hearts of Jesus and Mary as "modern innovations."[102] It was a strange accusation since Berington's revision of the prayer book, Fletcher's writings, and Lingard's letters to the *Catholic Magazine* all pleaded for devotional changes and supported the introduction of new forms. Paradoxically, in arguing for a return to "pristine simplicity," the Cisalpines baptized reform and anathematized development. Third, Cisalpinism was born and bred in an atmosphere of negative apologetic. At times Lingard's penal mentality as much as his acceptance of religious pluralism forced his liberal approach to reconciliation. Fourth, the advocacy of an unostentatious piety rested not only on critical principles but also on a more defensive attachment to an older way of life. Berington and Butler, despite an attitude of social openness, remained attached to a "ghetto" spirituality. In a similar fashion Lingard closed his eyes to the need for imaginative display among Irish immigrants and the more public demands of a postemancipation piety. Fifth, there was a definite disparagement of the "unseen world" in the Cisalpine mind. The sermons of James Archer and Thomas White (which Lingard published) were overmoralistic. They accepted the Enlightenment's sharp distinction between reason and revelation. As a result, the mysteries of faith were to be accepted, not pondered; the Christian life was confined to the sphere of the practical.[103] The historian's piety mirrored the limitations of the eighteenth century. Finally, the culture of the Enlightenment was unduly critical of baroque Catholicism. Thus, when religious romanticism began to dominate the climate of opinion, an approach such as Lingard's could only become more and more obsolete. Lingard definitely underestimated the value and importance of popular devotions. His letters testify to the fact that, as religious needs and the presuppositions supporting them shifted, his "reform" hardened into a mentality of opposition.

The argument here, however, is that despite these negative elements, the Cisalpine devotional mentality remained positive. Lingard's "reason" and "religion" summarized what he considered to be the essentials of Catholic doctrine, the dictates of a pluralistic society, and the consequences of an Enlightenment anthropology. Ultimately he and others rejected much of religious romanticism because its "form" did not correspond to their "feelings." Indeed, their understanding of "true devotion" could not accommodate a piety centered on external devotions. What "form" did correspond to Lingard's "feelings"? Was his piety rationalistic or did it leave room for the affections? The answers to these questions unveil the heart of Cisalpine spirituality.

An Integral Vision: Cisalpine Spirituality

For the most part, history has remained silent about the positive core of Cisalpine spirituality. But several important indications remain. In a letter of September 1831 Lingard referred to a manuscript written as a release from historical studies. The work was designed to "teach some Catholics to understand the [prayers] which they are in the habit of repeating, though some parts of them are to the repeaters an unknown tongue." Lingard wanted to print his small work as an appendix to a prayer book or as a separate tract. Unfortunately, his publisher refused to issue it unless Lingard affixed his name, which he refused to do. Presumably, therefore, his short explanation of the life of prayer remained unpublished. Today, among the extant Lingard manuscripts at Ushaw College is one entitled "Practice of Living in Union with Jesus Christ." It is undated but may be the work to which Lingard alluded in 1831. If it is, then he evidently reworked it, since one of the books he refers to was first published in 1839. Whenever it was written, the pamphlet embodies much of Lingard's inner life, and its private nature may be why he refused to sign it. To the contemporary historian it is a manuscript of prime importance, for it provides a perspective from which to view Cisalpine spirituality, its content, and its intellectual roots.[104]

After a few preliminary observations on the necessity of a firm resolution to do good and an exact fidelity to secular and religious duties, Lingard's manuscript defines the essence of the devout life: "The sum of it is that perfection consists in the entire renunciation of ourselves, & 2. in the full & pure union of ourselves with the divine will—viz. in being in union with God." To achieve this, a person must first of all have an "habitual conviction, founded on divine hope, that you are in Jesus, & Jesus in you"; that "without him you can do nothing"; that "whatever good you do *he* does it in you & with you, not separately but conjointly, not partially but entirely." The conviction is established by meditating on certain passages of the Scriptures (e.g., "I am the vine, you, the branches.") and realizing that in every activity—praying, reading, studying, or walking—"Jesus in his divine nature is within you, moving, ruling, performing all. . . ." The key to this divine indwelling is the friendship Jesus offers to the Christian. A person can truly and sincerely say to Jesus: "I to my beloved,

& my beloved to me." If he has a desire for this friendship, he cannot be deprived of it. The foundation of confidence is the love of Christ: "He is earnestly *desirous* of entering into & perfecting the relations of an eternal friendship with you" (Luke 12:49; John 15:17; Rom. 5:8–10). In summary, this union with Jesus is accomplished by his promise and the Christian's fulfillment of the offices of true friendship:

> True and disinterested friendship is (1) an attachment between two persons springing from a mutual esteem & respect for the good & amiable qualities that exist in each; detecting & producing (2) a frequent & familiar intercourse, as far as circumstances will permit; (3) a communion of goods; (4) the exclusion of all selfishness; (5) a much tried (prayer) confidence [?]; (6) & a disposition to share & relieve each others [sic] sufferings & sorrows; (7) an inclination & endeavour to imitate & copy each others' manners, conduct, & virtues; (8) a constant interchange of acts of kindness & good offices; (9) with an habitually sincere & earnest desire to promote to the fullest extent each others' interest & happiness, & to prevent or remove as far as possible every misfortune & evil. Weigh well the foregoing explanation; every part of it is of the utmost importance.

In the practical order, on the side of the Christian, there are eight ways in which this friendship is realized: (1) Meditation and spiritual reading on the passion of Christ, "especially his tender mercy & goodness to *you* in rescuing you, at the price of his own suffering & death, from your worst enemy, in placing you in the number of his friends. . . ." (2) The habitual recollection of "his perpetual and intimate presence within you." A person should be in *continual* intercourse with this friend. (3) By frequent considerations and acts of the will, a person must try to produce the habitual feeling that he is devoted to his Savior and friends. (4) The maintenance of an affectionate and unbounded confidence in Jesus based on his mercy and the individual's disposition. This general sentiment can be expressed in the repetition of different aspirations, e.g., "I have cast all my care upon him, for he hath a care of me." (5) By intention (at times *actual*, usually *virtual*) and *internal* virtue "you must endeavour *to unite yourself closely with Jesus in thought & will, in whatever you do, & in whatever you suffer.*" A person should consider himself as constantly making little presents to his Savior. (6) The diligent exercise of charity to others. Here it is helpful if a person offers daily prayers and actions (e.g., instruction, advice, consolation, alms deeds, bearing with faults, forgiving injuries) for the relief and comfort of the souls in purgatory and the members of the church on earth. (7) Conscious imitation of the Savior. A person should regulate all his thoughts, desires, affections, and exterior conduct according to what Jesus would say or do. (8) "*A lively interest in whatever concerns the glory, or casts dishonour on your Saviour & friend.*" Such a lively interest is shown by instruction for the poor and ignorant, attention to religious duties, the sanctifications of Sundays and holidays, and the decoration of chapels.

The "Practice of Living in Union with Jesus Christ" warns the reader that the devout life consists of two agents: Jesus is the principal one; the Christian's duty is to *watch* and to render the foregoing practice habitual and easy. Perseverance is the key; feelings of satisfaction or devotion come on Jesus' good time. The whole doctrine is summarized in the prayer that the Christian is encouraged to make before the crucifix:

> Jesus, my Saviour, I know—for your holy word declares it—that you earnestly desire to contact & maintain with me a true, affectionate & eternal friendship. I also know that if I will consent to devote myself entirely to you—that is, if I perform all I have to do with *the firm intention* of promoting your honour & glory & the good of your children—you engage on *your* part to take all that concerns me into your own hands, & to watch over me with so much care that *not one hair of my head shall perish:* . . . From this moment, therefore, throughout my life & forever, I am no longer my own, but yours. These hands & feet are yours—these eyes and this tongue are yours—the intellectual & active powers of my soul now belong to you. I devote & dedicate all to you

forever: & from this moment I direct all my actions, my words, & thoughts to promoting your honour & glory, & for your sake the good of your children.

The foregoing is only a brief excerpt from this concise and surprisingly fervent document. For the purposes of this study, two important characteristics should be noted. First, Lingard's exposition was completely Christocentric. The object of the devout life was union with God through the practice of the presence of Jesus and the imitation of his life. Everything else was secondary. It was this orientation, as much as his desire to placate Protestants and to separate essentials from accidentals, that caused Lingard to oppose proliferation of relics of the saints, the use of scapulars and medals, and excessive emphasis on the Blessed Mother. Lingard indicated his Christocentricity in a letter to John Walker: "I am greatly pleased with the seven offices D.N.I.C. By them we shall return towards the religious devotion of our ancestors. For many hundred years, the Passion of Christ was the great object of devotion among our countrymen: in defiance of the spirit of innovation it kept its place till about the middle of the last century as you will find by the office of the holy cross in prayer books up to that time; but ever since we have been running from the Son to the Mother, till devotion to the B.V. has usurped the place of the prayers which had for their object the passion of Christ." Also, when Robert Tate published an edition of Lingard's *Manual of Prayers* in 1844, Lingard noted with satisfaction that it included the litany of the passion. Again he wrote to Walker: "I wish much to encourage devotion to the passion. It was a favorite devotion once."[105] Lingard would have agreed with John Fletcher, who explained that all the titles in the Litany of Loreto referred to the great mystery of the redemption "and to the relationship solely, which, in consequence of this stupendous benefit, the Blessed Mother stands in, towards her divine Son."[106]

Second, the model of the devout life that Lingard proposed rested on the interior, permanent experience of presence. Ontologically, the divine indwelling provided the foundation.

On man's part, habitual recollection, continual prayer, and individual disposition were central. The conjunction of the two elements emphasized internalization, the conformity of the human will with the will of God. It focused attention on personal relationship and not on the practices of asceticism. Penance and sacramental activity were taken for granted, but pure love was the goal. In this view, forms became accidental; discursive meditations became a means not to action but to contemplation—the realization of union. Thus the devout life involved nothing extraordinary in the way of mortifications, fastings, or forms of prayer. In the practical order its essence was the sanctification of the ordinary, the sacrament of the "present" as a gift to God. With such an understanding Lingard naturally opposed particular devotions, methodical meditation, and the ascetical or imaginative practices associated with Luigi Gentili's retreats. After Walker had attended one of these Lingard wrote: "But do tell me what sent you to Loughbro'. What does Dr. Gentili there? Where was your cell 7 inches square? How did your piety feel at five every morning?" When formal meditation was introduced at Ushaw, he remarked: "Pray, have you also reduced meditation to an art? Spiritus ubi vult, spirat, and will not be bound by the Ushaw rules."[107]

This model of the devout life was not unique. James Archer's sermons may have emphasized the moral dimension of the Christian life. He himself probably depreciated mystical experiences. Still, he defined true devotion as "that habitual disposition of souls which is formed by divine love." Archer saw four elements in this disposition: the continual sense of the presence of God; sentiments of gratitude for his benefits; ardent desires of being inseparably united to him; placid resignation to every appointment of his providence. Devotion, then, in Archer's view did not require a retreat from the world or a gloomy and melancholy temper of mind. It was a spirit, not a particular act. He remarked on prayer: "Your mistake lies in supposing prayer to be an arrangement of choice ideas and profound speculations. You think that prayer is a science; whereas it is no more than the simple effusions of the heart, the unadorned and artless language of the affections. You imagine that to pray is to recite a set form of sentences. . . . The continual prayer which Jesus commands is not a recital of words, but the cries of a heart weeping over its own distresses, and animated with glowing desires of the good things of eternity." This "prayer" did not exclude domestic concerns, business or parental activities, the functions of civil life, the attentions of politeness, or the duties of state.[108]

Similarly, Charles Butler and Joseph Berington showed a continual interest in the interior life of the spirit. Butler was much more mystically oriented than Archer. He wrote complimentary lives of Fénelon, Thomas à Kempis, and Henri Marie de Boudon. In his life of Vincent de Paul, a man often associated with practical Christianity, he included a section on the "presence of God," the sacramental dimension of the ordinary.[109] He agreed with Alban Butler's stress on the prayer of contemplation as opposed to the exertions of meditation. In describing the piety of his uncle, Butler also presented his own ideal: "He exhorted everyone to a perfect discharge of the ordinary duties of his situation, to a conformity to the divine will both in great and little occasions, to good temper and mildness in his intercourse with his neighbour, to an habitual recollection of the divine presence, to scrupulous attachment to truth, to retirement, to extreme sobriety."[110] Lastly, the Catholic lawyer printed "An Essay on Mystical Theology, or the Science of Sacred Contemplation." His description relegated the imagination to a secondary place and emphasized habitual devotion. Continual prayer was something that Berington also recognized. A daily reading of *The Imitation of Christ* fed his spiritual life.[111]

Perhaps the best witness to this type of spirituality was volume 3 of John Fletcher's *Sermons on Various Religious and Moral Subjects*. This Cisalpine systematically applied the Christocentric and mystical elements of "true devotion" to the sacramental and penitential dimensions of Christian life. His approach was neither too rigoristic nor too lax. It represented a real synthesis of Christian humanism. For Fletcher, the essence of piety was union with Christ; the eucharist was the medium of incorporation. Like Lingard, he acknowledged the importance of frequent communion—not just at great feasts but during every season of the year. "*To Dwell* in Christ is manifestly the greatest of all possible advantages, and the first of all possible honours;—the sure token of divine friendship here; the sure pledge of the divine mercy hereafter." "The Eucharist is an immense,—a boundless, bottomless, ocean of grace." "Mystery of love! What feelings, and reflections art thou formed to light up in the heart, in which sensibility and reason are not extinguished."[112]

In a similar vein, penance became an act of reconciliation by which sins were effaced, grace diffused, and the Holy Spirit fixed his abode in the heart. To prove the malice of sin a person first had to appreciate the sanctity of the union "which, by the mystery of the Incarnation, God has formed with his human creatures." The state of sin "is a state of unhappiness; because it is a state, which disunites the soul from God." Also, the mass made the Christian people into "a holy nation, a royal priesthood." "Yes; the mystery of our altars is, indeed, the Marriage Feast provided, and served up to us, by the hands of the divine liberality. It is here, that the great Sovereign of the universe,—Himself the giver, and the gift,—bestows upon us all the delicacies and delights, which omnipotence itself, under the influence of benevolence, can create. He here *marries* us, as it were, to Himself,—taking us to Himself, and giving himself to us; uniting us to his love; and imparting to us his treasures. Such is the Mass." The obligation of attending mass rested not on law but on the proper understanding of this "mystery of faith." Fletcher summarized his attitude when he wrote: "The whole system of our divine religion is a system of love. It has love for its foundation; love for its end; love for its fruit; and love for its reward. Its great design and endeavour are to unite man to God by the bonds of gratitude; and man to man by the ties of goodwill."[113] This exposition was unique in its thoroughness, but it remained in definite continuity with the spirituality of the other Cisalpines. Both Butler and Lingard acknowledged the force and beauty of Fletcher's vision.[114]

This notion of true devotion, shared in various degrees by Lingard, Archer, Butler, Berington, and Fletcher, was at the core of the Cisalpine mentality. Its importance and their total vision of reform can be grasped properly only when the Cisalpines are placed in the perspective of the development of Catholic spirituality in the seventeenth and eighteenth centuries. Generally, after 1650 there was a shift in the tone of spirituality from more mystical considerations to more practical ones. The spread of rationalism, the Cartesian anthropological split between sense and sensibility, and the Enlightenment's emphasis on utility encouraged, on the one hand, a moralistic approach to piety, and, on the other hand, an overemotional emphasis. Intellectually "clear and distinct ideas" became the order of the day; affectively, imagination and enthusiasm became more and more suspect. Within the Catholic tradition, Louis Bourdaloue, one of the most influential French classical preachers and someone well known to the Cisalpines, testified to this gradual subordination of a man's inner experience of God to *le bon sens*. According to Henri Bremond, Bourdaloue's philosophy of prayer followed the tradition of *ascéticisme*. It tended to assimilate simple contemplation with the more spectacular graces associated with the mystical life. As a result, common prayer (more generally, Christian spirituality or *devotio*) became an exercise in ascesis; its end was not the experience of union with God but the performance of meritorious acts. Thus, habitual grace, the Trinitarian indwelling, was deemphasized, and practical preoccupations replaced the ancient-medieval theocentric vision. Oddly enough, as if to indicate the split between mind and heart, Bourdaloue witnessed to the "mystic way" in his own personal life.[115]

The Quietist controversy in the late seventeenth century encouraged this general tendency. The following years witnessed to *la deroute des mystiques*. Alban Butler believed that "the condemnation which had been passed in it [the Quietist dispute], on the abuses of devotion, had brought devotion itself into discredit, and thrown ridicule on the holiness of an interior life." Charles Butler concurred when he noted that after the dispute between Bossuet and Fénelon contemplative writers had abstained from detailed descriptions and had confined themselves to exhortations on habitual recollection, humility, self-denial, and detachment from wordly objects. All these men believed that a man's inner experience of the divine had been forced underground. Recent historical studies by Louis Cognet have confirmed their judgments. The effect on Catholic spirituality was devastating.[116]

Parallel with this impasse created by *ascéticisme* and the suspicion of any form of illuminism was the failure of many theologians to elucidate a theology that recognized the importance of both nature and grace and gave a genuinely unified role to the subjective and objective elements of the Christian life. Thus René Taveneaux writes of the Jansenists: "This aspiration for the absolute, marked as it was with undeniable grandeur, bore within itself, it is true, seeds of fragility. The desire to preserve the christian from the aggressiveness of evil leads to surrounding daily life with barriers, interdicts, and petty or rigid prescriptions. Foreign to the Port-Royal of the beginnings, this narrow moralism became a frequent occurrence among its inheritors of the XVIII century." Emile Appolis documents what he calls the rise of "moral *bénignisme*," the volatilization of sin. In this current the reporting of outward actions replaced personal contact with God; penitence did not have to stem from love of God; the sacraments could be given with no account of a change of life. Here, *ex opere operato* tended to be overemphasized at the expense of *ex opere operantis*.[117]

In all of these movements there occurred the gradual separation of individual piety from cultural, liturgical, and dogmatic realities. Personal life, life in the world, and religious belief—the union of which is integral spirituality—split. A similar disjunction reflected itself in the separation of reason and revelation and the church's institutional withdrawal from the constitutional patterns of society. In terms of the inner life, R. R. Palmer summarizes the withdrawal this way: "But what was it to be supernatural, when justice and goodness were a part of nature? It might mean two things: to be saintly, aloof, and holy, living in a righteousness not of this world; or to be ritualistic, performing the acts that were prescribed by the church, and acquiring the grace which the sacraments imparted, and which, though not necessary to make a man just or good, promoted him into heaven." Religious romanticism was largely a reaction to this state of affairs.[118]

After 1680 a movement for renewal, a Catholic Enlightenment, arose in the midst of these developments. Cisalpinism should be seen from the perspective of this current of reform. In his sermons James Archer argued for the necessity of outward observances, but he also castigated abuses. What he wanted was "enlightened piety," "reasonable service." His humanism showed through when he spoke of the delights of receiving communion and defined the Christian as the "temple of the living God." Archer's view of devotion, like John Fletcher's, recalled that of Francis de Sales. In a similar fashion Charles Butler manifested a deep appreciation of Renaissance humanism. He was well aware of the currents of mysticism from Johannes Tauler and *The Imitation of Christ* to Jean Joseph Surin. John Fletcher also appealed to the reform tradition that combined humanism and mysticism. In 1837 and 1844 he published some of the writings of Fénelon. *The Catholic's Prayer Book* utilized the same authority. Lingard's "Practice of Living in Union with Jesus Christ" referred to the following: Bernard of Clairvaux's *Tractatus de Gratia* (1127), *The Imitation of Christ*, Alfonso Rodríguez's *Practice of Christian Perfection* (1609), Lorenzo Scupoli's *Spiritual Combat* (1589) the *Ascensio Mentis ad Deum* (1615) of Bellarmine, Liguori's "Method of Conversing Continually and Familiarly with God" (1753), the writings of Teresa of Ávila, and, most important, the *Introduction to the Devout Life* (1608) and *Love of God* (1616) of Francis de Sales. What this tradition represented, in various degrees, was the combination of Catholicism with the forces of humanism, individualism, the emergence of the laity, and the mystic's interior relationship to God. Thomas à Kempis, Francis de Sales, and Fénelon, in the history of spirituality, stood for a synthetic vision.[119]

The English Catholic spiritual heritage also contributed to the Cisalpine mentality. Butler remarked in his "Mystical Theology" that Augustine Baker was very popular in England. Through Baker and Alban Butler the Cisalpines would have been familiar with the medieval mysticism of Walter Hilton, Richard Rolle, and *Cloud of Unknowing* (ca. 1370). The *Manual of Devout Prayers and Exercises* (1598) and *The Primer: or, Office of the Blessed Virgin Marie* (1559), standard works in post-Reformation England, continued this older tradition of piety, which was highly personal and empirical, and emphasized the centrality of Jesus. In the seventeenth century a strong Christocentricity, "unostentatious tenderness," and focus on the duties of ordinary life marked John Gother's works. Richard Challoner's *Garden of the Soul* continued the same approach and relied heavily on the *Introduction to the Devout Life.* (1608). Perhaps because English Catholicism was so closely knit, unmarked by the theological wranglings of the Jesuits and Jansenists and placed in the midst of an Enlightenment that was not anticlerical, it managed to preserve this older, more unified approach to spirituality.[120]

All these currents naturally coalesced with the Cisalpine anthropology. The result was a synthesis, however incomplete, of the subjective and the objective, an integral spirituality. A strong personalism and an openness to the world are manifested throughout Cisalpine reflections. Cisalpine spirituality confirmed, and, in turn, was supported by, the communal emphasis in ecclesiology, the speculative distinction between essentials and accidentals, the recognition of the role of the laity, the Christocentric emphasis in ecumenism, the respect for the individual conscience and the rights of criticism, the desire to unite priest and people in the liturgy, the hostile attitude toward particular devotions, and the support of the popular diffusion of Scripture. In this sense, Joseph Berington's daily reading of *The Imitation of Christ* influenced his *Reflections Addressed to Hawkins.* Charles Butler's spirituality supported his life as a lawyer. John Lingard's definition of "church," recognition of the importance of the communion of saints, and emphasis on the redemptive union between Christ, the individual, and all Christians, were interrelated. Ultimately, Christian life meant "praying with attention and devotion," the correspondence of form and feeling, the necessity of *rationabile obsequium.* Once again

Cisalpinism proved to be a vision of Catholicism and not a negative ideology.

In conclusion, it should be noted that the Cisalpine approach to reform failed precisely because of this unity. Before 1829 it had no chance to develop. After emancipation it collapsed when the Enlightenment's notion of "intelligibility"—with its positive and negative characteristics—ceased to respond to social, intellectual, and religious needs. New, more speculative questions were being posed; a different religious anthropology needed articulation. This work has not concerned itself with the triumph of religious romanticism, which belongs to the history of the Catholic revival. The conflict between the approaches of Wiseman and Lingard to biblical criticism was one indication of the change in outlook. A similar difference marked their attitudes toward the Oxford Movement and the fundamentals of Christian doctrine. In the area of spirituality a new form and feeling also took shape. The second generation of Cisalpines spent much of their life during the 1840s and early 1850s fighting a battle that had already been lost. To a large extent, they ignored the coherent set of principles that Berington, Butler, and Lingard had accepted. The unified view would emerge again only in Liberal Catholicism. In 1845 F. C. Husenbeth wrote the *Life of the Rev. Robert Richmond*. At that time he remarked to Lingard: "My earnest wish then is, that the Life of Mr. R. may open the eyes of some, and make them value and admire the plain, solid, sensible career of a hard working, unpretending missioner; and may tend to convince them that English priests really did understand the care of souls before the importation of so many new men and new theories. Yes, my dear Sir, I am a fervent *laudator temporis acti*: I am known among my friends for a tenacious memory for old things, and a fond clinging to old maxims, ways, and practices."[121]

Laudator temporis acti. Lingard could easily have applied the phrase to himself. The intellectual and pastoral reform of the English Catholic Enlightenment had ceased to attract believers.

epilogue

JOHN LINGARD was the last representative of the English Catholic Enlightenment. He died August 17, 1851. His life was shaped by and reflected all of the major social and intellectual forces that had nurtured the Cisalpine mentality. Lingard fought for political emancipation with the tools of the Whig tradition: separation of church and state and religious freedom. Although he was not personally involved in the disputes of the 1790s, his controversies with Milner and his views on the election of bishops indicate that he shared with earlier Cisalpines the principled acceptance of a natural rights philosophy. Theologically, this Catholic writer recognized the necessity of a *rationabile obsequium*. "Reasonable service" involved—in a pluralistic and constitutional society—an irenical apologetics and an acceptance of a Gallican ecclesiology. *A History of England* witnessed to the growing impact of secularization and acknowledgment of a scientific methodology. Finally, Lingard attempted to elucidate an integral spirituality, a Catholic doctrinal, liturgical, and devotional reform that would complement his own religious anthropology. But this vision, born of the conjunction of so many forces, had no future in the climate of the romantic revival.

The preceding chapters have argued that John Lingard's mentality was not unique, that he himself belonged to the movement known as Cisalpinism. In varying degrees the members of the Catholic Committee and Lingard's own friends, Joseph Berington, Charles Butler, John Fletcher, and John Kirk, shared a common outlook. Ultimately their view was positive. At its core it represented both a social and theological anthropology and a project of intelligibility. Seen from the cultural point of view, Cisalpinism tried to achieve a synthesis between an individual's outer institutional relationships and his inner spiritual life. In England the central factor in this movement was the acceptance of a Lockean view of the individual. Socially, the Cisalpine definition of man included the rights of the individual, the notion of contract, the importance of a limited government, and the necessity, in a religiously heterogeneous society, of freedom of conscience. In theological terms, this anthropology reflected itself in a revision of the pyramidal structure of the Tridentine church and an ecumenical program. A project of intelligibility naturally followed. If culture were to serve religion, and religion, culture, then politics, theology, and religious practice had to be persuasively presented to both an educated elite and a growing body of "reasonable men." Broadly speaking, Berington, Butler, and especially Lingard represented a religious attempt to grapple with the social and intellectual transformations of the modern world. It is in this light that one should see their total program. As Berington said: "I am a rational Catholic."[1] So, too, was John Lingard. For Cisalpinism as a whole, the struggle to make the Gospel culturally intelligible was the clarion call of the English Catholic Enlightenment.

notes

Abbreviations to Archival Repositories

AAB	Archives of the Archbishop of Birmingham
AAW	Archives of the Archbishop of Westminster
PF/SRC	Archives of Propaganda Fide, Scritture Riferite nei Congressi, Anglia
SEC/AAW	Saint Edmund's College Archives/Archives of the Archbishop of Westminster
UCA	Ushaw College Archives
VEC/S	Archives of the Venerable English College, Rome, Scritture

Preface

1. The following are some representative titles: W. J. Amherst, *The History of Catholic Emancipation and the Progress of the Catholic Church in the British Isles (Chiefly in England) from 1771 to 1820*, 2 vols. (London: K. Paul Trench & Co., 1886); Philip Hughes, *The Catholic Question, 1688-1829: A Study in Political History* (London: Sheed and Ward, 1929); David Mathew, *Catholicism in England, 1535-1935* (London: Longmans, Green, and Co., 1936); Denis Gwynn, *The Second Spring, 1818-1852: A Study of the Catholic Revival in England* (London: Burns & Oates, 1942).
2. Eamon Duffy, "Joseph Berington and the English Catholic Cisalpine Movement, 1772-1803" (Ph.D. diss., Selwyn College, Cambridge, 1972); J. C. H. Aveling, *The Handle and the Axe* (London: Blond & Briggs, 1976).
3. John Bossy, *The English Catholic Community, 1570-1850* (New York: Oxford University Press, 1976).
4. Bernard Plongeron, "Recherches sur l'Aufklärung Catholique en Europe Occidentale (1770-1830)," *Revue d'histoire moderne et contemporaine* 16 (1969): 560.

Introduction

1. Emile Appolis, Le "Tiers Parti" Catholique au XVIII* siècle (entre Jansénistes et Zelanti) (Paris: A. & J. Picard, 1960).
2. Bernard Plongeron, Théologie et politique au siècle des lumières (1770-1820) (Geneva: Librairie Droz, 1973); Plongeron, "Recherches sur l'Aufklärung Catholique"; Plongeron, "Questions pour l'Aufklärung Catholique en Italie," Il pensiero politico 3 (1970): 30-58.
3. H. R. Trevor-Roper, The European Witch-Craze of the Sixteenth and Seventeenth Centuries, and Other Essays (New York: Harper and Row, 1969), passim.
4. Mario Rosa, "Italian Jansenism and the Synod of Pistoia," trans. Edward A. Carpenter, Concilium 17 (1966): 34-49, quotation from p. 42.
5. Maurice Vaussard, "Un Janséniste de grande classe: Benedetto Solari," Revue d'histoire ecclésiastique 68 (1973): 429-56.
6. Marina Caffiero, "Cultura e religione nel settecento italiano: Giovanni Cristofano Amaduzzi e Scipione di Ricci," Rivista di storia della chiesa in Italia 28 (1974): 94-126.
7. Charles Van Der Plancke, "Une conscience d'église à travers le Catéchèse janseniste du XVIII* siècle," Revue d'histoire ecclesiastique 72 (1977): 5-39.
8. The definition of generation is taken from Plongeron, "Recherches sur l'Aufklärung catholique," p. 574, who follows the view of Y. Renouard. For biographical information on these people, see Joseph Gillow, A Literary and Biographical History, 5 vols. (London: Burns & Oates, 1885-1902); Godfrey Anstruther, The Seminary Priests: A Dictionary of the Secular Clergy of England and Wales, 1558-1860, vol. 4, 1716-1800 (Great Wakening, Essex: Mayhew, McCrammon, 1977). The best work on Joseph Berington is by Eamon Duffy, "Berington and the Cisalpine Movement"; the best on Lingard is Martin Haile and Edwin Bonney, Life and Letters of John Lingard, 1771-1851 (London: Herbert & Daniel, n.d.).
9. Charles Butler to John Kirk, 16 Sept. 1819, AAW, Poynter Papers, A67.
10. For background, see Haile and Bonney, Life and Letters of Lingard, Chap. 2; David Milburn, A History of Ushaw College (Durham: Ushaw College, 1964), pp. 10-25; Brendan Hogan, "The Philosophical Tradition of Douai," Ushaw Magazine 63 (1953): 145-59; Donald R. Kelley, Foundations of Modern Historical Scholarship (New York: Columbia University Press, 1970).
11. See Duffy, "Berington and the Cisalpine Movement," chap. 2.
12. See Theses Philosophicae, Crook and Ushaw, 1796-1797, UCA, sec. XVIII, D.5.8.
13. L. Mahieu, "La philosophie à l'université de Douai au XVIII* siècle," Mélanges de science religieuse 14 (1957): 71-82.
14. Michael Sharratt, "Copernicanism at Douai," Durham University

Journal 67, n.s. 36 (1974): 41–48; Sharratt, "Alban Butler: Newtonian in Part," *Downside Review* 96 (1978): 103-11.
15. Antonio Bottieri to John Kirk, 1782, AAB, C833.
16. John Lingard to John Walker, 13 Aug. 1845, UCA, Lingard Correspondence, 19: 1099.
17. The following analysis is based on the Theses Theologicae contained in UCA, sec. XVIII, D.5.17: 1 (1728), George Kendal presiding; 2 (1764), Mathew Gibson; 10 (1772), James Nicolas; 13 (1776), Richard Southworth; and, in D.5.11: (1796), Thomas Eyre.
18. Ibid., 13 (1776), Richard Southworth, p. 8, italics mine. For biographical information see Gillow, *Literary and Biographical History*; and Anstruther, *Seminary Priests*. The standard work on Milner is Frederick Charles Husenbeth, *The Life of the Right Rev. John Milner, D.D.* (Dublin: James Duffy, 1862).
19. Ex Theologia Universa, SEC/AAW, Ser. 9, no. 1, 223, items 17 and 18.
20. [John Lingard] "Irenaeus," introd. to [William Talbot] "Christianus," *The Protestant Apology for the Roman Catholic Church* (Dublin: H. Fitzpatrick, 1809).
21. John Fletcher, *Reflections on the Spirit etc. etc. of Religious Controversy* (London: Keating, Brown and Keating, 1804), p. 166.
22. Charles Butler, *Reminiscences of Charles Butler, Esq. of Lincoln's Inn*, 3d ed., 2 vols. (London: John Murray, 1822), 1: 5. For Butler's background, see Nigel J. Abercrombie, "The Early Life of Charles Butler (1750–83)," *Recusant History* 14 (1978): 281–92.
23. See the excerpts from the *Annali* in Kirk's hand AAB, C840; and the letters of Bottieri to Kirk, Oct. 1782, 22 Feb. 1783, and 1785, AAB, C832, C838, C855.
24. The standard works are by Bernard Ward, *The Dawn of the Catholic Revival in England*, 2 vols. (London: Longmans, Green, and Co., 1909); Ward, *The Eve of Catholic Emancipation*, 3 vols. (London: Longmans, Green, and Co., 1911–12).
25. The following exposition is highly indebted to Bossy, *English Catholic Community*.
26. Joseph Berington, *The State and Behaviour of English Catholics from the Reformation to the Year 1780* (London: n.p., 1780).

Chapter 1

1. Joseph Berington to John Kirk, 28 and 19 Apr. 1807, AAB, C1751, C1750.
2. For an excellent survey of the history of religious liberty in England, see Ursula Henriques, *Religious Toleration in England, 1787–1833* (London: Routledge and Kegan Paul, 1961). On Catholic emancipation, see Amherst, *History of Catholic Emancipation*; Hughes, *Catholic Question in English Politics*; Ward, *Eve of Catholic Emancipation*. On the role of the Dissenters, see Raymond G. Cowherd,

The *Politics of English Dissent* (New York: New York University Press, 1956); J. H. Hexter, "The Protestant Revival and the Catholic Question in England, 1778–1829," *Journal of Modern History* 8 (1956): 297–319.

3. Shute Barrington, *A Charge Delivered to the Clergy of the Diocese of Durham, 1801,* (London: W. Bulmer & Co., 1802); "A Liege Subject," letter, *Newcastle Courant*, 23 May 1807. An understanding of the historical evolution of the Roman Catholic position on church-state relationships is absolutely necessary for a proper perspective on Lingard's apologetic. The best and most provocative general survey is Luigi Sturzo, *Church and State*, trans. Barbara Barclay Carter, 2 vols. (Notre Dame, Ind.: University of Notre Dame Press, 1962). For shorter accounts, see Yves Congar, "Eglise et état," in *Catholicisme*, ed. G. Jacquement, 6 vols. to date (Paris: Letouzey et Ané, 1947–), 3: 1430–41; Hans Bornewasser, "State and Politics from the Renaissance to the French Revolution," trans. Theodore L. Westow, *Concilium* 47 (1969): 73–91; Joseph Lecler, "Religious Freedom: An Historical Survey," trans. Theodore L. Westow, ibid., 18 (1966): 3–20; John Courtney Murray, "St. Robert Bellarmine on the Indirect Power," *Theological Studies* 9 (1943): 491–535.

4. "A Liege Subject," letter, 23 May 1807, reprinted in *Letters on Catholic Loyalty Originally Published in the "Newcastle Courant"* (Newcastle: Edw. Walker, 1807), pp. 5–7.

5. Bishop Douglass, Diary, pt. 2, 18 Apr. and 12 May 1807, SEC/AAW, ser. 6, no. 9, 48.

6. Address, 20 May 1807, in *Letters on Catholic Loyalty*, pp. 14–22. The three answers were the response of the universities of Paris, Louvain, Alcalá, Douai, Salamanca, and Valadolid to a 1788 request by William Pitt for a sample of Catholic opinion on "the existence and extent of the Pope's dispensing power."

7. Lingard, letter, 6 June 1807, in Ibid., pp. 26–28. The quotation was taken from *Roman Catholic Principles in Reference to God and Country* (ca. 1680). Joseph Berington had republished this long-forgotten treatise as an appendix to his *Reflections Addressed to the Rev. John Hawkins* (Birmingham: M. Swinney, 1785). Since that time it became the standard Cisalpine formulary of the Catholic faith. Lingard's reference to it signified his basic acceptance of the position.

8. Charles Butler to unknown, 3 Mar. 1809, in Butler, Letter Books, BM, Add. Mss. 25127, pp. 38b–39b. For background, see Ward, *Dawn of the Catholic Revival*, 1: 126–51.

9. Barrington, *Charge Delivered to the Clergy of the Diocese of Durham*, p. 22.

10. Shute Barrington, *The Grounds on Which the Church of England Separated from the Church of Rome. Stated in a Charge Delivered to the Clergy of the Diocese of Durham, 1806* (London: F. and C. Rivington, 1807), quotation from p. 19.

11. See [Henry Coates] "Elijah Index," *A Protestant's Reply to the*

Author of a Pamphlet, Entitled, "Remarks on a Charge Delivered to the Clergy of the Diocese of Durham, by Shute, Bishop of Durham, 1806" (Newcastle: Edw. Walker, 1807); [Coates] "Elijah Index," Reply to the Reviewer of a Pamphlet, Entitled "Remarks . . ." (Newcastle: S. Hodgson, 1807); Henry Phillpotts, A Letter to the Author of "Remarks . . ." (Newcastle-upon-Tyne: D. Akenhead and Sons, 1807); Phillpotts, A Second Letter to the Author of Remarks . . . (Newcastle-upon-Tyne: D. Akenhead and Sons, 1808); John Lingard, A General Vindication of the Remarks . . . (Newcastle: S. Hodgson, 1808), pp. 60–61.
12. N. J. Hollingsworth, *A Defense of the Doctrine and Worship of the Church of England* (Durham: G. Walker, 1809), p. xiii; see also Hollingsworth, *Three More Pebbles Fresh from the Brook; or, The Romish Goliath Slain with His Own Weapon: Being an Answer to "Remarks on 'The Grounds on Which the Church of England Separated from the Church of Rome, . . .'"* (Durham: G. Walker [1809?]), pp. 22–39.
13. John Lingard, *Remarks on a Charge Delivered to the Clergy of the Diocese of Durham, by Shute, Bishop of Durham, 1806*, 3d ed., enlarged (Newcastle: Edw. Walker, 1807), pp. 10–11.
14. John Lingard, *Remarks on a Late Pamphlet Entitled "The Grounds on Which the Church of England Separated from the Church of Rome"* (London: W. Clowes, 1809), pp. 5–7.
15. Bishop Douglass, Diary, pt. 2, Jan. 1808, SEC/AAW, ser. 6, no. 9, 48.
16. For Ponsonby's statement, see Ward, *Eve of Catholic Emancipation*, 1: 63. On the general subject of the veto, see Charles Butler, *Historical Memoirs of the English, Irish, and Scottish Catholics since the Reformation*, 3d ed., 4 vols. (London: John Murray, 1822), 4: 110–76; Ward, *Eve of Catholic Emancipation*, 1: 49–82, 99–157; Hughes, *Catholic Question in English Politics*, pp. 252–74; Amherst, *History of Catholic Emancipation*, 2: 1–50; John Milner, *Origin and Progress of the Veto* (London: n.p., 1810). As one example of a veto scheme, George Ponsonby suggested that when an Irish Catholic bishop died, the bishops in the province would submit three names to the pope as possible successors. Once the pope approved all three, the lord lieutenant of Ireland would choose one, or, if he objected to all three, the process would begin again. See Ward, *Eve of Catholic Emancipation*, 1: 62.
17. Charles Butler to Francis Moylan, 1 Apr. 1809, in Butler, Letter Books, BM, 25127, pp. 59b–61b. John Milner supported the veto at first but quickly forbade all consideration of it when he realized the extent of the opposition in Ireland. Butler correctly explained this opposition: the Irish naturally ask why they should trust their church to the hands of a monarch whose confidential ministers exhibit a distrust of that Church. Butler to George Canning, 8 Nov. 1809, in ibid., pp. 156b–159.
18. The following exposition is taken directly from Lingard's introduc-

tion to Talbot's *Protestant Apology for the Roman Catholic Church*. For convenience, page references will be given in the text.
19. Sturzo, *Church and State*, 2: 324; for a survey of the history of religious toleration, see pp. 273–313, 314–65; Henriques, *Religious Toleration in England*, passim.
20. John Lingard, *A Review of Certain Anti-Catholic Publications* (London: Joseph Booker, 1813), p. 58.
21. John Lingard, *Examination of Certain Opinions, Advanced by the Right Rev. Dr. Burgess, Bishop of St. David's* (Manchester: Wardle and Bentham, 1813), p. 6.
22. George Tomline, *A Charge Delivered to the Clergy of the Diocese of Lincoln, 1812*, 2d ed. (London: Luke Hansard, 1813), p. 15. See also Lord Kenyon, *Observations on the Roman Catholic Question*, 4th ed. (London: J. J. Stockdale, 1812), p. 7.
23. Lingard, *Anti-Catholic Publications*, pp. 28–29.
24. Ibid., pp. 5, 48.
25. Ibid., p. 47; see also Lingard, *Examination of Certain Opinions*, p. 6. For Lingard's connection of the rights of citizenship with the ownership of property, see his *Anti-Catholic Publications*, p. 28.
26. Lingard, *Anti-Catholic Publications*, p. 44; on persecution, see pp. 17–18.
27. Ibid., p. 16.
28. For these events, see John Gillow to William Poynter, 2 Feb. 1814, AAW, Poynter Papers, A57; Thomas Smith to Poynter, 13 [15?] Feb. 1814, ibid., A60; *Orthodox Journal* 2 (1814): 13, 243; John Lingard, "To the Right Honourable the Commons of the United Kingdom of Great Britain and Ireland in Parliament Assembled," AAW, Poynter Papers, A60. Lingard's proposal of a veto plan seems to contradict his usual assumption of the ideal of church-state separation. Actually, the proposal was only a practical accommodation to the High Church Tory unitary view and did not imply an acceptance of that position. In this respect, the key words in the petition were: "Whatever your petitioners may think of the grounds of this jealously . . . ." Earlier, in *Anti-Catholic Publications*, Lingard had noted that the government could claim no right to an interference in episcopal elections. The only advantage that could result from a negative would be the quieting of Protestant apprehensions (p. 42).
29. Lingard, "To the Right Honourable the Commons," AAW, Poynter Papers, A60.
30. Thomas Smith to William Poynter, 15 Feb. 1814 and 26 Jan. 1812, AAW, Poynter Papers, A60, A51.
31. Ward, *Eve of Catholic Emancipation*, 2: 239–41.
32. Poynter to Lingard, 25 Jan. 1817, AAW, Poynter Papers, B20; Lingard to Poynter, 28 Jan. 1817, ibid., A61.
33. Lingard to Poynter, 10 Feb. 1817, ibid., A61.
34. John Lingard, *Observations on the Laws and Ordinances, Which*

Exist in Foreign States, Relative to the Religious Concerns of Their Roman Catholic Subjects (Dublin: Richard Coyne, 1817). This pamphlet was also published anonymously in London under the name "A British Roman Catholic." What follows is a summary of this very detailed and rich book. Although it is systematized, I do not believe the basic argument has suffered. For convenience, page references will be given in the text. John Milner also wrote a reply to the report, entitled *An Humble Remonstrance to the Members of the Hon. House of Commons*, by a Native Roman Catholic Prelate (London: Keating, Brown and Co.), 1816.

35. Lingard, *Laws and Ordinances*, p. 16. Lingard referred to the American experience one other time in his pamphlets. In *Anti-Catholic Publications* he wrote: "If, then, the authority of those who framed the American constitution, be of any weight, let it be taken entire, and it will be found to contain the most pointed condemnation of all that for which the anti-catholics contend" (p. 32).

36. Lingard to Poynter, 10 Mar. 1817, AAW, Poynter Papers, A61. Thomas Smith objected to some of Lingard's expressions. William Gibson's opinions were either incomprehensible or inconsequential. See Smith to Poynter, 25 Mar. 1817, AAW, Poynter Papers, A60; Poynter to Lingard, 29 Mar. 1817, ibid., B20.

37. The argument on these events is extremely detailed and need not concern us. See Joseph P. Chinnici, "John Lingard and the English Catholic Enlightenment" (D. Phil. diss., Greyfriars, Oxford, 1976), pp. 30–33. For documentary evidence, see Lingard to Poynter, 16 and 22 Feb. 1817, AAW, Poynter Papers, A61; Poynter to Robert Gradwell, 1817, ibid., B20; Lingard to Poynter, 26 Feb. 1817, ibid., A61; Poynter to Lingard, 1817 and 22 Mar. 1817, ibid., B20; Lingard to Poynter, 26 Mar. and 1 Apr. 1817, ibid., A61; Smith to Poynter, 4 Apr. 1817, ibid., A60. On the 1821 debate, see Lingard to Poynter, 18 and 31 Mar. 1821, ibid., A61; Kirk to Lingard, 23 Mar. 1821, ibid., A67; Smith to Poynter, 27 Mar. 1821, ibid., A60.

38. A copy of the petition is attached to Lingard to Edward Blount, 17 Dec. 1824, AAW, Poynter Papers, A58. In Lingard's Scrapbook there is another petition to the House of Commons from the people of the area around Lancaster. It is undated and presumably remained unsent. In this petition Lingard asked that Catholics be restored to the "full and free enjoyment of religious liberty" and be permitted to "worship God according to the dictates of their conscience." UCA, sec. XVIII, F.2.6.

39. On the Gallican background, see F. Cabrol, "Bossuet, ses relations avec l'Angleterre," *Revue d'histoire ecclésiastique* 27 (1931): 535–71; Yves Congar, "Gallicanisme," in *Catholicisme*, ed. Jacquement, 4: 1731–39; M. Dubruel, "Gallicanisme," in *Dictionnaire de théologie catholique*, ed. A. Vacant, E. Mangenot, and E. Amann, 15 vols. (Paris: Letouzey et Ané, 1903–50), 6: 1096–1137; Aime-Georges

Martimort, *Le Gallicanisme de Bossuet* (Paris: Editions du Cerf, 1953); Milburn, *Ushaw College*, pp. 10–25.
40. James Brennan, "A Gallican Interlude in Ireland," *Irish Theological Quarterly* 24 (1957): 219–37, 283–309.
41. Catholic Committee, *First Blue Book* (London: n.p., 1789); *Second Blue Book* (London: n.p., 1791); *Third Blue Book* (London: J. P. Coghlan, 1792). For background, see Duffy, "Berington and the Cisalpine Movement"; Ward, *Dawn of the Catholic Revival*, passim.
42. John Throckmorton, *A Letter Addressed to the Catholic Clergy of England on the Appointment of Bishops*, by a layman, 12 June 1790 (n.p. [1790?]), pp. 53, 117, 129; Throckmorton, *A Second Letter Addressed to the Catholic Clergy of England on the Appointment of Bishops* (London: n.p., 1791), pp. lxxvii, xcix, passim.
43. Joseph Strickland, *Remarks upon a Letter, Addressed by a Layman, to the Catholic Clergy of England, 29 June 1790 (n.p. [1790?])*; Strickland, *An Apology for Not Subscribing to the Oath* (n.p. [1790?]).
44. John Milner, *Letters to a Prebendary*, 2d ed. (Cork: n.p., 1802), pp. 23, 33, 34; Charles Plowden, *Considerations on the Modern Opinion of the Fallibility of the Holy See in the Decision of Dogmatical Questions* (London: n.p. 1790).
45. Francis Plowden, *Jura Anglorum: The Rights of Englishmen* (London: n.p. 1792); John Fletcher, *Thoughts on the Rights, and Prerogatives of the Church and State* (London: A. J. Valpy, 1823); *Declaration* (n.p., 1826), sec. 8. These works varied, but all denied the temporal power of the papacy.
46. See Sturzo, *Church and State*, 2, passim; Henriques, *Religious Toleration in England*, chap. 2.
47. Milner, *Letters to a Prebendary*, p. 422, n. 2.
48. Berington, *State and Behaviour of English Catholics*, p. 73.
49. Joseph Berington, *An Address to the Protestant Dissenters Who Have Lately Petitioned for a Repeal of the Corporation and Test Acts* (Birmingham: M. Swinney, 1787), p. 41; Berington, *The Rights of Dissenters from the Established Church, In Relation, Principally, to English Catholics* (Birmingham: M. Swinney, 1789), p. 34.
50. It is from this perspective that the *First, Second*, and *Third Blue Books* should be interpreted. For a contrasting opinion, see Duffy, "Berington and the Cisalpine Movement," passim.
51. [Fletcher], *Spirit of Religious Controversy*, pp. 234–38; Fletcher, *Sermons on Various Religious and Moral Subjects for All the Sundays after Pentecost*, 3 vols. (Newcastle: Edw. Walker, 1810–16), 1: 131–43.
52. See John Chetwode Eustace, *Answer to the Charge Delivered by the Lord Bishop of Lincoln to the Clergy of That Diocese, 1812* (London: J. Booker, 1813); James Archer, *Sermons on Various Moral and Religious Subjects, For All the Sundays and Some of the Principal Festivals of the Year*, 3d ed., 3 vols. (London: Jos. Booker,

1817), 1: 184–206; James Wheeler, *Sermons on the Gospels, for Every Sunday throughout the Year, With an Appropriate Sermon for the First and Last Sunday*, 2 vols. (London: Jos. Booker, 1834), 2: 275–87.
53. Berington to Kirk, n.d., AAB, C2222.
54. Charles Butler to Edward Jerningham, 13 Feb. 1809, in Butler, Letter Books, BM, 25127, p. 29b; Butler to My Lord, 19 May 1809, in ibid., p. 85.
55. Fletcher, *Rights, and Prerogatives of Church and State*, p. 104.
56. James Wheeler, *A Letter from the Rev. J. Wheeler, to Sir John Lawson, Bart., Containing a Proposed Arrangement, In Which All Due Provision Is Made Both for the Inviolable Maintenance of the Civil and Religious Establishments of the Country* (Richmond: M. Bell, 1810).
57. See n. 28, above.
58. John Throckmorton, *Considerations Arising from the Debates in Parliament on the Petition of the Irish Catholics* (London: J. Budd, 1806), pp. 148 ff. On the unpopularity of Throckmorton's position, see Ward, *Eve of Catholic Emancipation*, 1: 64–66. The Cisalpine position should also not be confused with that of Charles O'Conor, whose opinions were much more radical. See ibid., 145–47; Charles Butler to My Lord, 1812, in Butler, Letter Books, BM, 25128, pp. 71–72; Butler to John Coxe Hippisley, 25 Sept. 1812, in ibid., pp. 115–16.
59. See Congar, "Eglise et état," pp. 1430–41; Emile Ollivier, *L'église et L'état au concile du Vatican* (Paris: Garnier Frères, 1879), 1: chap. 2; Sturzo, *Church and State*, 2: 306; André Latreille, "L'intolerance religieuse sous l'ancien régime," in *Unité chrétienne et tolérance religieuse* (Paris: Éditions du Temps Present, 1950), pp. 73–103.
60. Plongeron, "Recherches sur l'Aufklärung catholique," pp. 599–604.
61. Milner, *Letters to a Prebendary*, pp. 432–33.
62. See Henriques, *Religious Toleration in England*, chap. 2; Cowherd, *Politics of English Dissent*, chap. 2; Hughes, *Catholic Question in English Politics*, pp. 77–94.
63. Berington, *State and Behaviour of English Catholics*, p. 140; see also Berington, *A Letter to Dr. Fordyce* (London: G. Robinson, 1779), p. 62.
64. Fletcher, *Sermons on Various Religious and Moral Subjects*, 1: 343, 360.
65. Fletcher, *Spirit of Religious Controversy*, pp. 220–66; on Archer, Eustace, and Wheeler, see n. 52, above.
66. Butler to Silvertop, 9 Mar. 1818, in Butler, Letter Books, BM 25129, pp. 133b–135; Ward, *Eve of Catholic Emancipation*, 2: 236.
67. Smith to Poynter, 26 Jan. 1812, AAW, Poynter Papers, A51.
68. Quoted in Haile and Bonney, *Life and Letters of Lingard*, pp. 230–31.
69. Smith to Poynter, 29 Sept. 1826, AAW, Poynter Papers, A60. The

wording of the petition had been suggested as early as April. See Edward Glover to Edward Blount, 26 Apr. 1826, ibid., A58.
70. James Yorke Bramston to Poynter, 10 Oct. 1826, ibid., A60. Poynter agreed with Bramston. See Oct. 1826, ibid., A58, where Poynter adds his remarks to a copy of the petition.

Chapter 2

1. General Board of British Catholics, Newcastle Declaration, *Orthodox Journal* 4 (1816): 28–30, 72–75. For background see Ward, *Eve of Catholic Emancipation*, 2: 233–54.
2. For Andrews's arguments, see his letters, *Orthodox Journal* 4 (1816): 1–11, 28–30, 49, 81–85.
3. See the following, all in the *Orthodox Journal* 4 (1816): John Milner, "Pastoral Instruction for Lent," p. 53; letters from E. L., p. 55; "A Catholic Priest," pp. 57–60; "A Roman Catholic," pp. 60–61; "Pastorini" [Milner], pp. 67–69; "A Catholic Priest of the Old School," pp. 94–97; "Another Catholic Priest," pp. 97–98; "A Parish Priest," pp. 100–01; J. S., pp. 177–78; M. B., p. 180; "Clericus," pp. 277–80; "A Parish Priest," pp. 305–10; "A Priest of the Old School," pp. 312–13. Subsequent citations will include author and page number only.
4. Henriques, *Religious Toleration in England*, p. 97.
5. "A Catholic Priest," pp. 59–60; "Clericus," p. 280; "Another Catholic Priest," p. 98.
6. "A Parish Priest," pp. 100–01; "A Priest of the Old School," p. 312; "A Parish Priest," p. 309.
7. See Duffy, "Berington and the Cisalpine Movement"; Ward, *Dawn of the Catholic Revival*. Some of Duffy's material has been published in article form: "Ecclesiastical Democracy Detected: I (1779–1787)," *Recusant History* 10 (1970): 193–209; "Ecclesiastical Democracy Detected: II (1787–1796)," ibid., pp. 309–31; "Doctor Douglass and Mister Berington—An Eighteenth-Century Retractation," *Downside Review* 88 (1970): 246–69.
8. Ward, *Dawn of the Catholic Revival*, 1: 205–08.
9. Catholic Committee, "To the Right Reverend Charles, Lord Bishop of Rama, Vicar Apostolic of the Western District;—William, Lord Bishop of Acanthos, Vicar Apostolic of the Northern District;—John, Lord Bishop of Centuria, Vicar Apostolic of the Southern District, of England," in *Second Blue Book*, p. 16, italics mine. The document was signed by Charles Berington, Joseph Wilkes, Lord Stourton, Lord Petre, Henry Charles Englefield, John Lawson, John Throckmorton, William Fermor, John Towneley, and Thomas Hornyold. See also Ward, *Dawn of the Catholic Revival*, 1: 252–57.
10. Quoted in Ward, *Dawn of the Catholic Revival*, 1: 328–29.
11. Ward, *Dawn of the Catholic Revival*, 1: 332.

12. "Clericus," p. 280; Milner, *Letters to a Prebendary*, p. 442, n. 2.
13. Quoted in Plongeron, "Recherches sur l'Aufklärung catholique," p. 578. For further reflections on the *rationabile obsequium*, see Plongeron, *Théologie et politique au siècle des lumières*, pp. 82-83, passim.
14. Charles Plowden, *Remarks on the Writings of the Rev. Joseph Berington Addressed to the Catholic Clergy of England* (London: J. P. Coghlan, 1792), p. 7. For other examples of this argument, see John Milner, *The Divine Right of Episcopacy Addressed to the Catholic Laity of England in Answer to the Layman's Second Letter to the Catholic Clergy of England* (London: J. P. Coghlan, 1791), pp. 15-16; Charles Plowden, *Remarks on a Book Entitled "Memoirs of Gregorio Panzani"* (London: J. P. Coghlan, 1794), p. 69.
15. John Lingard, *The Antiquities of the Anglo-Saxon Church*, 2 vols. (Newcastle: Edw. Walker, 1806), 2d ed. (London: Keating, Brown and Keating, 1810); for Milner's reaction, see Lingard to Orrell, 20 May 1807 [copy], UCA, Lingard Correspondence, 1: 25; Charles Butler to Lingard, Dec. 1808, in Butler, Letter Books, BM, 25127, pp. 176-78. It is interesting to note that Haile and Bonney, in their quotation of this letter, omit the last paragraph. *Life and Letters of Lingard*, pp. 108-09. On Lingard's troubles with Milner, see Lingard to Poynter, 12 Aug. 1822, AAW, Poynter Papers, A61.
16. Croskell to Lingard, 4 Jan. 1816 [copy], UCA, Lingard Correspondence, 23: unnumbered.
17. Berington, *State and Behaviour of English Catholics*, pp. 70, 153-54. The argument here is not that Berington derived his ecclesiological principles solely from his political beliefs but only that the two were interrelated. The quotation seems to reflect the influence of Edmund Richer's *Libellus de Ecclesiastica et Politica Potestate* (1611).
18. Berington, *Reflections Addressed to Hawkins*, pp. 68-70. For further remarks on this see Duffy, "Ecclesiastical Democracy Detected: I."
19. Throckmorton, *Letter on the Appointment of Bishops*, p. 13. For the general history, see Ward, *Dawn of the Catholic Revival*, 1: 218-39. Duffy contends that this whole controversy was motivated by a desire to free Catholics from the charge of foreign domination and not by a zeal for "primitive discipline." He consistently maintains that the Cisalpine appeal to antiquity was rooted in the penal status quo. "Berington and the Cisalpine Movement," p. 205. I believe that the apologetic motive played a strong part but that the positive influence of a Lockean anthropology should not be disregarded. As a result, our emphases and interpretations differ.
20. John Milner, *The Clergyman's Answer to the Layman's Letter on the Appointment of Bishops* (n.p., 1790); Charles Plowden, *Modern Opinion of the Fallibility of the Holy See*, pp. 115-33; Strickland,

Remarks upon a Letter on the Appointment of Bishops; Throckmorton, *Second Letter on the Appointment of Bishops*, quotations from pp. 3, 54, 98.
21. Milner, *Divine Right of Episcopacy*, quotations from pp. 3, 15, 18, 68. In this pamphlet Milner came dangerously close to equating the church with the papacy. But in describing the church as a "monarchy mixed with aristocracy," he seemed to adopt the usual Gallican doctrine. Milner's thought was ambiguous. Perhaps it should be recalled that the French doctrine differed from the ultramontane not on the hierarchical nature of the church but on how one conceived the organization of the hierarchy. Milner, reacting against Throckmorton, tended to overemphasize the papacy, but I do not believe that he would have gone as far as Charles Plowden. The latter wrote that "by the divine appointment of Christ, there is no *proper and essential jurisdiction* in the church, which is not *properly* and *essentially* subordinate to that of the Pope, and actually derived from him." *Remarks on the Writings of Berington*, pp. 18–19. For background, see Dubruel, "Gallicanisme," p. 1099.
22. Joseph Berington, *The Memoirs of Gregorio Panzani* (Birmingham: n.p., 1793), quotaton from p. 42; the "four evils" can be found on pp. 461–63.
23. Plowden, *Remarks on "Memoirs of Panzani,"* pp. 292–93.
24. John Sturges, *Reflections on the Principles and Institutions of Popery*, 2d ed. (Winchester: J. A. Robbins, 1800). Joseph Berington's thoughts were printed in a letter to the *Gentleman's Magazine* 69 (1799): 653–54.
25. Joseph Berington and John Kirk, *The Faith of Catholics* (London: Joseph Booker, 1813), p. 145; John Milner, *A Letter to the Catholic Clergy of the Midland District*, 21 Jan. 1823 (n.p., 1823), p. 3.
26. Lingard, *Antiquities of the Anglo-Saxon Church*, 1810 ed., p. 57.
27. Lingard to John Jones, 9 Oct. 1833, SJ, Lingard Correspondence, vol. 9. See also Bernard Ward, *The Sequel to Catholic Emancipation*, 2 vols. (London: Longmans, Green, and Co., 1915), 1: 55–56. Ward omitted the last two sentences in the second paragraph quoted.
28. John Lingard to Cardinal Acton, 15 Feb. 1839, PF/SRC, 9: 560–61.
29. Milner, *Letters to a Prebendary*, pp. 23–45; Charles Plowden, *Modern Opinion of the Fallibility of the Holy See*, nos. 1 and 2.
30. Throckmorton, *Second Letter on the Appointment of Bishops*, p. 72. This summary of the Cisalpine view is based on the *First, Second*, and *Third Blue Books* and the reading of a great deal of correspondence. See Butler to Berington, 13 Nov. 1817, in Butler, Letter Books, BM, 25129, pp. 82b–85; Berington to Butler, 25 Nov 1817, AAB, C2217; Throckmorton to Butler, 25 Nov. 1817, ibid. C2216; Butler to John Kirk, 8 Jan. 1818, in Butler, Letter Books, BM, 25129, pp. 107–08, 118b–19; Kirk to Butler, 14 Feb. 1818, AAW,

Poynter Papers, A67; Butler to Lingard, 12 Mar. 1818, in Butler, Letter Books, BM, 25129, pp. 137b–39; Lingard to Butler, 15 Mar. 1818, AAW, Poynter Papers, A61; Kirk to Butler, 24 Mar. 1820, ibid., A67.
31. John Milner, *A Sermon Preached in the Roman Catholic Chapel at Winchester* (London: J. P. Coghlan [1789]), pp. 13–14. See also Milner, *Certain Considerations on Behalf of the Roman Catholics*, 7 Mar. 1791 (n.p. [1791?]). Milner *Pastoral Letter of John Bishop of Castabella*, 27 Dec. 1803 (London: Keating, Brown, and Co., 1803).
32. Butler, probably 1807, AAW, Poynter Papers, misplaced; for Lingard, see introd. to *Protestant Apology*, p. cxxv.
33. Charles Plowden, *Modern Opinion of the Fallibility of the Holy See*, p. 128; John Kirk to William Poynter, 19 June 1821, AAW, Poynter Papers A67.
34. See Robert Gradwell, Journal, 10 May 1824, AAW, Poynter Papers, E7.
35. John Milner, *A Serious Expostulation with the Rev. Joseph Berington upon His Theological Errors concerning Miracles* (London: J. P. Coghlan, 1797), pp. 73–85.
36. William Eusebius Andrews, "Jansenism in England," *Orthodox Journal* 8 (1820): 232–41, quotation from p. 237.
37. For some background to these ideas, see Jean Delumeau, *Le Catholicisme entre Luther et Voltaire* (Paris: Presses Universitaires de France, 1971), pp. 156–91; Edmond Préclin, *Les Jansénistes du XVIIIe siècle et la constitution civile du clergé* (Paris: Librairie Universitaire, J. Gamber, 1929); L.-J. Rogier, G. de Bertier de Sauvigny, and Joseph Hajjar, *Siècle des lumières, révolutions, restaurations*, trans. from the Dutch by Fr. van Groenendaeal (Paris: Editions du Seuil, 1966), pp. 137–61. A good summary of the Cisalpine view may be found in Duffy, "Berington and the Cisalpine Movement," pp. 190–205. Duffy isolates three major sources for Throckmorton's Letters: Josephinism and Jansenism; domestic sources: the history of the Elizabethan appellants, defenders of James I's oath, the Irish Remonstrance, and Blackloe's cabal; the Gallicans, Fleury, Pierre de Marca. Duffy's factual analysis is true, but the interpretation disregards the impact of English constitutional theory from Locke onwards.
38. See Jean Orcibal, "L'Idée d'église chez les Catholiques du XVIIIeme siècle," in *Comitato internazionale di scienze storiche x congresso internazionale di scienze storiche, Roma 4–11 Settembre 1955 relazioni*, ed. G. C. Sansoni (Florence: Biblioteca Storica Sansoni, 1955), 4: 111–35.
39. *Third Blue Book*, cited in Ward, *Dawn of the Catholic Revival*, 2: 145–46; Pistoia is quoted in Charles A. Bolton, *Church Reform in 18th Century Italy* (The Hague: Martinus Nijhoff, 1969), p. 72; Berington to John Douglass, 10 Apr. 1798, AAW, Douglass Papers,

XLVII, 157. See also Charles Walmesley to Douglass, 2 Mar. 1795, ibid., XLVI, 28. For further information on the Synod of Pistoia, see J. Carreyre, "Pistoie," *Dictionnaire de théologie catholique*, ed. Vacant, Mangenot, and Amann, 12: 2134–2230.

40. A good summary of Febronianism and its relationship to Joseph II's reform can be found in Georges Goyau, *L'Allemagne religieuse* (Paris: n.p., 1905), chap. 1, 2. See also Robert Duchon, "De Bossuet À Febronius," *Revue d'histoire ecclésiastique* 65 (1970): 375–422. For an explicit rejection of the *nova disciplina*, see Charles Butler, *A Continuation of the Rev. Alban Butler's "Lives of the Saints to the Present Time"* (London: Keating and Brown, 1823), app., pp. xl–xli, xlix–li.
41. See Richard Simpson, "Milner and His Times," *Home and Foreign Review* 2 (Apr. 1863): 531–57; M. D. R. Leys, *Catholics in England, 1559–1829* (London: Longmans, 1961), pp. 136–39; Mathew, *Catholicism in England*, pp. 146–48; Ward, *Dawn of the Catholic Revival*, 1: 88–89.
42. Plongeron, *Théologie et politique au siècle des lumières*, pp. 112–13.
43. "Pastorini" [Milner], pp. 67–69.
44. "Clericus," pp. 277–80. The quotation is from R. R. Palmer, *Catholics and Unbelievers in Eighteenth Century France* (Princeton: Princeton University Press, 1939), p. 83. The position of the English Catholics was very similar to that of their French counterparts. Palmer's book provides excellent background.
45. Lingard, introd. to *Protestant Apology*, p. cv.
46. Ibid., pp. xix, xcv.
47. See Lingard, *Antiquities of the Anglo-Saxon Church*, 1810 ed., p. 184; Joseph Berington, *An Essay on the Depravity of the Nation* (Birmingham: Myles Swinney, 1788); Butler, "On the Reunion of Christians," in *An Historical and Literary Account of the Formularies, Confessions of Faith, or Symbolic Books of the Roman Catholic, Greek, and Principal Protestant Churches* (London: A. J. Valpy, 1816), p. 199.
48. Francis Veron, *The Rule of Catholic Faith Sever'd from the Opinions of the Schools, Mistakes of the Ignorant, and Abuses of the Vulgar*, trans. E. S. (Paris: John Billaine, 1660), chap. 2. On Veron, see Pierre Feret, *La faculté de théologie de Paris et ses docteurs les plus célèbres*, 4 (Paris: Picard et Fils, 1906): 53–92.
49. Henry Holden, *Divinae fidei analysis seu de fide Christianae resolutione* (Paris: n.p., 1652), trans. W. G. under the title *The Analysis of Divine Faith; or, Two Treatises of the Resolution of Christian Belief with an Appendix on Schism* (Paris: n.p., 1658), quotation from p. 2. On Holden, see George H. Tavard, *La tradition au XVIIe siècle en France et en Angleterre* (Paris: Éditions du Cerf, 1969), pp. 420–38.
50. Holden, *Analysis of Divine Faith*, bk.1, chap. 1, lessons i, ii, iii; chap. 4, lesson 1.

51. Edward Hawarden, *The Rule of Faith Truly Stated* (n.p., 1721). On Hawarden, see Gillow, *Literary and Biographical History*, 3: 167–82.
52. Hawarden, *Rule of Faith*, p. 175. This statement of Hawarden's principles is based on the summary of "A Catholic Priest," pp. 57–60.
53. See Roger Aubert, *Le problème de l'acte de foi* (Louvain: n.p., 1945), pp. 647–78.
54. "Clericus," pp. 227–80; "A Parish Priest," p. 305.
55. Petition dated 17 June 1814 PF/SRC, 6: 457.
56. See selected articles from the reply of William Sharrock to Propaganda Fide, 1803 [copy], VEC/S, MIL, 54.4, 14, q. 65; John Milner to Propaganda Fide, 22 Aug. 1803 [copy], ibid., 12, q. 65, 66; Luke Concanen to Milner, 29 Sept. 1807, AAB, A833; Milner to Propaganda Fide, 22 Aug. 1803 [copy], VEC/S, MIL, 54.5, 13, q. 57; John Kirk to William Poynter, 3 May 1823, AAW, Poynter Papers, A67.
57. Butler to unknown, 1817, in Butler, Letter Books, BM, 25129, p. 32.
58. Butler to Lingard, Dec. 1809, in ibid., 25127, pp. 177–78. Haile and Bonney omitted the second sentence quoted and "confining within them" in the third sentence. *Life and Letters of Lingard*, pp. 108–09.
59. Lingard, *Antiquities of the Anglo-Saxon Church*, 1810 ed., pp. 13–14; Lingard, introd. to *Protestant Apology*, p. clxvii; Lingard, first preface to *A Collection of Tracts on Several Subjects Connected with the Civl and Religious Principles of Catholics* (London: Keating & Brown, 1826); Lingard, *General Vindication of the Remarks . . .* p. 93 n.
60. John Milner to Propaganda Fide, 22 Aug. 1803 [copy], VEC/S, Mil, 54.4, 12, q. 65, 66. See also Milner, "Status Ecclesia Catholicae in Anglia," 23 Sept. 1812, PF/SRC, 6: 345–46; Joannis Milner a Litta, Prefect, 26 July 1814, ibid., 6: 453–56; Milner to Prefect of S. P. Fide, 12 June 1820, ibid., 7: 481–83; Charles O'Conor to Poynter, 2 Feb. 1806, AAW, Poynter Papers, A52.
61. Francis Plowden to Miss Stonor, 24 Mar. 1817 [copy], in Butler, Letter Books, BM, 25129, pp. 6B–8; Robert Plowden to Messrs. Keating and Co., 26 Aug. 1820, AAW, Poynter Papers, A61; Thomas Smith to Poynter, 28 July 1827, ibid., A60; J. Corbishley to Rev. Mr. Hurst, 28 July 1810, UCA, Lisbon College Archives. I am indebted for this last rerference to J. Derek Holmes.
62. John Lee to John Kirk, 27 June 1821, AAW, Poynter Papers, A67.

Chapter 3

1. For background to these developments, see Owen Chadwick, *From Bossuet to Newman: The Idea of Doctrinal Development* (Cambridge: University Press, 1957); George H. Tavard, *Holy Writ or Holy Church: The Crisis of the Protestant Reformation* (London:

Burns & Oates, 1959); Tavard, *Tradition au xviie siècle*; Yves M.-J. Congar, *Tradition and Traditions*, trans. Michael Naseby and Thomas Rainborough (London: Burns & Oates, 1966); Tavard, "Tradition in Early Post-Tridentine Theology," *Theological Studies* 23 (1962): 377–405.
2. Lingard introd. to *Protestant Apology*, p. lxxxiv; Berington and Kirk, *Faith of Catholics*, p. 1.
3. Berington and Kirk, *Faith of Catholics*, p. viii. It should be noted that Berington translated Veron's principle: "All that, and that only, is of Catholic Faith, which God has revealed. . . ." The original Latin had *revelatum in verbo Dei*. By omitting *in verbo Dei* Berington, I believe, wanted to avoid the false identification of the word of God with only the written word. He would have understood the phrase in a much broader way.
4. John Lingard, *Strictures on Dr. Marsh's "Comparative View of the Churches of England and Rome"* (London: J. F. Dove, 1815), p. 4.
5. Berington and Kirk, *Faith of Catholics*, p. xii. Berington had expressed similar views much earlier in *Reflections Addressed to Hawkins*, pp. 39–57.
6. Berington to Kirk, 5 Nov. 1810, AAB, C1857.
7. Berington and Kirk, *Faith of Catholics*, p. xlii. In *Dr. Marsh's "Comparative View"* Lingard called the explanation of tradition and church authority in *The Faith of Catholics* "perspicacious" and "elegant" (p. 23). He also recommended it in private letters. See Lingard to Thomas Sherburne, 30 Sept. 1816, UCA, Lingard Correspondence, Misc. Letters and Scraps.
8. See the introduction to Berington and Kirk, *Faith of Catholics*; Lingard, *"Dr. Marsh's "Comparative View,"* passim; for comments on the source of revelation, see pp. 12–16. The quotation is from Berington and Kirk, *Faith of Catholics*, p. xix.
9. Berington and Kirk, *Faith of Catholics*, pp. xiii, xvii, xv; Lingard to John Walker, 2 Aug. 1837, UCA, Lingard Correspondence, 16: 906.
10. *Declaration*, secs. 1–3; Berington to Kirk, 28 June [1826], AAW Poynter Papers, A68; Tavard, *Tradition au XVIIe siècle*, pp. 155–94.
11. George Tavard, "Christopher Davenport and the Problem of Tradition," *Theological Studies* 24 (1963): 278–90; Tavard, "Scripture and Tradition among Seventeenth-Century Recusants," ibid. 25 (1964): 343–85.
12. John Milner, *The End of Religious Controversy* (London: n.p., 1818), 101–03; Lingard, introd. to *Protestant Apology*, p. xx; Lingard, *Dr. Marsh's "Comparative Views,"* p. 59.
13. Berington and Kirk, *Faith of Catholics*, pp. xxi, 386–95; Lingard, *Antiquities of the Anglo-Saxon Church*, 1806 ed., 1: 273–74. See also Lingard to Walker, 3 Apr. 1842 and May 1845, UCA, Lingard Correspondence, 18: 1021, 1061b. Charles Butler also emphasized

the unchangeableness of the deposit of faith. See Butler to Francis Plowden, n.d., in Butler, Letter Books, BM, 25129, pp. 8–10b.
14. Lingard, introd. to *Protestant Apology*, p. xxiv; nn. xcvii–xcviii.
15. See ibid., pp. xcviii, lxxv; Berington, *Memoirs of Panzani*, p. 43 n. For background, see Martimort, *Gallicanisme de Bossuet*, passim; Chadwick, *From Bossuet to Newman*, passim.
16. Holden, *Analysis of Divine Faith*, p. 98. See also Tavard, *Tradition au XVIIe siècle*, pp. 420–38.
17. Milner, *Certain Considerations on Behalf of the Roman Catholics*.
18. Tavard, "Scripture and Tradition among Seventeenth-Century Recusants"; Berington and Kirk, *Faith of Catholics*, pp. 130, 354; Lingard, *Dr. Marsh's "Comparative Views,"* pp. 49–53, 66; Lingard, introd. to *Protestant Apology*, p. clv.
19. Lingard, introd. to *Protestant Apology*, p. lxx. The following exposition is largely from this work; for convenience, page references will be given in the text. Lingard referred to Ussher's 1624 "Sermon on the Universality of the Church of Christ, and the Unity of the Catholic Faith Professed Therein."
20. Robert Bellarmine, *De Ecclesia* q. 1, a. 2, conclusion, t. 1, p. 24, in Dubruel, "Gallicanisme," p. 1098; Edmund Richer, *Libellus de Ecclesiastica et Politica Potestate* (Cologne: n.p. 1701), bk. 3, p. 21; Holden, *Analysis of Divine Faith*, pp. 109, 108.
21. Jacques Bénigne Bossuet, *Conference avec M. Claude ministre de Charenton sur la matiere de l'eglise* (Paris: n.p., 1682), p. 7. On Bossuet's ecclesiology, see Martimort, *Le Gallicanisme de Bossuet*, pp. 175–82. Martimort specifically notes that Bossuet and the Gallican tradition avoided the excesses of Richer. For Berington, see *Reflections Addressed to Hawkins*, pp. 37–38. Also see John Lingard, *Catechetical Instructions on the Doctrines and Worship of the Catholic Church*, 3d ed. (London: Charles Dolman, 1841), p. 33, where Lingard defines "church" as "the congregation of all the faithful under their invisible head Jesus Christ."
22. Lingard, *Antiquities of the Anglo-Saxon Church*, 1806 ed., 1: 232.
23. See also Lingard, *Collection of Tracts*, p. 153.
24. Lingard, introd. to *Protestant Apology*, pp. cli–clii. The quotation was taken from Bossuet's *Exposition*, sec. 21.
25. Martimort, *Le Gallicanisme de Bossuet*, pp. 175–82, 277–90, 549–63; Congar, "Gallicanisme," pp. 1731–39.
26. Berington, *Reflections Addressed to Hawkins*, pp. 69–70. For the detailed background of Berington's statement see Duffy's two articles entitled "Ecclesiastical Democracy Detected."
27. John Carroll to Berington, 29 Sept. 1786, AAB, C892. See also J. Foothead to John Kirk, 17 Mar. 1787, ibid., C901; Berington to John Chadwick, 29 July 1786, UCA, President's Archives, C5; Duffy, "Berington and the Cisalpine Movement," p. 218. The creed is taken from [Berington], *An Appeal to the Catholics of England*

by the Catholic Clergy of the County of Stafford (Wolverhampton; privately printed, 1792). For background, see Marie Rowlands, "The Staffordshire Clergy, 1688–1803," *Recusant History* 9 (1968); 219–41. I disagree with Rowlands's claim that the Cisalpines denied their opinions were Gallican. Some did, perhaps, but not all; Berington was certainly aware that his opinions were Gallican.

28. Berington's interpretation is from the Staffordshire clergy's *Short and Plain Statement of Facts* (1798), p. 15, as quoted by Duffy, "Berington and the Cisalpine Movement," p. 272; Berington to Kirk, 26 Dec. 1794, AAB, C1310; Berington, letter, *Gentleman's Magazine* 69 (1799): 653–54; Berington and Kirk, *Faith of Catholics*, p. xiv, where Berington responds to Poynter; Berington to Kirk, 29 June 1812, AAB, C1912.

29. Butler, *Formularies, Confessions of Faith, or Symbolic Books*, p. 12; for Butler's recommendation of Bossuet, see Butler to Royal Highness, 20 Apr. 1812, in Butler, Letter Books, BM, 25128, pp. 2b–3; Butler to Lord of Moira, July 1812, in ibid., pp. 42–42a; Butler to John Throckmorton, 31 Aug. 1812, in ibid., pp. 85–86; the long quotation is from Butler, *The Historical Memoirs of the Church of France in the Reigns of Lewis the Fourteenth, Lewis the Fifteenth, Lewis the Sixteenth, and the French Revolution* (London: W. Clarke & Sons, 1817), pp. 37–38. On the pope's primacy of jurisdiction, see ibid., p. 35; Butler, *Miscellaneous Tracts* (n.p., 1813), in which Butler printed "A Letter on the Spiritual Supremacy of the Pope" written to George Bruning, 24 Feb. 1799.

30. See Poynter's remarks on O'Conor's pamphlet *Columbanus*, Nov. 1811, AAW, Poynter Papers, A52. The Cisalpine view was typical in many respects of the English Catholics. See Bishop Stonor on the supremacy of the pope, AAB, A94. Berington told John Evans not to confound infallibility and supremacy: the first applied only to the church, the assembly of the faithful. Berington to John Evans, 1810, AAB, C1863.

31. The argument is taken from Lingard's "Remarks on the Bishop of Durham's Explanation of the Antepenultimate Answer in the Church Catechism," printed in his *Collection of Tracts*, pp. 243–57.

32. Lingard, introd. to *Protestant Apology*, pp. iv–v.

33. Lingard, *Antiquities of the Anglo-Saxon Church*, 1806 ed., 1: 339–56 n. M, quotation from p. 344.

34. Ibid., 1: 351–52.

35. See Veron, *Rule of Catholic Faith*, chap. 5; Holden *Analysis of Divine Faith*, 2: sec. 4, no. 4, pp. 237–48; Bossuet, *An Exposition of the Doctrine of the Catholic Church in Matters of Controversy* (London: n.p., 1685), chap. 13; Edward Hawarden, *The True Church of Christ*, 2 vols. (n.p., 1714–15), 2: 143–247; *An Essay towards a Proposal for Catholick Communion, by a Minister of the Church of England* (London: n.p., 1704), pp. 98–115; Lingard, *A General Vindication of the Remarks* . . . printed in his *Col-*

lection of Tracts, p. 83, the quotation from p. 81 n. See also Lingard, introd. to *Protestant Apology*, p. lxxxiii.
36. Berington and Kirk *Faith of Catholics*, p. 244. Berington, though, did maintain that "transubstantiation" denoted the change effected but did not define the manner of change. See Berington to unknown, n.d., AAB, C1713. For Milner's opinions, see Lingard to Poynter, 12 Aug. 1822, AAW, Poynter Papers, A61.
37. This summary is taken from Lingard, introd. to *Protestant Apology*, pp. xxv–xviii. For convenience, subsequent page references will be in the text.
38. Lingard, introd. to *Protestant Apology*, p. cliii. It should be noted that Lingard was much more conciliatory in his interpretation of the Twentieth and Twenty-eighth Articles than Christopher Davenport had been in *Deus, Natura, Gratia* (1634). See John Berchmans Dockery, *Christopher Davenport, Friar and Diplomat* (London: Burns & Oates, 1960), pp. 136–49.
39. Charles Butler, *An Address to the Protestants of Great Britain and Ireland* (London: Luke Hansard & Sons, 1813), p. 17; Butler, *Formularies, Confessions of Faith, or Symbolic Books;* John Fletcher, *A Comparative View of the Grounds of the Catholic, and Protestant, Churches* (London: A. J. Valpy, 1826).
40. Butler to Charles Hornyold, 12 July 1817, in Butler, Letter Books, BM, 25129, p. 54.

Chapter 4

1. For Berington, see John Kirk, *Biographies of English Catholics in the Eighteenth Century*, ed. John Hungerford Pollen and Edwin Burton (London: Burns & Oates, 1909), pp. 17–20; Butler gives the best survey of his own works in the introduction to the third volume of *Historical Memoirs respecting the English, Irish, and Scottish Catholics, From the Reformation to the Present Time* (London: John Murray, 1819–21); for Kirk, Fletcher, and Lingard, see Gillow, *Literary and Biographical History*, 4: 37–50; 2: 298–300; 4: 254–78.
2. John Lingard, Journal, UCA, sec. XVIII, F.2.11.a.
3. Claude Fleury, "Premier discours," in *Discours sur l'histoire Ecclésiastique* (Nismes: Pierre Beaume, 1785). See also David Knowles, *Great Historical Enterprises* (London: Thomas Nelson and Sons, 1963).
4. Edmund Jones, "John Lingard and the Simancas Archives," *Historical Journal* 10 (1967): 57–76. Donald F. Shea, *The English Ranke: John Lingard* (New York: Humanities Press, 1969), completely disregards the contribution of the French tradition to Lingard's mentality. The book is extremely inaccurate.
5. Lingard, *Antiquities of the Anglo-Saxon Church*, 1810 ed., pp. iv, 103, 105, 262, 268, passim; Lingard, *A History of England, From the*

First *Invasion by the Romans to the Accession of William and Mary in 1688*, 8 vols. (London: J. Mawman, 1819–30), 4: v.
6. Butler to Lingard, Dec. 1809, in Butler, Letter Books, BM, 25127, pp. 176–78. Haile and Bonney omitted "and the offense . . . of Vendome" in the second sentence quoted, and "from the omission . . . are crowded" in the third. *Life and Letters of Lingard*, pp. 108–09.
7. Joseph Berington, *The History of the Lives of Abeillard and Heloisa* (Birmingham: M. Swinney, 1787), pp. xxiv–xxv; Berington, *The History of the Reign of Henry II, and of Richard and John, His Sons* (Birmingham: M. Swinney, 1790), xviii. On Berington, see also Thomas Preston Peardon, *The Transition in English Historical Writing, 1760–1830* (New York: Columbia University Press, 1933), pp. 151–56. For Butler, see his *Historical Memoirs*, 1819–21 ed., 3: 87; 4: 287–97.
8. Lingard, *Antiquities of the Anglo-Saxon Church*, 1810 ed., pp. iii, 46, 146, 256, quotation from p. 394.
9. Lingard to Kirk, 18 Dec. 1819 and Mar. [1821], AAW, Poynter Papers, A67; Lingard to J. Mawman, 10 May 1823, UCA, Lingard Correspondence 9: 470; Lingard to John Walker, 23 Oct. 1849, ibid., 19: 1160.
10. Charles Butler, review of *Antiquities of the Anglo-Saxon Church*, 1807, AAW, Poynter Papers, misplaced.
11. Lingard to Mawman, 23 Nov. 1820, UCA, Lingard Correspondence, 9: 458.
12. Lingard, *History of England* 1: 45. For modern evaluations of Lingard's work, see G. P. Gooch, *History and Historians in the Nineteenth Century* (London: Longmans, Green and Co., 1913), p. 291; Herbert Butterfield, *Man on His Past* (Cambridge: University Press, 1955), p. 191; B. H. G. Wormald, "The Historiography of the English Reformation," in *Historical Studies*, ed. T. Desmond Williams (London: Bowes and Bowes, 1958), 1: 50–58; Jones, "Lingard and the Simancas Archives"; S. M. Toyne, "Guy Fawkes and the Powder Plot," *History Today* 1 (1951): 16–25.
13. Lingard to Mawman, 14 Feb. 1824, UCA, Lingard Correspondence, 9: 474.
14. Lingard, *History of England*, 3: 325 n. 94; 1: iii.
15. John Miller, *Popery and Politics in England, 1660–1688* (Cambridge: University Press, 1973), pp. 79–80, 89; Chadwick, *From Bossuet to Newman*, chap. 3.
16. Berington to Kirk, 10 Dec. 1823, AAW, Poynter Papers, A67.
17. M. A. Tierney, "Memoir of the Rev. Dr. Lingard," in Lingard, *The History of England, From the first Invasion by the Romans to the Accession of William and Mary in 1688*, 6th ed. (London: Charles Dolman, 1854), 1: 33–34.

18. Butler to Rev. B. Barrett, 22 Dec. 1808, Butler, Letter Books, BM, 25127, p. 3b.
19. Lingard to Orrell, 20 May 1807 [copy], UCA, Lingard Correspondence, 1: 25; Richard Thompson to Lingard, n.d., ibid., 1: 69; Lingard, *Antiquities of the Anglo-Saxon Church*, 1806 ed., 1: 40–41.
20. Richard Southworth to Rev. Joseph Hodgson, 30 July 1807, AAW, Poynter Papers, A52; Thomas Eyre to Hodgson, n.d., ibid.
21. Lingard to Robert Gradwell, 3 or 4 June 1819, VEC/S, LIN, 66.8, 6.
22. See the following letters, all in the *Orthodox Journal* 7 (1819): J. M., pp. 228–231; "Candidus," pp. 266–69; J. M., pp. 302–06; "Candidus," pp. 349–53; "No Unbeliever," pp. 355–357; "Minimus," p. 376; "Amicus Justitiae," pp. 379–80; "No Unbeliever," pp. 393–96; "Judex," pp. 423–28; "Narrator," pp. 460–62; T., pp. 468–69; *Orthodox Journal* 8 (1820): "Amicus Justitiae," pp. 21–22; "Candidus," pp. 22–27; Editor, pp. 27–34; "Candidus," pp. 85–86.
23. It is extremely difficult to say who "Candidus" was. I have decided in favor of Lingard mostly on the basis of the internal evidence. The important point is that "Candidus," if he did not write directly under Lingard's inspiration, surely represented the historian's opinions. For various opinions see Husenbeth, *Life of Milner*, pp. 393–407; Gillow, *Literary and Biographical History*, 4: 276–77; Kirk to Poynter, 9 Aug. 1819, AAW, Poynter Papers, A67; John Lee to Kirk, 15 May 1820, ibid. See also W. E. Andrews to Rev. Mr. Morris, 16 Mar. 1820, ibid.; Lee to Kirk, 5 May 1820, ibid.; Haile and Bonney, *Life and Letters of Lingard*, p. 172. The unprinted letter from "Amicus Justitiae," 9 Mar. 1820, can be found in AAW, Poynter Papers, A67; from "Philorthodoxos," 16 Mar. 1820, in ibid.
24. J. M., pp. 229, 305; T., p. 468; J. M., pp. 229–30; T., p. 468; J. M., p. 305; "Judex," pp. 423–28; "No Unbeliever," p. 395.
25. "Amicus Justitiae," pp. 379–80, 21–22; "Candidus," p. 350.
26. Lingard, *History of England*, 1: 63; J. M., pp. 229–30; "Candidus," p. 268; J. M., p. 305; "Amicus Justitiae," pp. 21–22.
27. Editor, p. 33; William Eusebius Andrews to Mr. Last, 16 Mar. 1820, AAW, Poynter Papers A67.
28. "No Unbeliever," p. 356; Editor, p. 28.
29. Editor, pp. 28–30; "Candidus," 85–86; J. M., p. 306; Lingard to Gradwell, 17 May 1820, UCA, Lingard Correspondence, 2: 104.
30. John Talbot to Kirk, 21 Feb. and 16 Nov. 1820, AAW, Poynter Papers, A67; Talbot to Kirk, 28 Nov. 1820, UCA, Lingard Correspondence, 24: 1595.
31. Lingard to Kirk, 10 Dec. 1820, AAW, Poynter Papers, A67; see also Lingard to Kirk, 25 Nov. 1820, ibid.
32. Milner's comments are contained in a letter from Thomas Smith to the Cardinal Prefect of Propaganda, 2 July 1823, PF/SRC, 8:

66–67. See also Robert Gradwell, Journal, 30 Dec. 1823 and 8 Jan. 1824, AAW, Poynter Papers, E7; Gradwell to Poynter, 15 Jan. 1824, ibid., GL.
33. Gradwell to Poynter, 3 Jan. 1824, AAW, Poynter Papers, GL; See also Poynter to Kirk, 15 May 1822 [1823?], ibid., Poynter Papers, A67; Lingard to Poynter, 26 May 1823, ibid., A61; Kirk to Poynter, 31 May 1823 and 16 June 1822, ibid., A67; T. M. McDonnell to Kirk, 15 July 1825, AAW, Poynter Papers, A68.
34. Thomas White to Lingard, 7 Oct. 1828, UCA, Lingard Correspondence, 1: 86.
35. Ward, *Eve of Catholic Emancipation*, 3: 98–104; Milner, "A Letter to the Catholic Clergy of the Midland District," 21 Jan. 1823, AAW, Poynter Papers, A68.
36. Lingard, *Histoire d'Angleterre, depuis la première invasion des Romains*, trans. Le Chevalier de Roujoux, 2d ed., 14 vols. (Paris: n.p., 1825–31). For examples of Roujoux's attitude, see 1: 249; 3: 172, 316–37; 4: 118; 5: 25, 356.
37. R., review of *Histoire d'Angleterre*, *Le mémorial catholique* 6 (1826): 288–96; 7 (1827): 21–36, 106–24, 169–90, 260–72. For convenience, subsequent page references will be given in the text.
38. Ibid. 10 (1828): 168–73. This letter was expanded and translated into Italian: [Giacoma Ventura?] "Bastia," *Osservazioni sulla storia d'Inghilterra del Dottor Lingard dirette in forma di lettera al sig. editore del memoriale cattolico* (n.p., 1828), For convenience, subsequent page references will be given in the text.
39. Lingard to John Bradley, 27 Jan. 1829, UCA, Lingard Correspondence, 6: 277; Gradwell to Lingard, 23 Jan. 1829, SJ, Lingard Correspondence.
40. Gradwell to Lingard, 23 Jan. 1829, SJ, Lingard Correspondence.
41. Lingard, *Storia d'Inghilterra del Dottore Giovanni Lingard*, trans. from the English by Domenico Gregori, 2d ed., 8 vols. (Rome: n.p., 1828–33). The notes are scattered throughout these volumes.
42. Lingard to John Walker, 13 May 1848, UCA, Lingard Correspondence 20: 1277.
43. Lingard, "Notes on Italian translation," UCA, Miscellaneous Letters and Scraps. Cf. Lingard, *Storia d'Inghilterra*, 3: 44–49.
44. Lingard to Wiseman, 22 Jan. 1836, UCA, Lingard Correspondence, 6: 345; Joseph de Maistre, *Du Pape, suivi de L'Eglise Gallicane dans son rapport avec Le Souverain Pontife*, 2 vols. (Brussels; n.p., 1828), 1: xxvii, chap. 8. See also Lingard to Robert Tate, 10 Dec. [1836], UCA, Lingard Correspondence, 11: 629. For background, see "L'ecclesiologie au XIXe siècle," *Revue des sciences religieuses* 34 (1960), especially Roger Aubert, "La géographie ecclésiologique au XIXe siècle," pp. 11–55; Wilfrid Ward, *William George Ward and the Catholic Revival* (London: Macmillan and Co., 1893), pp. 82–129.

Chapter 5

1. John Bew to John Kirk, 31 Dec. 1819, AAW, Poynter Papers, A67. For background, see John D. Gay, *The Geography of Religion in England* (London: Duckworth, 1971), chap. 5; Gwynn, *Second Spring*; Ward, *Sequel to Catholic Emancipation*, vol 1; Sheridan Gilly, "The Roman Catholic Mission to the Irish in London," *Recusant History* 10 (1969): 123-45; J. Derek Holmes, "Catholics and Politics at the Time of Emancipation," *New Blackfriars* 54 (1973): 365-73.
2. For biographical information on what I call "the second generation of Cisalpines," see entries in Gillow, *Literary and Biographical History*. For John Walker, see *Tablet*, 5 July 1873, p. 21.
3. Lingard to Walker, 22 July 1850, UCA, Lingard Correspondence, 22: 1442.
4. *Catholic Magazine* 1 (1831): 1-5.
5. See the following letters, all in the *Catholic Magazine* 1 (1831-32): Henry Weedall, pp. 345-51; H. Y. [Lingard], pp. 484-87; F. C. H. [Husenbeth], pp. 548-50; "Philalethes," pp. 550-52; R. S. Y. [Robert Tate], pp. 625-28; Editor, pp. 686-89; Y., pp. 766-71; *Catholic Magazine* 2 (1832): H. Y., pp. 35-44. Subsequent citations will include author and page number only. See also Lingard to [Daniel Rock], 11 Jan. 1832, UCA, Lingard Correspondence, 7: 368.
6. Y., p. 770.
7. F. C. H., pp. 548-50; "Philalethes," pp. 550-52. See also Lingard to Tate, 14 Dec. 1831, UCA, Lingard Correspondence, 11: 624.
8. H. Y., pp. 35-44; quotations from pp. 36-37. See also Lingard to John Kirk, 29 Nov. 1831, UCA, Lingard Correspondence, 3: 170.
9. See the following, all in the *Catholic Magazine* 3 (1833): "Proselytos" [Lingard], "Proselytos on His Conversion," pp. 17-22, 126-33, 302-09; letters from "Lauretanus" [Joseph Curr], pp. 202-28; "Pastor" [Husenbeth], pp. 209-13; *Catholic Magazine* 4 (1833): "Pastor," pp. 36-40; Mariano Gil de Tejada, pp. 229-35; "Proselytos," pp. 111-13. Subsequent citations will include author and page number only. For the identification of the men in this controversy, see F. C. Husenbeth to John Walker, 6 Dec. 1864, UCA, Walker Correspondence, folder 12, 48.
10. Lingard to Robert Tate, n.d., UCA, Lingard Correspondence, 11: 625.
11. "Proselytos," pp. 17-22; quotations from pp. 17, 19, 22.
12. "Lauretanus," p. 203; "Pastor," pp. 38, 212.
13. "Proselytos," pp. 303, 113.
14. Nicholas Wiseman to Tandy, 2 Feb. 1834, UCA, Wiseman Papers, 788; Lingard to Tate, n.d., ibid., Lingard Correspondence, 11: 625. See also Kirk to Wiseman, 9 Apr. 1834, UCA, Wiseman Papers, 203.

15. See the following letters, all in the *Catholic Magazine* 5 (1834): "Sacerdos" [Lingard], pp. 85-87, 232-34, 591-95; "Angla" [Lingard], pp. 88-89, 220-23; "Catechistes" [Lingard], "On the Catechism," pp. 89-93, 142-46, 203-06; "Missionarius," pp. 155-59, 380-81; John Woods, pp. 168-70; W. E. Andrews, 282-85; "Paulinus," pp. 325-30, 440-47, 517-24; "Anglus" [Lingard], pp. 448-49; "Catechistes Junior" [Lingard], "On the Catechism," 457-61, 508-13, 715-19; Editors, pp. 524-26. Subsequent citations will include author and page number only. For the identification of Lingard's letters to the *Catholic Magazine*, see Haile and Bonney, *Life and Letters of Lingard*, pp. 387-88. Internal evidence indicates that "Catechistes Junior" was Lingard.
16. "Catechistes," p. 89; "Catechistes Junior," p. 457; "Sacerdos," pp. 86-87; "Angla," pp. 88-89; "Anglus," pp. 448-49; "Sacerdos" [Lingard], p. 233.
17. "Missionarius," pp. 155-59; for the opinion of Lingard on devotions, see "Angla," p. 221.
18. Andrews, pp. 282-85; "Paulinus," pp. 325-30; Woods, pp. 168-70.
19. See Ward, *Sequel to Catholic Emancipation*, vol. 1; Wilfrid Ward, *The Life and Times of Cardinal Wiseman*, 2 vols. (London: Longmans, Green, and Co., 1897), vol. 1. Perhaps the best account is Claude R. Leetham, *Luigi Gentili, A Sower for the Second Spring* (London: Burns & Oates, 1965). The career of Husenbeth provides a good example of Lingard's influence on the clergy. He began his public career as an ardent supporter of Milner. During the 1830s and 1840s he corresponded with Lingard, and his views became much more liberal. Yet, in 1862, eleven years after Lingard's death, Husenbeth wrote an extremely complimentary biography of Milner. For some interesting reflections on Husenbeth's personality, see [M. A. Bacon], "A Biographical Sketch of Husenbeth," Cambridge University Library, Add. Mss., 6245, 72.
20. For some opinions see W. T. [on German biblical criticism], *Catholic Magazine* 2 (1832): 669-81; 4 (1833): Editor [on the Catechisms], ibid. 4 (1833): 265-74.
21. Milner to Douglass, 29 Oct. 1796, AAW, Douglass Papers, XLVI, 251; Douglass to Berington, 10 Dec. 1796, ibid., 267; Berington to Douglass, 12 Dec. 1796, ibid., 268.
22. John Milner, *A Serious Expostulation with the Rev. Joseph Berington upon His Theological Errors concerning Miracles* (London: J. P. Coghlan, 1797), p. 18; Butler, *The Book of the Roman Catholic Church*, 2d ed. (London: John Murray, 1825), p. 47, referring to Lingard's *Antiquities of the Anglo-Saxon Church*, chap. 12 n. 6.
23. John Fletcher, *The Catholic's Prayer Book* (London: A. J. Valpy, 1830), pp. iii-vi; Berington, *Essay on the Depravity of the Nation*, p. 34; Berington to Kirk, 25 Oct. 1808, AAB, C1796; Berington to Kirk, 26 Aug. 1817, AAW, Poynter Papers, A67.

24. See an article on church and state, *Catholic Magazine* 1 (1831): 340–45; Editor, comment on *Mirari Vos*, ibid. 2 (1832): 735–38; editorial, ibid., p. 753; T. M. McDonnell, letter, ibid., pp. 797–99.
25. Plongeron, "Recherches sur l'Aufklärung Catholique," p. 593.
26. Wiseman to the earl of Shrewsbury [3 Jan. 1842], UCA, Wiseman Papers, 464; Wiseman to D. A. Durtnall, 25 Nov. 1833, ibid., 197. The usual view of the Second Spring is supported by Ward, *Life and Times of Wiseman*, vol. 1, and Brian Fothergill, *Nicholas Wiseman* (London: Faber and Faber, 1963). The classic formulation can be found in John Henry Newman's 1852 sermon at the First Provincial Synod of Westminster. Newman entitled it "The Second Spring," and the tradition of English Catholic historiography has generally accepted his picture of the *gens lucifuga*. See John Henry Newman, *Sermons and Essays* (London: Catholic Truth Society, 1907).
27. Lingard to Walker, 18 Feb. [1850], UCA, Lingard Correspondence, 22: 1409.
28. Alexander Geddes, *Prospectus of a New Translation of the Holy Bible* (Glasgow: privately printed, 1786), p. 110; Geddes, *Doctor Geddes' Address to the Public, on the Publication of the First Volume of His New Translation of the Bible* (London: n.p., 1793); for Berington's opinions, see *Reflections Addressed to Hawkins*, pp. 39–57. See also Butler, *Horae Biblicae* (Oxford: J. White, 1799). For opposition, see John Milner to Propaganda Fide, 12 June 1820, PF/SRC, 7: 481–83.
29. [Lingard], *A New Version of the Four Gospels*, by a Catholic (London: Joseph Booker, 1836); Lingard to Silvertop, 24 June 1839, UCA, Lingard Correspondence, 7: 376. The following exposition is taken directly from Lingard's *A New Version of the Four Gospels*. For convenience, page references will be given in the text.
30. Nicholas Wiseman, "Catholic Versions of Scripture," *Dublin Review* 2 (1837): 475–92, quotation from p. 492.
31. Nicholas Wiseman, "Remarks on the 'New Version of the Gospels by a Catholic,'" UCA, Wiseman Papers, sec. XVIII, Black Box, introd., comments on p. 415.
32. Ibid., comment on p. 113. It is interesting to note that Charles Butler had also translated "full of grace" by "most favoured of God." He had to defend this translation to Vicar Apostolic Poynter. See Butler to Poynter, 9 Apr. 1823, AAW, Poynter Papers, A58.
33. See Lingard to Walker, 26 Jan. [no year], UCA, Lingard Correspondence, 16: 902; Lingard to Silvertop, 24 June 1839, ibid., 7: 376; Tierney to Lingard, 7 Oct. 1836, SJ, Lingard Correspondence; Lingard to Walker, 7 Jan. 1839, UCA, Lingard Correspondence, 16: 908.
34. John Lingard, *Catechetical Instructions on the Doctrines and Wor-*

ship of the Catholic Church, 3d ed. (London: Charles Dolman, 1841); Lingard to Husenbeth, 24 Dec. 1830, UCA, Lingard Correspondence, 2: 133; Lingard to Tate, 22 June 1835, ibid., 11: 627.

35. Lingard, "A First or Shorter Catechism," *Catholic Magazine* 5 (1834): 89, 142, 203; Lingard to James Yorke Bramston, 24 Jan. 1836, AAW, Poynter Papers, A79; Richard Thompson to Thomas Griffiths, 18 May 1836, AAW, Griffiths Papers, A80.
36. For examples, see Lingard to Bramston, 24 Jan. 1836, AAW, Griffiths Papers, A79; Griffiths's notes on Lingard's work, ibid.; Lingard to Tate [1 Dec. 1838], UCA, Lingard Correspondence, 11: 637; Lingard to Walker, n.d., ibid., 16: 930.
37. See Lingard to Husenbeth, 6 Aug. 1840, UCA, Lingard Correspondence, 2: 142; Lingard to George Oliver, 9 Nov. 1840, ibid., 8: 420; Lingard to Tate [7 Feb. 1840], ibid., 11: 648; Lingard to Walker, 9 May 1840, ibid., 17: 958.
38. Lingard to Lord Shrewsbury, 5 June [1839? 1840?], ibid., 6: 336.
39. The following analysis rests on a comparison between Lingard's work and the different editions of the *Catechism: An Abridgment of Christian Doctrine with Proofs of Scripture for Points Controverted. Catechistically Explained, by Way of Question and Answer* (Douai: n.p., 1661); *An Abridgment of Christian Doctrine, With Proofs of Scripture for Points Controverted. Catechistically Explained by Way of Question and Answer* (London: T. Meighan, 1756); *An Abridgment of Christian Doctrine Revised and Approved by Wm. G. V. A. and Published for the Use of the N----N District* (Newcastle-upon-Tyne: n.p., 1812); *An Abridgment of Christian Doctrine, Revised, Improved, and Recommended by Authority, for the Use of the Faithful in the Four Districts in England*, 3d ed. (York: C. Croshaw, 1832).
40. Lingard, *Catechetical Instructions*, pp. 71–72; Lingard to Walker, 19: 1182, n.d. and [1840?], UCA, Lingard Correspondence, 16: 937.
41. Lingard, *Catechetical Instructions*, pp. 73, 95, 78. Cf. *Abridgment of Christian Doctrine*, 1812 ed., pp. 17–18; 1832 ed., pp. 29, 31.
42. Lingard, *Catechetical Instructions*, pp. 138, 81. Cf. *Abridgment of Christian Doctrine*, 1812 ed., p. 18; 1832 ed. See also Lingard to Walker, [16 Feb. 1850], UCA, Lingard Correspondence, 22: 1408.
43. Bernard Groethuysen, *The Bourgeois, Catholicism vs. Capitalism in Eighteenth Century France*, trans. Mary Ilford (London: Barrie & Rockliff, 1968). For the social background of the English Catholics, see Leys, *Catholics in England*, pp. 169–85; Bossy, *English Catholic Community*.
44. Archer, *Sermons on Various Moral and Religious Subjects*, 1: 89–107; Fletcher, *Sermons of Various Religious and Moral Subjects*, 3: 377–475.
45. *Abridgment of Christian Doctrine*, 1812 ed., p. 2; 1832 ed., p. 4.
46. "Catechistes Junior," pp. 457–61; Lingard, *Catechetical Instructions*,

pp. 4–5, 99. Cf. *Abridgment of Christian Doctrine*, 1661 ed., p. 177; 1756 ed., p. 92.
47. Lingard to Charles Newsham, n.d., UCA, Lingard Correspondence, 10: 534. See also Lingard, *Catechetical Instructions*, p. 129, and Cf. *Abridgment of Christian Doctrine*, 1812 ed., p. 13; 1832 ed., p. 23.
48. Lingard to Newsham, 29 Oct. [1842], UCA, Lingard Correspondence, 10: 565.
49. Lingard to Newsham, n.d., *ibid.*, 10: 534; Lingard, *Catechetical Instructions*, p. 7. Cf. *Abridgment of Christian Doctrine*, 1661 ed., p. 5. The 1812 and 1832 editions also did not mention "supernatural quality."
50. Lingard, *Catechetical Instructions*, pp. 15, 37. Cf. *Abridgment of Christian Doctrine*, 1812 ed., p. 9; 1832 ed., pp. 9, 16. The 1756 edition also avoided the use of the word "nature." For this and other interesting comments on the 1756 edition's catechism, see J. D. Crichton, "Religious Education in England in the Penal Days (1559–1778)," in *Shaping the Christian Message*, ed. Gerard S. Sloyan (New York: Macmillan Co., 1959), pp. 63–90.
51. Lingard, *Catechetical Instructions*, pp. 42, 23. Cf. *Abridgment of Christian Doctrine*, 1812 ed., pp. 11, 6; 1832 ed., pp. 19, 11.
52. Lingard, *Catechetical Instructions*, p. 89. Cf. *Abridgment of Christian Doctrine*, 1832 ed., p. 34. See also Lingard to Walker, n.d., UCA, Lingard Correspondence, 16: 944.
53. For example, Lingard, *Catechetical Instructions*, p. 10 n. 4, on the creation of the world and the problems raised by geology; ibid. p. 17, where Lingard states that Christians keep the memory of Christ's birth on Christmas Day. Earlier catechisms had said that Christ was born on Christmas Day. *Abridgment of Christian Doctrine*, 1812 ed., p. 5; 1832 ed., p. 9.
54. See Griffiths's comments on Lingard's catechism, AAW, Poynter Papers, A79; Lingard to Walker, n.d., UCA, Lingard Correspondence, 17: 990. Cf. Lingard, *Catechetical Instructions*, p. 112, with *Abridgment of Christian Doctrine*, 1812 ed., p. 22; 1832 ed., p. 40.
55. See Griffiths's notes, AAW, Poynter Papers, A79. The earlier catechisms had treated these subjects.
56. Lingard to Bramston, 24 Jan. 1836, AAW, Griffiths Papers, A79; Lingard, *Catechetical Instructions*, p. 40.
57. For example, Lingard, *Catechetical Instructions*, p. 99 compared with *Abridgment of Christian Doctrine*, 1661 ed., 180; 1756 ed., p. 109. The 1812 ed. (p. 21) and 1832 ed. (p. 38) also did not mention the matter and form of baptism.
58. Lingard to Newsham, 29 Oct. 1842, UCA, Lingard Correspondence, 10: 565; Lingard to Tate, n.d., ibid., 11: 636; see also Lingard to Tate, n.d., ibid., 637.
59. Lingard, *Catechetical Instructions*, pp. 119–20; Lingard to Tate, n.d., UCA, Lingard Correspondence, 11: 636. For earlier conflicts

over the nature of indulgences, see John Kirk to Charles Butler, 5 Jan. 1823, AAW, Poynter Papers, A67; Poynter to Kirk, 14 Aug. 1820, ibid.
60. Lingard, *Catechetical Instructions*, p. 103. Cf. *Abridgment of Christian Doctrine*, 1812 ed., p. 21; 1832 ed., p. 38.
61. Lingard, *Catechetical Instructions*, pp. 2, 8–9.
62. Lingard to Walker, 10 Apr. 1843, UCA, Lingard Correspondence, 21: 1339.
63. Lingard, *Catechetical Instructions*, pp. 37–38; Lingard to Walker, 8 Sept. 1843 and n.d., UCA, Lingard Correspondence, 21: 1354, 19: 1182; the quotation is from Lingard to Husenbeth, 11 Aug. 1840, ibid., 2: 143.
64. Lingard, *Catechetical Instructions*, pp. 39, 51–52, 134–36, 128–30.
65. Ibid., pp. 41–44, 122–23, 114–115, 111. I believe that Lingard's exposition of the sacrament of penance may also account for the attitude of the Cisalpine, John Bew, at Oscott College. Husenbeth reported that when Bew instructed the students on penance, he did not give any advice peculiar to ecclesiastics, i.e., he wanted them to administer the sacrament rather than to judge the penitent. Both Lingard and Bew were proponents of "enlightened piety." On Bew, see Frederick Charles Husenbeth, *The Life of the Right Reverend Monsignor Weedall* (London: Longman, Green, Longman, and Roberts, 1860), p. 36.
66. Lingard, *Catechetical Instructions*, p. 133, italics mine.
67. Lingard to Husenbeth, 3 Nov. 1842, UCA, Lingard Correspondence, 1842, 2: 149. See also Lingard to Husenbeth, 19 Nov. 1840, ibid., 146; Lingard to Tate, n.d., ibid., 11: 660.
68. Lingard to Newsham, n.d., ibid., 10: 534.
69. Lingard to Tate, 7 Feb. 1840, UCA, Lingard Correspondence, 11: 648; Lingard to Walker, n.d., ibid., 17: 990; Husenbeth to Tierney, 10 Sept. 1851, SJ, Lingard Correspondence; Tierney, "Memoir of Lingard," in Lingard, *History of England*, 1854 ed., 1: 28; Lingard to [Silvertop?], 13 Feb. 1844, UCA, Lingard Correspondence, 7: 379; Lingard to Walker, 3 July 1845, ibid., 18: 1059; Gil de Tejada, pp. 229–35; "Paulinus," pp. 440–47; Thompson to Bramston, 23 Jan. 1836, AAW, Griffiths Papers, A79.
70. See Lingard to Tate, 13 Dec. 1842, UCA, Lingard Correspondence, 11: 662; Lingard to Walker, 11 May 1844, ibid., 19: 1085.
71. Wiseman, "Anglican Claim of Apostolical Succession," *Dublin Review* 7 (1839): 139–80. See also Ward, *Life and Times of Wiseman*, 1: chap. 10. For the ecumenical views of Lamennais, see J.-R. Derré, "L'Oecuménisme mennaisien," in *Les Catholiques libéraux au XIXe siècle*, ed. Jacques Gadille (Grenoble: Presses Universitaires de Grenoble, 1974), 53–66. Lingard strongly objected to this type of ecumenism. See Lingard to Walker, [27 Oct.] 1841, UCA, Lingard Correspondence, 17: 1006.
72. Wiseman, "Cenni sullo stato religioso dell' Inghilterra tratti da

particolari lettere scritte di recente," 12 Jan. 1839, PF/SRC, 9: 525–26.
73. "The Late Dr. Lingard," *Tablet*, 26 July 1851, pp. 473–74.
74. Lingard to Tate, 22 June 1835, UCA, Lingard Correspondence, 11: 627.
75. John Lingard, *A Manual of Prayers on Sundays and during Mass* (Lancaster: C. Clark, 1833); Lingard to Jones, 21 Nov. 1833, SJ, Lingard Correspondence.
76. Lingard, *Manual of Prayers*, pp. 1–16. Cf. Richard Challoner, *The Garden of the Soul* (London: T. Meighan, 1751).
77. Lingard, *Manual of Prayers*, pp. 17–37; Lingard to Jones, 21 Nov. 1833, SJ, Lingard Correspondence.
78. Lingard to John Walker, 16 Nov. 1843, UCA, Lingard Correspondence, 21: 1361.
79. "Proselytos," p. 19; Lingard to Walker, 18 Dec. 1842, UCA, Lingard Correspondence, 18: 1045. On this and many of his other views on the liturgy Lingard was in the dominant tradition of English Catholic piety. See Marion Norman, "John Gother and the English Way of Spirituality," *Recusant History* 11 (1972): 306–19.
80. Lingard to Walker, 24 July 1844, UCA, Lingard Correspondence, 19: 1097. See also Lingard to Walker, 5 May 1845, ibid., 18: 1051.
81. See Lingard to Walker, n.d., and 16 Nov. 1843, ibid., 16: 900, 21: 1361. See also Gradwell, Journal, 12 Aug. 1825, AAW, Poynter Papers, E8. Gradwell wrote: "He [Lingard] recommends to the students to study simplicity of style, good reading and good delivery in the Church service, which is too much neglected; and rather to read well than preach ill."
82. See *Catholic Magazine* 1 (1831–32): H. Y., "On the Litanies," pp. 546–47; "Translation of Psalms," pp. 670–77, 730–39; ibid. 2 (1832): "Psalms," pp. 161–69, 327–33; Lingard, *Manual of Prayers*, pp. 39–48. For background and the difference between Wiseman and Lingard, see Lingard to Walker, 11 Dec. 1842, UCA, Lingard Correspondence, 21: 1329; Nicholas Wiseman, "Prayer and Prayer Books," *Dublin Review* 26 (1842): 448–85.
83. Lingard to Walker, n.d., UCA, Lingard Correspondence, 19: 1099. See also Lingard to Walker, 21 Aug. 1850, ibid., 22: 1445. George Brown, one of Lingard's friends, also thought that the burial service should be in English. See George Brown to Wiseman, 2 Oct. 1836, UCA, Wiseman Papers, 258.
84. Lingard to Walker, 26 Mar. 1850, UCA, Lingard Correspondence, 22: 1415.
85. Berington, *Reflections Addressed to Hawkins*, pp. 72–73; [Berington], "A Few Remarks Addressed to Shute, Bishop of Durham, on His Charge to the Clergy of His Diocese Lately Published, by a Catholic," AAB, C1749, p. 24.
86. For backgronud to *The Garden of the Soul*, see Edwin H. Burton,

The Life and Times of Bishop Challoner (1691–1781), 2 vols. (London: Longmans, Green, and Co., 1909), 1: 127–36 Cf. *The Garden of the Soul* (London: Keating, Brown, and Co., 1806), with *The Garden of the Soul* (Derby: Thomas Richardson and Son, 1842).
87. *Gother's Prayers for Sundays & Festivals* (Wolverhampton: J. Smart, 1800), p. iv. For background, see Husenbeth, *Life of Milner*, pp. 108–09. Milner thought these prayers gave too much scope "to the reasoning part of these devotions, at the expense of the affective part" (p. 110).
88. So complains Richard Thompson to Gradwell, 18 Sept. 1830, AAW, Griffiths Papers, A71.
89. *Prayers before and after Mass* (London: J. Booker, 1826). I have found no documentary evidence that indicates the source of this liturgical attitude. It was certainly not unusual in eighteenth-century France and bore some resemblance to the innovations of the Jansenists. For background, see Henri Bremond, *Histoire litteraire du sentiment religieux en France depuis la fin des guerres de religion jusqu's nos jours*, 9 (Paris: Bloud et Gay, 1932): chap. 2, sec. 3–4; Préclin, *Jansénistes du XVIIIe siècle*, bk. 2, chap. 2; René Taveneaux, *La vie quotidienne des Jansénistes aux XVIIe et XVIIIe siècles* (Paris: Librairie Hachette, 1973), pp. 127–33, 219–25.
90. Lingard, *Catechetical Instructions*, pp. 125, 126. This was the same as *Abridgment of Christian Doctrine*, 1832 ed., p. 21, but the 1812 ed., p. 12, defined prayer as "raising up our minds to God."
91. Lingard to Newsham, n.d., UCA, Lingard Correspondence, 10: 534, italics mine.
92. "Angla," pp. 220–23.
93. Fletcher, *Catholic's Prayer Book*, p. 75. For Lingard's approval, see "Proselytos," pp. 302–09.
94. For background, see Lingard to unknown, 23 Oct. 1821, UCA, Lingard Correspondence, 1: 2; Lingard to Poynter, 3 July 1822, AAW, Poynter Papers, A61; Lingard to Husenbeth, 24 July and 14 Oct. 1848, UCA, Lingard Correspondence, 2: 127, 128; Lingard to Walker, 31 Oct. 1844, ibid., 19: 1119.
95. Lingard to Walker, 28 May 1841 and 8 Nov. 1847, UCA, Lingard Correspondence, 17: 992, 20: 1261; Walker to Lingard, 20 Mar. 1851, ibid., 1: 78; Lingard to Walker [18 July 1844], ibid., 19: 1090. For background, see J. Derek Holmes, "John Henry Newman's Attitude towards History and Hagiography," *Downside Review* 92 (1974): 248–64.
96. See Charles Butler, *An Account of the Life and Writings of the Rev. Alban Butler* (Edinburgh: Keating & Brown, 1800); Charles Fell, *The Lives of Saints* (London: Thomas Meighan, 1729), 1: i–xx; Charles Butler, *Continuation of Butler's "Lives of the Saints to the Present Time."*

97. Lingard to Tate, n.d., UCA, Lingard Correspondence, 11: 630; Lingard to Walker [30 June 1842], ibid., 18: 1029.
98. Lingard to Walker, 21 May 1841 and 16 Feb. 1850, ibid., 17: 988, 22: 1408; Lingard to Newsham, 4 May 1842, ibid., 10: 562; Lingard to Tate, n.d., ibid., 11: 642; Lingard to Price, 6 Sept. [no year] [copy], ibid., 15: 874; Lingard to Walker, 13 Oct. 1843, ibid., 18: 1039.
99. Lingard to Walker, 16–17 Aug. 1841, 24 Apr. [1847], [5 June 1849] [copy], 28 May 1841, ibid., 17: 999, 20: 1239, 19: 1146, 17: 992.
100. Berington, *Reflections Addressed to Hawkins*, pp. 72–74; John Bew, "Prospectus for Oscott," AAW, Douglass Papers, XLV, ser. 2, 19. For the meaning of Bew's "enlightened piety," see "Responsa R.P.D. Joannis Milner . . . a Sac. Congregatione de Propaganda Fide . . . die 22 Augusti, 1803," VEC/S, MIL, 54.4, 12, response to qs. 65, 66; Memoriale R. D. Joannis Milner, 10 Nov. 1802, PF/SRC, 6: 102–07; Milner to Litta, 22 Jan. 1818, ibid., 7: 41. Kirk to Poynter, 31 Aug. 1823, AAW, Poynter Papers, A67; Archer, *Sermons on Various Moral and Religious Subjects*, 2: 1–17; Fletcher, *Sermons on Various Religious and Moral Subjects*, 3: 54; for Butler, see Lingard to Walker [11 Nov.?] 1840, UCA, Lingard Correspondence, 17: 970.
101. Berington, *Reflections Addressed to Hawkins*, p. 20; Butler to Kirk, 15 Oct. 1823, AAW, Poynter Papers, A67.
102. Berington, *Memoirs of Panzani*, p. xxxii. Significantly enough, Milner was the first to popularize devotion to the Sacred Heart in England. See *Bishop Milner's Devotion to the Sacred Heart of Jesus: With the Indult of His Holiness Pope Pius VII in Favour of That Devotion* (London: Robert Washbourne, 1867); Husenbeth, *Life of Milner*, p. 279.
103. A classic example of the Enlightenment problem can be found in Thomas White, *Sermons for the Different Sundays, and Principal Festivals of the Year*, selected and arranged by John Lingard, 2 vols. (London: Jos. Booker, 1828), 2: 334: "The mysteries of faith, such as the unity and trinity of God, etc. we are only bound to know in speculation, that is, to believe them; but our knowledge of the sacraments must be practical, in order to receive them with advantage to our souls."
104. Lingard to Gradwell, 21 Sept. [1831?] AAW, Griffiths Papers, A72; John Lingard, "Practice of Living in Union with Jesus Christ," UCA, Miscellaneous Box. The following exposition is taken from this manuscript.
105. Lingard to Walker [Feb. 1843], and Good Friday 1844, UCA, Lingard Correspondence, 21: 1341, 19: 1100. Tate reedited Lingard's *Manual of Prayers* in 1837 and 1844. Lingard was not always pleased with the editions. See Lingard to Tate, n.d., ibid., 11: 632; Lingard to Walker, n.d., ibid., 16: 928. Tate added

a larger number of prayers, devotions to the Blessed Mother, prayers at benediction, and several litanies. The additions were a good example of the difference between Lingard and the second generation of Cisalpines. The latter were much more strongly influenced by religious romanticism.

106. Fletcher, *Catholic's Prayer Book*, pp. 326–29.
107. Lingard to Walker, 13 and 28 Oct. 1843, UCA, Lingard Correspondence, 18: 1039, 21: 1360. For further remarks on the spirituality of retreats, see Lingard to Walker, 8 June 1849 and 20 Nov. 1841, ibid., 19: 1147, 17: 1008; Lingard to Tate, 7 Oct. 1848, ibid., 12: 742, where Lingard complains about Wiseman's Roman manner of giving retreats. On Charles Newsham's ultramontane revision of Ushaw spirituality, see Milburn, *Ushaw College*, pp. 175–76.
108. Archer, *Sermons on Various Moral and Religious Subjects*, 2: 5, 50–51; see also pp. 1–17.
109. For an example of Butler's view, see his *Lives of Dom Armand-Jean de Bouthillièr de Rancé, Abbot Regular and Reformer of the Monastery of La Trappe; And of Thomas à Kempis, The Reputed Author of "The Imitation of Christ."* (London: Luke Hansard & Sons, 1814). On Butler's disagreement with Archer, see Butler to Fletcher, 12 Sept. 1812, in Butler, Letter Books, BM, 25128, pp. 110b–12.
110. Butler, *Life and Writings of Alban Butler*, p. 54. Cf. Charles Butler to Fletcher, 12 Sept. 1812, in Butler, Letter Books, BM, 25128, pp. 110b–12.
111. Butler, "An Essay on Mystical Theology, or the Science of Sacred Contemplation," in *Miscellaneous Tracts*, pp. 1–22; Kirk, *Biographies of English Catholics*, p. 18.
112. Fletcher, *Sermons on Various Religious and Moral Subjects*, 3: 225, 275, 11. For Lingard's opinions on communion, see Lingard to Walker, 27 Dec. 1848, UCA, Lingard Correspondence, 20: 1296. "Frequent communion" did not mean daily communion, a practice introduced during the Second Spring. The approach of Fletcher and Lingard was more relaxed than that of the recusant Catholics who communicated possibly five or six times a year. See Marie Rowlands, "The Education and Piety of Catholics in Staffordshire in the 18th Century," *Recusant History* 10 (1969): 67–78.
113. Fletcher, *Sermons on Various Religious and Moral Subjects*, 3: 135, 119, 318, 401.
114. For Butler's opinion, see Gillow, *Literary and Biographical History*, 2: 299. Lingard expressed his approval as "Angla," p. 221.
115. For some interesting reflections on these developments, see Jacques Le Brun, "Politics and Spirituality: The Devotion to the Sacred Heart," trans. John Griffiths, *Concilium* 69 (1971): 29–43. For general intellectual background, see Basil Willey, *The Seventeenth*

Century Background (New York: Doubleday, 1953); Willey, The Eighteenth Century Background (Boston: Beacon Press, 1961). Bremond, Histoire litteraire, 8: 310–60.
116. Butler, *Life and Writings of Alban Butler*, pp. 42–43; Butler, *Miscellaneous Tracts*, pp. 20–21; Louis Cognet, *Crépuscule des mystiques* (Tournai, Belgium: Desclée, 1958); L.-J. Rogier, *Le siècle des lumières et la révolution (1715–1800)*, trans. from the Dutch by Van Groenendael, in *Nouvelle histoire de l'eglise*, 4, (Paris: Éditions du Seuil, 1966), pp. 122–32; Alexander Dru, introd. to Maurice Blondel, *The Letter on Apologetics and History and Dogma*, trans. Alexander Dru and Illtyd Trethowan (London: Harvill Press, 1964).
117. Taveneaux, *Vie quotidienne des Jansénistes*, p. 251; Appolis, "*Tiers Parti*" *Catholique*, chap. 1.
118. Palmer, *Catholics and Unbelievers*, p. 52.
119. Archer, *Sermons on Various Moral and Religious Subjects*, 1: 125–47, 334–59, 360–74; Butler, *Miscellaneous Tracts*, pp. 1–22; Butler, *The Life of Fénelon, Archbishop of Cambray* (London: Longman, Hurst, Rees, and Orme, 1810); for Fletcher, see Gillow, *Literary and Biographical History*, 2: 298–300.
120. Butler, "An Essay on Mystical Theology" in *Miscellaneous Tracts*, pp. 20–21; Anthony Low, *Augustine Baker* (New York: Twayne Publishers, 1970); Joseph Gillow, *The Origin and History of the Manual* (London: Westminster Press, 1910); Norman, "Gother and English Spirituality." On Challoner, see Burton, *Life and Times of Challoner*, 1: chaps. 8, 21.
121. Husenbeth to Lingard, 21 May 1845, UCA, Lingard Correspondence, 18: 1055.

Epilogue

1. Berington, *Reflections Addressed to Hawkins*, p. 22.

BIBLIOGRAPHY

Primary Sources: Archives

Archives of the Archbishop of Birmingham (AAB), Cathedral House, Birmingham.
Ser. A and C, 1786–1829.

British Museum (BM), London.
Manuscript Department, Add. Mss. 25127–29, Charles Butler, Letter Books.

Cambridge University Library, Cambridge.
Manuscript Department, Add. Mss. 6241–47, Frederick Charles Husenbeth, Selected Letters.

Archives of Propaganda Fide (PF/SRC), Rome.
Scritture Riferite nei Congressi, Anglia: vol. 6 (1801–17); vol. 7 (1818–22); vol. 8 (1823–33); vol. 9 (1834–41).

Saint Edmund's College Archives (SEC/AAW), Old Hall Green, now at the Archives of the Archbishop of Westminster.
Ser. 6: no. 9, 48, Bishop Douglass, Diary (1792–1811).
Ser. 9: no. 1, 223, Ex Theologia Universa; no. 3, 143, Theological Papers, Crookhall & Ushaw (1795–1824); no. 65, 111, Theological Mss., XVIII–XIX Century; no. 69, 132, Ms., The Sacrament of the Lord's Supper; no. 71, 98, Church History, 1: 400–1121; no. 72, 99, Church History, 2.

Ser. 12: no. 4, 166, Miscellaneous Papers re Catholic Affairs 18th & 19th Century; no. 5, 154, Miscellaneous Papers, 19th & 20th Century; no. 6, 155, Miscellaneous Papers, 18th–19th–20th Centuries.
Ser. 21: no. 20.2, John Lingard, Letters to G. Dunn of Newcastle; no. 1–3, Catholic Relief and Emancipation.

Archives of the Society of Jesus (SJ), Farm Street, London.
Lingard Correspondence: vol. 9 (1818–60).

Ushaw College Archives (UCA), Ushaw College, Durham.
Smith of Brooms: Correspondence (1793–1839).
Joseph Gillow: Correspondence with Edwin Bonney.
M. Hallé [Martin Haile]: Correspondence with Edwin Bonney.
John Lingard: Correspondence and Papers, vols. 1–22; A–Lan; Leigh–Youens (typescript): In this collection there are 1596 letters to and from John Lingard, dating from the early years of the nineteenth century until his death in 1851. Lingard destroyed most of his letters, so this collection is not entirely representative; the vast majority date from 1830 to 1851. Typescripts were made of all the letters at the request of Philip Hughes, who at one time wished to publish the entire collection. Marvin R. O'Connell, professor of church history at the University of Notre Dame, Indiana, has a copy of the collection. The originals or copies made by John Walker may be found in the archives of Ushaw College, the Archdiocese of Westminster, the Society of Jesus, Farm Street, London, and the Venerable English College, Rome. References in this work are to the typescripts of the letters, but unless otherwise noted, these have been checked against the originals.
Correspondence with John Coulston, Ushaw College Library, Black Box, sec. XVIII.
Miscellaneous Letters and Scraps.
Miscellaneous Papers, President's Archives, File 4.
Lingard Transcripts and Gradwell Correspondence.
Assorted Papers: Anglo-Saxonicae Ecclesiae redditus pro

anno 1806; *A History of England*, proof sheets; Commonplace Book with extracts from Anglo-Saxon History; Commonplace Book; Short Diary (1800); Journal of Tour to Naples (Summer 1817); Notebooks 1 & 2, mostly verse; Notebook entitled "Catechism"; Notebook transcriptions of certain psalms; "Practice of Living in Union with Jesus Christ"; Scrapbook.

Liverpool Diocesan Archives, 100–200.

President's Archives: PA/D, Letters to Vicar Apostolic William Gibson; PA/G, M. A. Tierney to Charles Newsham; PA/O, Richard Thompson to Charles Newsham, John Walker to Charles Newsham; PA/R, Rev. Richard Thompson Papers.

Theses Philosophicae, Crook and Ushaw, sec. XVIII, D.5.8.

Theses Theologicae, sec. XVIII, D.5.17.

Theses Theologicae, 1796, sec. XVIII, D.5.11.

Ushaw College History.

John Walker: Correspondence: vol. 1, to J. H. Newman, Charles Newsham, George Errington, John Penswick, Alexander Goss, A. W. Pugin, and John Briggs; Folders 1, 5, 6, 7, 10, 12, 13, 14.

John S. Wallis: Correspondence with Canon John Walker.

Bishop Thomas Walsh: Correspondence with the earl of Shrewsbury.

Bernard Ward: Correspondence with Edwin Bonney.

Nicholas Wiseman: Correspondence, 147–550; Unindexed Papers, Black Box, sec. XVIII.

Archives of the Venerable English College (VEC/S), Rome.
Scritture: 54 CLI (Lord Clifford), JCH (John Coxe Hippisley), MIL (Bishop John Milner); 55 PAX (Bishop William Poynter, Appendix), POY (Bishop William Poynter); 56 CPL (Gradwell Family Letters); 59 Unindexed Robert Gradwell Papers; 66 KIR (John Kirk), LIN (John Lingard); 67 BUT (Charles Butler), SMI (Bishop Thomas Smith, Northern District), THO (Richard Thompson–Robert Gradwell), WHI (Thomas White); 70 WAL (Bishop Thomas Walsh); 72 BAI (Bishop Peter Augustine Baines), McD (Thomas Mi-

chael McDonnell); 75 Unindexed Nicholas Wiseman Papers; 76 BRO (Bishop George Brown).

Archives of the Archbishop of Westminster (AAW), Archbishop's House, Westminster, London.
Bishop John Douglass Papers: XLIV (1792–93); XLV (1793–94); XLVI (1795–96); XLVII, (1797–98).
Bishop Thomas Griffiths Papers: 141, 1833–35; A71–A88, Main Series (1830–40); B–4, Griffiths, Diary and Letter Book; W1/2, Episcopal Correspondence (1820–50); Z40, Griffiths, Diary (1834–36).
Bishop William Poynter Papers: A51–A52, Correspondence of Poynter and Douglass, Political Activities (1808–12); A56, Propaganda (1812–27); A57, Propaganda (1812–27); A57–A58, Political Activities (1812–27); A59, Vicars Apostolic–Western District (1812–27), Milner (1812–26), Midland (Walsh) (1826–27); A60, Vicars Apostolic–Northern District (1812–27), Scottish and Irish (1812–27); A61, Coadjutor (1825–27), Clergy in Other Districts (1812–27); A62–A63, London District Clergy and Parishes (1812–27); A63, Vicar General (1812–25); A66, Colleges, Rome (1815–27); A67–A68, Kirk (1812–27); A68, Gandolfi (1814–20), Miscellaneous (1812–26); A68(i), Poynter (personal), Synods (1812–25), Pastorals (1813–27); B20 Poynter, Copy Book; E7, Gradwell, Journal (1817–25); E8, Gradwell, Journal (1825–28); GL Gradwell, Letters (1817–28).
Saint Edmund's College Archives: see above.

Primary Sources: Printed Works

An Abridgment of Christian Doctrine with Proofs of Scripture for Points Controverted. Catechistically Explained, by Way of Question and Answer. Douai: n.p., 1661.
An Abridgment of Christian Doctrine, With Proofs of Scripture for Points Controverted. Catechistically Explained by Way of Question and Answer. London: T. Meighan, 1756.
An Abridgment of Christian Doctrine Revised and Approved

by *Wm. G. V. A. and Published for the Use of the N———N District.* Newcastle-upon-Tyne: n.p., 1812.

An Abridgment of Christian Doctrine, Revised, Improved, and Recommended by Authority, for the Use of the Faithful in the Four Districts of England. 3d ed. York: C. Croshaw, 1832.

Archer, James. *A Letter from the Reverend James Archer to the Right Reverend John Milner, Vicar Apostolic of the Midland District.* London: Joseph Booker, 1810.

———. *Sermons on Various Moral and Religious Subjects, For All the Sundays and Some of the Principal Festivals of the Year.* 3d ed. 3 vols. London: Jos. Booker, 1817.

Baines, P. A. *A History of the Pastoral Addressed to the Faithful of the Western District, On the Occasion of the Fast of Lent, 1840.* Prior Park: W. Murray, 1841.

———. *A Letter Addressed to Sir. Chas. Wolseley, Bart., on the Lenten Pastoral of 1840.* Prior Park: privately printed, 1841.

Barrington, Shute. *A Charge Delivered to the Clergy of the Diocese of Durham, at the Ordinary Visitation of that Diocese, in the Year 1801.* London: W. Bulmer & Co., 1802.

———. *The Grounds on Which the Church of England Separated from the Church of Rome. Stated in a Charge Delivered to the Clergy of the Diocese of Durham, at the Ordinary Visitation of the Diocese, in the Year 1806.* London: F. and C. Rivington, 1807.

Berington, Joseph. *An Address to the President of Protestant Association: Including Remarks on Strictures Lately Published on "The State and Behaviour of English Catholics."* London: privately printed, 1782.

———. *An Address to the Protestant Dissenters Who Have Lately Petitioned for a Repeal of the Corporation and Test Acts.* Birmingham: M. Swinney, 1787.

[———]. *An Appeal to the Catholics of England by the Catholic Clergy of the County of Stafford.* Wolverhampton: privately printed, 1792.

———. *An Essay on the Depravity of the Nation with a View to the Promotion of Sunday Schools etc. of Which a*

More Extended Plan Is Proposed. Birmingham: Myles Swinney, 1788.

———. *The History of the Lives of Abeillard and Heloisa: Comprising a Period of Eighty-Four Years, from 1079 to 1163. With Their Genuine Letters from the Collection of Amboise.* Birmingham: M. Swinney, 1787.

———. *The History of the Reign of Henry II, and of Richard and John, His Sons.* Birmingham: M. Swinney, 1790.

———. *A Letter to Dr. Fordyce, In Answer to His Sermon on the Delusive and Persecuting Spirit of Popery.* London: G. Robinson, 1779.

———. *A Literary History of the Middle Ages; Comprehending an Account of the State of Learning, from the Close of the Reign of Augustus, to Its Revival in the Fifteenth Century.* London: J. Mawman, 1814.

———. *The Memoirs of Gregorio Panzani, Giving an Account of His Agency in England in the Years 1634, 1635, 1636 + an Introduction and a Supplement, Exhibiting the State of the English Catholic Church, And the Conduct of Parties, before and after That Period, to the Present Time.* Birmingham: n.p., 1793.

———. *Reflections Addressed to the Rev. John Hawkins. To Which Is Added, An Exposition of Roman Catholic Principles, In Reference to God and the Country.* Birmingham: M. Swinney, 1785.

———. *The Rights of Dissenters from the Established Church, In Relation, Principally, to English Catholics.* Birmingham: M. Swinney, 1789.

———. *The State and Behaviour of English Catholics from the Reformation to the Year 1780 with a View of Their Present Numbers, Wealth, Character, etc.* London: n.p., 1780.

———, and Kirk, John. *The Faith of Catholics, Confirmed by Scripture, and Attested by the Fathers of the First Five Centuries of the Church.* London: Joseph Booker, 1813.

Bossuet, Jacques Bénigne. *An Exposition of the Doctrine of the Catholic Church in Matters of Controversy.* London: n.p., 1685.

Butler, Charles. *An Account of the Life and Writings of the*

Rev. Alban Butler: Interspersed with Observations on Some Subjects of Sacred and Profane Literature, Mentioned in His Writings. Edinburgh: Keating & Brown, 1800.

———. The Book of the Roman Catholic Church: In a Series of Letters Addressed to Robt. Southey, Esq. LL.D. on His "Book of the Church." 2d ed. London: John Murray, 1825.

———. A Continuation of the Rev. Alban Butler's "Lives of the Saints to the Present Time": With Bibliographical Accounts of the Holy Family, Pope Pius VI, Cardinal Ximénes, Cardinal Bellarmine, Bartholomew de Martyribus, and St. Vincent of Paul, and Historical Minutes of the Society of Jesus. London: Keating and Brown, 1823.

———. An Historical and Literary Account of the Formularies, Confessions of Faith, or Symbolic Books of the Roman Catholic, Greek, and Principal Protestant Churches. London: A. J. Valpy, 1816.

———. The Historical Memoirs of the Church of France in the Reigns of Lewis the Fourteenth, Lewis the Fifteenth, Lewis the Sixteenth, and the French Revolution. London: W. Clarke & Sons, 1817.

———. Historical Memoirs respecting the English, Irish, and Scottish Catholics, From the Reformation to the Present Time. 4 vols. London: John Murray, 1819–21.

Butler, Charles. Historical Memoirs of the English, Irish, and Scottish Catholics since the Reformation; With a Succinct Account of the Principal Events in the Ecclesiastical History of This Country antecedent to That Period, and in the Histories of the Established Church, and the Dissenting and Evangelical Congregations. 3d ed. 4 vols. London: John Murray, 1822.

———. Horae Biblicae, Being a Connected Series of Miscellaneous Notes on the Original Texts, Early Versions, and Printed Editions of the Old and New Testaments. Oxford: J. White, 1799.

———. The Life of Fénelon, Archbishop of Cambray. London: Longman, Hurst, Rees, and Orme, 1810.

———. *The Lives of Dom Armand-Jean de Bouthillièr de Rancé, Abbot Regular and Reformer of the Monastery of La Trappe; And of Thomas à Kempis, the Reputed Author of "The Imitation of Christ." With Some Account of the Principal Religious and Military Orders of the Roman Catholic-Church.* London: Luke Hansard & Sons, 1814.

———. *Miscellaneous Tracts.* N.p., 1812.

———. *Reminiscences of Charles Butler, Esq. of Lincoln's Inn.* 3d ed. 2 vols. London: John Murray, 1822.

———. *A Short Reply to Doctor Phillpotts' Answer. (In His "Letter to a Layman") to Mr. Butler's Letter on the Coronation Oath.* London: John Murray, 1828.

———. *A Succinct History of the Geographical and Political Revolutions of the Empire of Germany, or the Principal States Which Composed the Empire of Charlemagne, from His Coronation in 814, to Its Dissolution in 1806; With Some Account of the Genealogies of the Imperial House of Hapsburgh, and of the Six Secular Electors of Germany, and of the Roman, German, French and English Nobility.* London: Longman, Hurst, Rees, Orme, and Brown, 1812.

Catholic Committee. *First Blue Book*, London: n.p., 1789.

———. *Second Blue Book*, London: n.p., 1791.

———. *Third Blue Book*, London: J. P. Coghlan, 1792.

Challoner, Richard. *The Garden of the Soul; or, A Manual of Spiritual Exercises and Instructions for Christians Who (Living in the World) Aspire to Devotions.* London: T. Meighan, 1751.

———. *Grounds of Catholic Doctrine by Bishop Challoner as Contained in the Professions of Faith, Published by Pope Pius IV. With an Introductory Preface, by the Rev. Richard Thompson.* Manchester: R. & W. Dean, 1802.

———. *A Short History of the Origin and Progress of the Protestant Religion, Extracted from Protestant Writers, by Way of Question and Answer.* London: Keating, Brown, and Keating, 1803.

[Coates, Henry] "Elijah Index." *A Protestant's Reply to the*

Author of a Pamphlet, Entitled, "Remarks on a Charge Delivered to the Clergy of the Diocese of Durham, by Shute, Bishop of Durham, at the Ordinary Visitation of That Diocese in the Year, 1806." Newcastle: Edw. Walker, 1807.

Dodd, Charles. The Church History of England. From the Year 1500, to the Year 1688. 3 vols. Brussels: n.p., 1737–42.

Encyclical Letter. Charles Bishop of Rama, Vicar Apostolic of the Western District; William, Bishop of Acanthos, Vicar Apostolic of the Northern District, and John, Bishop of Centuria, Vicar Apostolic of the Southern District. To All the Faithful, Clergy and Laity of their respective Districts. 19 Jan. 1791. N.p. [1791?].

An Essay towards a Proposal for Catholick Communion. By a Minister of the Church of England. London: n.p., 1704.

Eustace, John Chetwode. Answer to the Charge Delivered by the Lord Bishop of Lincoln to the Clergy of That Diocese at the Triennial Visitation in the Year 1812. London: J. Booker, 1813.

Fell, Charles. The Lives of Saints: Collected from Authentick Records of Church History; With a Full Account of the Other Festivals throughout the Year, The Whole Interspersed with Suitable Reflections. Vol. 1 London: Thomas Meighan, 1729.

Fletcher, John. The Catholic's Prayer Book; or, The Exercises of a Christian Life, According to the Doctrines of the True Church of Jesus Christ; and the Maxims, and Spirit, of His Gospel. London: A. J. Valpy, 1830.

———. A Comparative View of the Grounds of the Catholic, and Protestant, Churches. London: A. J. Valpy, 1826.

———. Letters on the Spanish Inquisition by the Count Joseph de Maître with Notes. London: W. Hughes, 1838.

———. The Prudent Christian; or, Considerations on the Importance and Happiness, of Attending to the Care of Our Salvation. London: Keating and Brown, 1834.

[———]. Reflections on the Spirit etc. etc., of Religious Controversy. London: Keating, Brown and Keating, 1804.

———. Sermons on Various Religious and Moral Subjects for

All the Sundays after Pentecost: With Illustrations. 3 vols. Newcastle: Edw. Walker, 1810–16.

———. *Thoughts on the Rights, and Prerogatives of the Church and State; With Some Observations upon the Question of Catholic Securities.* London: A. J. Valpy, 1823.

Fleury, Claude. *Discours sur l'histoire ecclésiastique.* Nismes: Pierre Beaume, 1785.

Gandolphy, Peter. *A Defense of the Ancient Faith, in Four Volumes; or, A Full Exposition of the Christian Religion, in a Series of Controversial Sermons.* London: Keating, Brown, and Keating, 1815.

Geddes, Alexander. *An Answer to the Bishop of Comana's Pastoral Letter.* By a Protesting Catholic. 26 Jan. 1790. London: n.p., 1790.

———. *Doctor Geddes' Address to the Public, on the Publication of the First Volume of His New Translation of the Bible.* London: n.p., 1793.

———. *A Modest Apology for the Roman Catholics of Great Britain.* London: n.p., 1800.

———. *Prospectus of a New Translation of the Holy Bible.* Glasgow: privately printed, 1786.

Gibson, Matthew. *A Pastoral Letter of Matthew, Bishop of Comana, Vicar Apostolic, Addressed to All the Clergy, Secular and Regular, and to All the Faithful of the Northern District.* 15 June 1790. London: n.p., 1790.

Gother, John. *Gother's Prayers for Sundays & Festivals, Adapted to the Use of Private Families or Congregations. To Which Is Added the Appendix, Containing Prayers before and after Mass, and Some Evening Devotions.* Wolverhampton: J. Smart, 1800.

———. *A Papist Mis-represented, and Represented; or, A Twofold Character of Popery.* N.p., 1665.

Hawarden, Edward. *The Rule of Faith Truly Stated, In a New and Easy Method; or, A Key to Controversy.* N.p., 1721.

———. *The True Church of Christ, Shewed by Concurrent Testimonies of Scripture and Primitive Tradition.* 2 vols. N.p., 1714–15.

Holden, Henry. *The Analysis of Divine Faith; or, Two Treatises of the Resolution of Christian Belief with an Appendix of Schism.* Translated by W. G. Paris: n.p., 1658.

———. *Divinae fidei analysis seu de fide Christianae resolutione.* Paris: n.p., 1652.

Hollingsworth, N. J. *A Defense of the Doctrine and Worship of the Church of England, As Maintained by the Bishops of London and Durham: And Particularly in the Two Last Charges by the Bishop of Durham: In Five Letters, Addressed to the Author of "A Letter to A Clergyman of the Diocese of Durham, In Answer to His Second Letter,"* etc. Durham: G. Walker, 1809.

———. *Three More Pebbles Fresh from the Brook; or, The Romish Goliath Slain with His Own Weapon: Being an Answer to "Remarks on 'The Grounds on Which the Church of England Separated from the Church of Rome, Reconsidered by Shute, Bishop of Durham'": In Three Letters to the Remarker.* Durham: G. Walker [1809?].

Huntingford, George Isaac. *The Petition of the English Roman Catholics Considered: In a Charge Delivered to the Clergy in the Diocese of Gloucester, at the Triennial Visitation of That Diocese in the Month of June, 1810.* 2d ed. London: Luke Hansard & Sons, 1812.

Husenbeth, Frederick Charles. *The Life of the Right Rev. John Milner, D. D., Bishop of Castabala.* Dublin: James Duffy, 1862.

———. *The Life of the Right Reverend Monsignor Weedall, D.D., Including Incidentally the Early History of Oscott College.* London: Longman, Green, Longman, and Roberts, 1860.

Kenyon, Lord. *Observations on the Roman Catholic Question.* 4th ed. London: J. J. Stockdale, 1812.

Kirk, John. *Biographies of English Catholics in the Eighteenth Century.* Edited by John Hungerford Pollen, and Edwin Burton. London: Burns & Oates, 1909.

Letters on Catholic Loyalty Originally Published in the "Newcastle Courant." Newcastle: Edw. Walker, 1807.

Lingard, John. "The Ancient Church of England and the

Liturgy of the Anglican Church." *Dublin Review* 11 (1841): 167–96.

———. *The Antiquities of the Anglo-Saxon Church.* 2 vols. Newcastle: Edw. Walker, 1806. 2d ed. London: Keating, Brown and Keating, 1810.

———. *Catechetical Instructions on the Doctrines and Worship of the Catholic Church.* 3d ed. London: Charles Dolman, 1841.

———. *A Collection of Tracts on Several Subjects Connected with the Civil and Religious Principles of Catholics.* London: Keating & Brown, 1826.

———. "Did the Anglican Church Reform Herself?" *Dublin Review* 8 (1840): 334–73.

———. *Documents to Ascertain the Sentiments of British Catholics, in Former Ages, respecting the Power of the Popes.* London: J. Booker, 1812.

———. "Dodd's Church History of England." *Dublin Review* 6 (1839): 395–415.

———. *Examination of Certain Opinions, Advanced by the Right Rev. Dr. Burgess, Bishop of St. David's In Two Recent Publications, Entitled, Christ, and Not Peter, the Rock, And Johannis Sulgeni versus hexametri in laudem Sulgeni patris.* Manchester: Wardle and Bentham, 1813.

———. *A General Vindication of the Remarks on the Charge of the Bishop of Durham containing a Reply to a Letter from a Clergyman of the Diocese of Durham, (Second Ed.). A Reply to the Observations of the Rev. Thos. Le Mesurier, Rector of Newton Longville. A Reply to the Strictures of the Rev. G. S. Faber, Vicar of Stockton upon Tees. And Some Observations on the More Fashionable Methods of Interpreting the Apocalypse.* Newcastle: S. Hodgson, 1808.

———. *Histoire d'Angleterre, depuis la première invasion des Romains.* Translated from the English by Le Chevalier de Roujoux. 2d ed. 14 vols. Paris: n.p., 1825–31.

———. *The History and Antiquities of the Anglo-Saxon Church, Containing an Account of Its Origin, Government, Doctrines, Worship, Revenues, and Clerical and*

Monastic Institutions. 2 vols. London: Charles Dolman, 1845.
———. *A History of England, From the First Invasion by the Romans to the Accession of William and Mary in 1688.* 8 vols. London: J. Mawman, 1819–30.
———. *The History of England, From the First Invasion by the Romans to the Accession of William and Mary in 1688.* 6th ed. Vol. 1. London: Charles Dolman, 1854.
———. *A Manual of Prayers on Sundays and during Mass.* Lancaster: C. Clark, 1833.
[———]. *A New Version of the Four Gospels; With Notes Critical and Explanatory.* By a Catholic. London: Joseph Booker, 1836.
———. *Observations on the Laws and Ordinances, Which Exist in Foreign States, Relative to the Religious Concerns of Their Roman Catholic Subjects.* Dublin: Richard Coyne, 1817.
[———]. Introduction to *The Protestant Apology for the Roman Catholic Church; or, The Orthodoxy, Purity, and Antiquity of Her Faith and Principles Proved, From the Testimony of Her Most Learned Adversaries,* by "Christianus" [William Talbot]. *Prefixed Is an Introduction, Concerning the Nature, Present State, and True Interests of the Church of England; And on the Means of Effecting a Reconciliation of the Churches: With Remarks on the False Representations, Repeated in Some Late Tracts, of Several Catholic Tenets, Particularly the Supremacy of the See of Rome.* By "Irenaeus" [John Lingard]. Dublin: H. Fitzpatrick, 1809.
———. *Remarks on a Charge Delivered to the Clergy of the Diocese of Durham, by Shute, Bishop of Durham, at the Ordinary Visitation of That Diocese in the Year 1806.* 3d ed., enlarged. Newcastle: Edw. Walker, 1807.
———. *Remarks on a Late Pamphlet Entitled "The Grounds on Which the Church of England Separated from the Church of Rome, Reconsidered by Shute, Bishop of Durham."* London: W. Clowes, 1809.
———. *A Review of Certain Anti-Catholic Publications: viz.*

A Charge Delivered to the Clergy of the Diocese of Gloucester, in 1810, by George Isaac Huntingford, D.D., F.R.S., Bishop of Gloucester (Reprinted in 1812).

A Charge Delivered to the Clergy of the Diocese of Lincoln in 1812, by George Tomline, D.D. F.R.S., Lord Bishop of Lincoln; And Observations on the Catholic Question, by the Right Hon. Lord Kenyon. London: Joseph Booker, 1813.

———. *Storia d'Inghilterra del Dottore Giovanni Lingard.* Translated from the English by Domenico Gregori. 2d ed. 8 vols. Rome: n.p., 1828–1833.

———. *Strictures on Dr. Marsh's "Comparative View of the Churches of England and Rome."* London: J. F. Dove, 1815.

———. *The Widow Woolfrey versus the Vicar of Carisbrooke; or, Prayer for the Dead, A Tract for the Times.* London: Catholic Institute of Great Britain, 1839.

Milner, John. *Audi Aleteram Partem.* N.p., 1792.

———. *A Brief Account of the Life of the Late R. Rev. Richard Challoner, D.D., Bishop of Derba, and Apostolical Vicar of the Southern District.* London: J. P. Coghlan, 1798.

———. *A Case of Conscience Solved; or, Catholic Emancipation Proved To Be Compatible with the Coronation Oath, In a Letter from a Casuist in the Country, to His Friend in Town. Dedicated to the Right Hon. W. Wyndham, N.P. etc. With a Supplement in Answer to Considerations on the Said Oath, by John Reeves, Esq.* London: C. Clarke, 1801.

———. *Certain Considerations on Behalf of the Roman Catholics, Who Have Conscientious Objections to Changing Their Name, and to the Form of Words in Which Certain Passages Appear in the Oath Contained in Mr. Mitford's Bill, Modestly Submitted to the Honourable Committee of the House of Commons.* 7 Mar. 1791. N.p. [1791?].

———. *The Clergyman's Answer to the Layman's Letter on the Appointment of Bishops.* N.p., 1790.

———. *The Divine Right of Episcopacy Addressed to the*

Catholic Laity of England in Answer to the Layman's Second Letter to the Catholic Clergy of England; With Remarks on the Oaths of Supremacy and Allegiance. London: J. P. Coghlan, 1791.

―――. The End of Religious Controversy, In a Friendly Correspondence between a Religious Society of Protestants and a Roman Catholic Divine. London: n.p., 1818.

―――. The Exclamations of the Soul to God; or, The Meditations of St. Teresa after Communion. London: n.p., 1790.

―――. Facts Relating to the Present Contest amongst the Roman Catholics of This Kingdom concerning the Bill To Be Introduced into Parliament for Their Relief. 24 Feb. 1791. N.p. [1791].

―――. An Historical and Critical Inquiry into the Existence and Character of Saint George. London: n.p., 1792.

―――. The History Civil and Ecclesiastical and Survey of the Antiquities of Winchester. 2 vols. Winchester: James Robbins, 1798.

[―――]. An Humble Remonstrance to the Members of the Hon. House of Commons, On the Nature and Object of the Report of Its Select Committee, For Inquiring into the Laws and Ordinances of Foreign States, Respecting Their Roman Catholic Subjects, etc. By a Native Roman Catholic Prelate. London: Keating, Brown, and Co., 1816.

―――. A Letter to the Catholic Clergy of the Midland District. 21 Jan. 1823. N.p., 1823.

―――. Letters to a Prebendary: Being an Answer to Reflections on Popery. By the Rev. J. Sturges, L.L.D., Prebendary and Chancellor of Winchester, and Chaplain to His Majesty. With Remarks on the Opposition of HOADLYISM to the Doctrines of the Church of England. 2d ed. Cork: n.p., 1802.

―――. Observations on the Means Necessary for Further Illustrating the Ecclesiastical Architecture of the Middle Ages. 15 Feb. 1800. N.p., [1800].

―――. Origin and Progress of the Veto. London: n.p., 1810.

―――. Pastoral Letter of John Bishop of Castabella, Vicar Apostolic. 27 Dec. 1803. London: Keating, Brown, and Co., 1803.

———. *A Serious Expostulation with the Rev. Joseph Berington upon His Theological Errors concerning Miracles, and Other Subjects.* London: J. P. Coghlan, 1797.
———. *A Sermon Preached in the Roman Catholic Chapel at Winchester, April 23, 1789, etc. Being the General Thanksgiving Day for His Majesty's Happy Recovery.* London: J. P. Coghlan [1789].
———. *A Short View of the Chief Arguments against the Catholic Petition Now before Parliament, And of Answers to Them, in a Letter to a Member of the House of Commons.* London: Keating, Brown and Co., 1805.
———. *Strictures on the Poet Laureate's Book of the Church.* London: Keating and Brown, 1824.
Newman, John Henry. *Sermons and Essays.* London: Catholic Truth Society, 1907.
Phillpotts, Henry. *A Letter to the Author of "Remarks on a Charge Delivered by Shute, Bishop of Durham, at the Ordinary Visitation of That Diocese in the Year 1806."* Newcastle-upon-Tyne: D. Akenhead and Sons, 1807.
———. *A Second Letter to the Author of Remarks on the Bishop of Durham's Charge, Occasioned by the Vindication of Those Remarks Lately Republished.* Newcastle-upon-Tyne: D. Akenhead and Sons, 1808.
Plowden, Charles. *Considerations on the Modern Opinion of the Fallibility of the Holy See in the Decision of Dogmatical Questions with an Appendix on the Appointment of Bishops.* London: n.p., 1790.
———. *Remarks on a Book Entitled "Memoirs of Gregorio Panzani."* London: J. P. Coghlan, 1794.
———. *Remarks on the Writings of the Rev. Joseph Berington Addressed to the Catholic Clergy of England.* London: J. P. Coghlan, 1792.
Plowden, Francis. *Jura Anglorum: The Rights of Englishmen.* London: n.p., 1792.
Prayers before and after Mass, Proper for Country Congregations. To Which Are Added Some Evening Prayers, for Sundays and Holidays. London: J. Booker, 1826.
Rathborne, Joseph. *Are the Puseyites Sincere? A Letter Most*

Respectfully Addressed to a Right Reverend Catholic Lord Bishop, on the Oxford Movement. London: T. James, 1841.
Remarks on Sir John Throckmorton's Considerations. Arising from the Debates in Parliament, On the Petition of the Irish Catholics. By a Friend to the Constitution. Reading: Smart and Cowslade, 1806.
Strickland, Joseph. *An Apology for Not Subscribing to the Oath, Proposed To Be Taken by the Catholics of England, This Present Year, 1790.* N.p. [1790?].
———. *Remarks upon a Letter, Addressed by a Layman, to the Catholic Clergy of England, on the Appointment of Bishops.* 29 June 1790. N.p. [1790?].
———. *A Second Apology for Disapproving of the Oath, Intended To Be Taken by the Catholics of England, This Present Year, 1790.* N.p., 1790.
Sturges, John. *Reflections on the Principles and Institutions of Popery with Reference to Civil Society and Government Especially That of This Kingdom, Occasioned by the Rev. John Milner's History of Winchester in Letters to the Rev. John Monk Newbolt, Rector of St. Maurice, Winchester.* 2d ed. Winchester: J. A. Robbins, 1800.
Throckmorton, John. *Considerations Arising from the Debates in Parliament on the Petition of the Irish Catholics.* London: J. Budd, 1806.
———. *A Letter Addressed to the Catholic Clergy of England on the Appointment of Bishops. By a Layman.* 12 June 1790. N.p. [1790?].
———. *A Second Letter Addressed to the Catholic Clergy of England on the Appointment of Bishops. In Which the Objections to the First Letter Are Answered.* London: n.p., 1791.
Tierney, M. A., ed. *Dodd's Church History of England from the Sixteenth Century to the Revolution in 1688. With Notes, Additions and a Continuation.* 5 vols. London: Charles Dolman, 1839–43.
Tomline, George. *A Charge Delivered to the Clergy of the Diocese of Lincoln at the Triennial Visitation of That*

Diocese in May, June, and July, 1812. 2d ed. London: Luke Hansard, 1813.

[Ventura, Giacoma?] "Bastia." *Osservazioni sulla storia d'Inghilterra del Dottor Lingard dirette in forma di lettera al sig. editore del memoriale cattolico.* N.p., 1828.

Veron, Francis. *The Rule of Catholic Faith Sever'd from Opinions of the Schools, Mistakes of the Ignorant, and Abuses of the Vulgar.* Translated by E. S. Paris: John Billaine, 1660.

Wheeler, James. *A Letter from the Rev. J. Wheeler, to Sir John Lawson, Bart., Containing a Proposed Arrangement, In Which All Due Provision Is Made Both for the Inviolable Maintenance of the Civil and Religious Establishments of the Country. And for the Complete Security of the Vital Interests of the Catholic Religion, with a View to the Attainment of Catholic Emancipation.* Richmond: M. Bell, 1810.

———. *Sermons on the Gospels, for Every Sunday throughout the Year, with an Appropriate Sermon for the First and Last Sunday.* 2 vols. London: Jos. Booker, 1834.

White, Thomas. *Sermons for the Different Sundays, and Principal Festivals of the Year: With a Few Additional Sermons on Various Subjects.* Selected and arranged by John Lingard. 2 vols. London: Jos. Booker, 1828.

Wiseman, Nicholas. "Catholic Versions of Scripture." *Dublin Review* 2 (1837): 475–92.

Primary Sources: Periodicals

Catholic Magazine and Review.
Catholic Miscellany and Monthly Repository of Information.
Catholicon.
Dolman's Magazine.
Dublin Review.
Home and Foreign Review.
Orthodox Journal, and Catholic Monthly Intelligencer.
Rambler.

Selected Secondary Studies: Printed Works and Dissertations

Altholz, Josef L. *The Liberal Catholic Movement in England.* Montreal: Palm Publishers, 1962.

Amherst, W. J. *The History of Catholic Emancipation and the Progress of the Catholic Church in the British Isles (Chiefly in England) from 1771 to 1820.* 2 vols. London: K. Paul Trench & Co., 1886.

Appolis, Emile. *Le "Tiers Parti" Catholique au XVIIIe siècle (entre Jansénistes et Zelanti).* Paris: A. & J. Picard, 1960.

Aubert, Roger. *Le problème de l'acte de foi.* Louvain: n.p., 1945.

Aveling, J. C. H. *The Handle and the Axe.* London: Blond & Briggs, 1976.

Bolton, Charles A. *Church Reform in 18th Century Italy.* The Hague: Martinus Nijhoff, 1969.

Bossy, John. *The English Catholic Community, 1570–1850.* New York: Oxford University Press, 1976.

Bremond, Henri. *Histoire litteraire du sentiment religieux en France depuis la fin des guerres de religion jusqu's nos jours.* Vols. 8 and 9. Paris: Bloud et Gay, 1928–32.

Burton, Edwin H. *The Life and Times of Bishop Challoner (1691–1781).* 2 vols. London: Longmans, Green, and Co., 1909.

Butterfield, Herbert. *Man on His Past.* Cambridge: University Press, 1955.

Chadwick, Owen. *From Bossuet to Newman: The Idea of Doctrinal Development.* Cambridge: University Press, 1957.

Chinnici, Joseph P. "John Lingard and the English Catholic Enlightenment." D.Phil. dissertation, Greyfriars, Oxford, 1976.

Clark, Ruth. *Strangers and Sojourners at Port Royal, Being an Account of the Connections between the British Isles and the Jansenists of France and Holland.* Cambridge: University Press, 1932.

Cognet, Louis. *Crépuscule des mystiques.* Tournai, Belgium: Desclée 1958.
———. *Post-Reformation Spirituality.* Translated by P. J. Hepburne-Scott. London: Burns and Oates, 1959.
———. *La spiritualité moderne, Vol. 1, L'essor: 1550–1650.* N.p.: Aubier, 1966.
Congar, Yves M.-J. *Tradition and Traditions.* Translated by Michael Naseby and Thomas Rainborough. London: Burns & Oates, 1966.
Cowherd, Raymond G. *The Politics of English Dissent.* New York: New York University Press, 1956.
Delumeau, Jean. *Le Catholicisme entre Luther et Voltaire.* Paris: Presses Universitaires de France, 1971.
Dockery, John Berchmans. *Christopher Davenport, Friar and Diplomat.* London: Burns & Oates, 1960.
Dru, Alexander. *The Church in the Nineteenth Century: Germany, 1808–1918.* London: Burns and Oates, 1963.
Duffy, Eamon. "Joseph Berington and the English Catholic Cisalpine Movement, 1772–1803." Ph.D. dissertation, Selwyn College, Cambridge, 1972.
Feret, Pierre. *La faculté de théologie de Paris et ses docteurs les plus célèbres.* Vol. 4. Paris: Picard et Fils, 1906.
Fothergill, Brian. *Nicholas Wiseman.* London: Faber and Faber, 1963.
Gadille, Jacques, ed. *Les Catholiques libéraux au XIXe siècle.* Grenoble: Presses Universitaires de Grenoble, 1974.
Gay, John D. *The Geography of Religion in England.* London: Duckworth, 1971.
Gillow, Joseph. *A Literary and Biographical History; or, Bibliographical Dictionary of the English Catholics from the Breach with Rome in 1534 to the Present Time.* 5 vols. London: Burns & Oates, 1885–1902.
———. *The Origin and History of the Manual.* London: Westminster Press, 1910.
Gooch, G. P. *History and Historians in the Nineteenth Century.* London: Longmans, Green and Co., 1913.
Goyau, Georges. *L'Allemagne religieuse.* Vol. 1. Paris: n.p., 1905.
Groethuysen, Bernard. *The Bourgeois: Catholicism vs. Cap-*

italism in Eighteenth Century France. Translated by Mary Ilford. London: Barrie & Rockliff, 1968.
Gwynn, Denis. *The Second Spring, 1818–1852: A Study of the Catholic Revival in England.* London: Burns & Oates, 1942.
Haile, Martin, and Bonney, Edwin. *Life and Letters of John Lingard, 1771–1851.* London: Herbert & Daniel, n.d.
Hale, J. R., ed. *The Evolution of British Historiography, Bacon to Namier.* London: Macmillan, 1967.
Henriques, Ursula. *Religious Toleration in England, 1787–1833.* London: Routledge and Kegan Paul, 1961.
Hughes, Philip. *The Catholic Question, 1688–1829: A Study in Political History.* London: Sheed and Ward, 1929.
Jacquement, G., ed. *Catholicisme: hier, aujourd'hui, demain.* 6 vols. to date. Paris: Letouzey et Ané, 1947.
Kelley, Donald R. *Foundations of Modern Historical Scholarship.* New York: Columbia University Press, 1970.
Knowles, David. *Great Historical Enterprises.* London: Thomas Nelson and Sons, 1963.
Leetham, Claude R. *Luigi Gentili, A Sower for the Second Spring.* London: Burns & Oates, 1965.
Leys, M. D. R. *Catholics in England, 1559–1829: A Social History.* London: Longmans, 1961.
Low, Anthony. *Augustine Baker.* New York: Twayne Publishers, 1970.
McElrath, Damian. *Richard Simpson, 1820–1876: A Study in XIXth Century English Liberal Catholicism.* Louvain: Universitaire de Louvain, 1972.
Machin, G. I. T. *The Catholic Question in English Politics, 1820 to 1830.* Oxford: University Press, 1964.
Martimort, Aimé-Georges. *Le Gallicanisme.* Paris: Presses Universitaires de France, 1973.
———. *Le Gallicanisme de Bossuet.* Paris: Éditions du Cerf, 1953.
Mathew, David. *Catholicism in England, 1535–1935.* London: Longmans, Green, and Co., 1936.
———. *Catholicism in England: The Portrait of a Minority, Its Culture and Tradition.* 2d ed. London: Eyre and Spottiswoode, 1948.

Milburn, David. *A History of Ushaw College*. Durham: Ushaw College, 1964.

Miller, John. *Popery and Politics in England, 1660–1688*. Cambridge: University Press, 1973.

Nedoncelle, Maurice. *Trois aspects du problemé Anglo-Catholique au XVIIe siècle*. Paris: Bloud et Gay, 1951.

Ollivier, Emile. *L'église et l'état au concile du Vatican*. 2 vols. Paris: Garnier Freres, 1879.

Palmer, R. R. *Catholics and Unbelievers in Eighteenth Century France*. Princeton: Princeton University Press, 1939.

Peardon, Thomas Preston. *The Transition in English Historical Writing, 1760–1830*. New York: Columbia University Press, 1933.

Perry, Elizabeth Israels. *From Theology to History: French Religious Controversy and the Revocation of the Edict of Nantes*. The Hague: Martinus Nijhoff, 1973.

Plongeron, Bernard. *Théologie et politique au siècle des lumières (1770–1820)*. Geneva: Librairie Droz, 1973.

Préclin, Edmond. *Les Jansénistes du XVIIIe siècle et la constitution civile du clerge: Le développement du richérisme. Sa propagation dans le bas clergé 1713–1791*. Paris: Librairie Universitaire, J. Gamber, 1929.

———. *L'union des églises gallicane et anglicane, une tentative au temps de Louis XIV, P.-F. le couraver (de 1681– à 1732) et Guillaume Wake*. Paris: Librairie Universitaire, J. Gamber, 1928.

Roche, J. S. *A History of Prior Park College and Its Founder Bishop Baines*. London: Burns, Oates, and Washbourne, 1931.

Rogier, L.-J.; Sauvigny, G. de Bertier de; and Hajjar, Joseph. *Siècle des lumières, révolutions, restaurations*. Translated from the Dutch by Fr. van Groenendaeal. Paris: Editions du Seuil, 1966.

Schiefen, Richard J. "The Organization and Administration of Roman Catholic Dioceses in England and Wales in the Mid-Nineteenth Century." Ph.D. dissertation, University of London, 1970.

Shea, Donald F. *The English Ranke: John Lingard*. New York: Humanities Press, 1969.

Sloyan, Gerard S., ed. *Shaping the Christian Message.* New York: Macmillan Co., 1959.
Sturzo, Luigi. *Church and State.* Translated by Barbara Barclay Carter. 2 vols. Notre Dame, Ind.: University of Notre Dame Press, 1962.
Sykes, Norman. *From Sheldon to Seeker: Aspects of English Church History, 1660–1768.* Cambridge: University Press, 1959.
Tavard, George H. *Holy Writ or Holy Church: The Crisis of the Protestant Reformation.* London: Burns & Oates, 1959.
———. *La tradition au XVIIe siècle en France et en Angleterre.* Paris: Éditions du Cerf, 1969.
Taveneaux, René. *La vie quotidienne des Jansénistes aux XVIIe et XVIIIe siècles.* Paris: Librairie Hachette, 1973.
Vacant, A.; Mangenot, E.; and Amann, É., eds. *Dictionnaire de théologie catholique, contenant l'expose des doctrines de la théologie catholique, leurs preuves et leur histoire.* 15 vols. Paris: Letouzey et Ané, 1903–50.
Ward, Bernard. *The Dawn of the Catholic Revival in England (1781–1803).* 2 vols. London: Longmans, Green, and Co., 1909.
———. *The Eve of Catholic Emancipation (1803–1829).* 3 vols. London: Longmans, Green, and Co., 1911–12.
———. *History of St. Edmund's College.* Old Hall, London: Kegan Paul, 1893.
———. *The Sequel to Catholic Emancipation (1830–1850).* 2 vols. London: Longmans, Green, and Co., 1915.
Ward, Wilfrid. *The Life and Times of Cardinal Wiseman.* 2 vols. London: Longmans, Green, and Co., 1897.
———. *William George Ward and the Catholic Revival.* London: Macmillan and Co., 1893.
Watkin, E. I. *Roman Catholicism in England from the Reformation to 1950.* London: Oxford University Press, 1957.
Willey, Basil. *The Eighteenth Century Background.* Boston: Beacon Press, 1961.
———. *The Seventeenth Century Background.* New York: Doubleday, 1953.

Selected Secondary Studies: Articles

Abercrombie, Nigel J. "The Early Life of Charles Butler (1750–83)." *Recusant History* 14 (1978):281–92.
Aubert, Roger. "La géographic ecclésiologique au XIXe siècle." In *"L'ecclesiologie au XIXe siècle," Revue des sciences religieuses* 34 (1960): 11–55.
———. "Religious Liberty from 'Mirari Vos' to the 'Syllabus.'" Translated by Eileen O'Gorman. *Concilium* 7 (1965): 89–105.
Bornewasser, Hans. "State and Politics from the Renaissance to the French Revolution." Translated by Theodore L. Westow. *Concilium* 47 (1969): 73–91.
Brennan, James. "A Gallican Interlude in Ireland." *Irish Theological Quarterly* 24 (1957): 219–37, 283–309.
Cabrol, F. "Bossuet, ses relations avec l'Angleterre." *Revue d'histoire ecclésiastique* 27 (1931): 535–71.
Caffiero, Marina. "Cultura e religione nel settecento italiano: Giovanni Cristofano Amaduzzi a Scipione di Ricci." *Rivista di storia della chiesa in Italia* 28 (1974): 94–126.
Duchon, Robert. "De Bossuet À Febronius." *Revue d'histoire ecclésiastique* 65 (1970): 375–422.
Duffy, Eamon. "Doctor Douglass and Mister Berington—An Eighteenth-Century Retractation." *Downside Review* 88 (1970): 246–69.
———. "Ecclesiastical Democracy Detected: I (1779–1787)." *Recusant History* 10 (1970): 193–209.
———. "Ecclesiastical Democracy Detected: II (1787–1796)." *Recusant History* 10 (1970): 309–31.
Gilly, Sheridan. "The Roman Catholic Mission to the Irish in London." *Recusant History* 10 (1969): 123–45.
Harris, P. R. "The English College, Douai, 1750–1794." *Recusant History* 10 (1969): 79–95.
Hennesey, James. "National Traditions and the First Vatican Council." *Archivum Historiae Pontificiae* 7 (1969): 491–512.
Hexter, J. H. "The Protestant Revival and the Catholic Question in England, 1778–1829." *Journal of Modern History* 8 (1956): 297–319.

Hogan, Brendan. "The Philosophical Tradition of Douai." *Ushaw Magazine* 63 (1953): 145–159.
Holmes, J. Derek. "Catholics and Politics at the Time of Emancipation." *New Blackfriars* 54 (1973): 365–73.
———. " 'Conciliarists' versus 'Papalians.' " *Annuarium Historiae Conciliorum* 5 (1973): 424–436.
———. "John Henry Newman's Attitude towards History and Hagiography." *Downside Review* 92 (1974): 248–64.
Hughes, Philip. "Historians Reconsidered I: John Lingard." *History Today* 1 (1951): 57–62.
Jones, Edmund. "John Lingard and the Simancas Archives." *Historical Journal* 10 (1967): 57–76.
Jupp, P. J. "Irish Parliamentary Elections and the Influence of the Catholic Vote, 1801– 1820." *Historical Journal* 10 (1967): 183–96.
Latreille, André. "L'Intolerance religieuse sous l'ancien régime." In *Unité chrétienne et tolérance religieuse*, pp. 73–103. Paris: Éditions du Temps Present, 1950.
Le Brun, Jacques. "Politics and Spirituality: The Devotion to the Sacred Heart." Translated by John Griffiths. *Concilium* 69 (1971): 29–43.
Lecler, Joseph. "Religious Freedom: An Historical Survey." Translated by Theodore L. Westow. *Concilium* 18 (1966): 3–20.
Leetham, Claude. "Gentili's Reports to Rome." *Wiseman Review* 237 (1963–64): 395–414.
Mahieu, L. "La philosophie à l'université de Douai au XVIIIe siècle." *Mélanges de science religieuse* 14 (1957): 71–82.
Murray, John Courtney. "St. Robert Bellarmine on the Indirect Power." *Theological Studies* 9 (1943): 491–535.
Norman, Marion. "John Gother and the English Way of Spirituality." *Recusant History* 11 (1972): 306–19.
Plongeron, Bernard. "Questions pour l'Aufklärung Catholique en Italie." *Il Pensiero Politico* 3 (1970): 30–58.
———. "Recherches sur l'"Aufklärung" catholique en Europe Occidentale (1770–1830)." *Revue d'histoire moderne et contemporaine* 16 (1969): 555–605.
Préclin, Edmond. "L'influence du Jansénisme Francais a l'étranger." *Revue historique* 182 (1938): 24–71.

Rosa, Mario. "Italian Jansenism and the Synod of Pistoia." Translated by Edward A. Carpenter. *Concilium* 17 (1966): 34–49.
Rowlands, Marie. "The Education and Piety of Catholics in Staffordshire in the 18th Century." *Recusant History* 10 (1969): 67–78.
———. "The Staffordshire Clergy, 1688–1803." *Recusant History* 9 (1968): 219–41.
Schiefen, Richard J. " 'Anglo-Gallicanism' in Nineteenth-Century England." *Catholic Historical Review* 63 (1977): 14–44.
Sharratt, Michael. "Alban Butler: Newtonian in Part," *Downside Review* 96 (1978): 103–11.
———. "Copernicanism at Douai." *Durham University Journal* 67, n.s. 36 (1974): 41–48.
Simpson, Richard. "Milner and His Times." *Home and Foreign Review* 2 (1863): 531–57.
Tavard, George H. "Christopher Davenport and the Problem of Tradition." *Theological Studies* 24 (1963): 278–90.
———. "Scripture and Tradition among Seventeenth-Century Recusants." *Theological Studies* 25 (1964): 343–85.
———. "Tradition in Early Post-Tridentine Theology." *Theological Studies* 23 (1962): 377–405.
Toyne, S. M. "Guy Fawkes and the Powder Plot." *History Today* 1 (1951): 16–25.
Vaussard, Maurice. "Un Janséniste de grande classe: Benedetto Solari." *Revue d'histoire ecclésiastique* 68 (1973): 429–56.
Watkin, Dom Aelred, and Butterfield, Herbert. "Gasquet and the Acton-Simpson Correspondence." *Cambridge Historical Journal* 10 (1950): 75–105.
Wormald, B. H. G., "The Historiography of the English Reformation." In *Historical Studies*, edited by T. Desmond Williams, 1:50–58. London: Bowes and Bowes, 1958.

index

Abridgment of Christian Doctrine, 154–158, 168
Ascéticisme, 184
Acton, Charles, 54
Address to the Protestants of Great Britain and Ireland (C. Butler), 105
Aelfric, 101–102
Age of Reason, 142
Ailly, Pierre d', 93
Alcuin, 102
Alexander, Noel (Natalis), 4, 34, 58, 89
Almain, Jacques, 34
Amort, Eusebius, 3
Analysis of Divine Faith (H. Holden), 63, 84, 87
Andrews, William Eusebius, 41, 58, 119, 121–122, 143
Antiquities of the Anglo-Saxon Church (J. Lingard), 48, 71, 82, 89, 103, 110–111, 113–114, 117–118, 126, 171
Apostolicum Ministerium (Benedict XIV), 47
Appolis, Emile, 3, 6, 8, 184
Archer, James, 37, 39, 157, 173, 175, 180–182, 185
Aristotle, 63
Arnauld, Antoine, 58
Asseline, Bishop of Boulogne, 103
Auctorem Fidei (Pius VI), 59
Augustine, 93

Baader, F. X. 146

Bailey, Thomas, 81, 84
Bailly, Louis, 156
Baines, Peter Augustine, 136
Baker, Augustine, 185
Barrington, Shute, 16, 18–20, 99–100
Bede, 101–102
Bellarmine, Robert, 76, 87, 185
Belsen, John, 81
Benedict XIV, 3, 47
Berington, Charles, 51
Berington, Joseph, 36, 70, 80, 82, 97–98, 99, 105–106, 120, 133–134, 138, 151, 170, 182, 187–189; *An Essay on the Depravity of the Nation*, 71; and biblical criticism, 148; and Gallican tradition, 8; and John Throckmorton, 11; approves Quesnel, 83; birth of, 6; Butler and Lingard, comparison with, 108, 111, 116; catechisms, criticism of, 145; Charles Plowden, reacts to, 48; Church, contractual view of, 50; Church-State separation, support of, 37; "Candidus," defended by, 120; crusades, comments on, 115; doctrinal development, rejection of, 82–84; Douai thesis accepting sensationalism, 7; ecclesiology of, 60, 93–95; education, 11; emancipation, struggle for, 14–15; eucharist, understanding of, 103; external devotions, opposition to, 173; *Faith of Catholics*, defends his introduction to, 78–79;

foreign enthusiasm, criticism of, 174; friend of George Silvertop, 27; ghetto spirituality, attraction to, 174–175; historical writings of, 107, 111; interior life, view of, 181; James II, interpretation of, 50; John Sturges, support of, 53; Lingard's *History of England*, criticism of, 116; materialism, acceptance of, 11; Middle Ages, attitude towards, 113; miracles, view of, 144–145; natural rights philosophy, acceptance of, 36; Oath of 1789, support of, 45; politics and theology of, 57; *Prayer Book for the Use of the London District*, author of, 145; Protestants, openness towards, 70; religious liberty, acceptance of, 38–39; republicanism of, 36; schism, rejection of, 59; Scipio Ricci, agreement with, 59; Scripture and tradition, his approach to, 79–80; spiritual life of, 186; teaching authority, view of, 79–80; theology, context of his, 76; toleration, view of, 13; tradition, view of, 85; rule of faith, acceptance of, 78; vernacular liturgy, support of, 168; writings, antipapal and anti-Jesuit tone of, 126; writings, purpose of, 16

Bew, John, 134, 173, 218n
Bingham, Joseph, 111
Blue Books (Catholic Committee), 35, 37, 58–59, 107
Blundell, Charles, 39
Board of English Catholics, 13, 27
Bollandists, 109–110, 171
Boniface VIII, 23
Book of Common Prayer, 99–100
Bossuet, Jacques Bénigne, 4, 8, 10, 33–34, 37, 58–59, 68, 73, 80–81, 83–84, 88, 93, 96, 98, 102, 105, 133, 183
Bossy, John, 12
Bottari, Giovanni, 4
Bottieri, Antonio, 8
Boudon, Henri Marie de, 181
Bourdaloue, Louis, 80, 183
Bramston, James Yorke, 39–40, 155, 159, 163
Bremond, Henri, 183
British Catholic Association, 39
Burke, Edmund, 52
Burnet, Gilbert, 111
Butler, Alban, 6–7, 110, 171, 181, 183, 185
Butler, Charles, 97–99, 120, 133–134, 138, 144, 151, 170, 174, 185–189; acknowledges impact of Quietist dispute, 183; advises Lingard, 49; and biblical criticism, 148; and Gallican tradition, 8; and ultramontanism, 18; *Antiquities of the Anglo-Saxon Church*, evaluation of, 56–57, 117; authority, view of, 49; Berington and Lingard, compared with, 108, 111, 116; birth of, 6; *Blue Books*, author of, 37; conscious of Protestant prejudice, 70; context of theology of, 76; defended by "Candidus," 120; ecclesiology of, 60, 95–96; education of, 11; ecumenism of, 106; emancipation, struggles for, 14, 17; Fletcher's spirituality, acknowledges force of, 182; Francis Plowden's objection to, 72–73; friend of George Silvertop, 27; ghetto spirituality, attachment to, 174–175; historical writings, characteristics of, 107–108, 111; interior life, view of, 181; law, practice of, 11; Lingard, encouragement of, 110, 119; Lingard and Gibbon, compares, 113; Middle Ages, attitude towards, 113; miracles, view of, 145; natural rights philosophy, acceptance of, 36; politics and theology of, 57; religious liberty, acceptance of, 39; renaissance humanism, appreciation of, 185; saints' lives, criti-

cal approach to, 171; suspicious of papal encroachments, 174; writings, purpose of, 16; veto, rejection of, 21

Caffiero, Marina, 5, 8
Calvinism, 86, 99-100
Calvinists, 62
Canisius, Peter, 76, 87
Cano, Melchior, 76
Caron, Redmond, 34
Carroll, John, 94
Carte, Thomas, 111-112
Cartesianism, 183
Carthage, Council of, 51
Catechetical Instructions (J. Lingard, 154-164, 168
catechisms, 142, 154-164
Catholic Board, 148
Catholic Committee, 13, 16, 35, 45, 47, 58, 95, 107, 188
Catholic Enlightenment, 3-4, 135, 145, 151, 185
Catholic Magazine, 136, 139, 141-142, 144-147, 163, 174
Catholic Relief Bill (1789), 45
Catholic's Prayer Book (J. Fletcher), 139, 143, 145, 185
Challoner, Richard, 8, 143, 148, 154, 168
Charles I, 128
Chateaubriand, 132
Chillingworth, William, 62, 65, 81
Church and State, 194n; and jurisdictionalism, 23-24, 30, 37; and the papacy, 17; Cisalpine view of, 16, 33, 59, 145; eighteenth century view of, 43; history of relations between, 30-32; Joseph Berington's views on, 36; Lingard's view of, 22, 30, 32, 130; separation of, 188; separation of, and rights of conscience, 38; union of, 22; union of, Catholic objections to, 20
Church of England, 99-106

Cisalpine Club, 13, 58, 134
Cisalpines, 66-67; accused of Jansenism, 57; and common Christian creed, 63; and diffusion of Scripture, 148-155; and historical mentality, 107; and liturgical reform, 166; and pastoral reform, 142; and private judgment, 43, 63; and reform of devotional life, 168-175; and Second Spring, 146-147, 149; antischolastic, 63; authority, protest arbitrary exercise of, 46; basic principles of, 146; Bossuet, influence of, 59; careers pursued in England, 11; characteristics of their mentality, 108, 132, 153, 155, 168, 174-175, 183, 188-189; Church and state, views on, 33-40; combine Gallican, Jansenist, and Lockean traditions, 60; common view of, 125; complete synthesis of, 97-98, 186; consciousness of change, 116; core of their thinking, 117; debates of 1790's, 36-37; development, idea of, 82; ecclesiology of, 47-48, 50-51, 86-98; emancipation, support of, 16; external devotions, opposition to, 173; faith and culture, attempt to unite, 74, 106; foreign enthusiasms, criticism of, 174; government, view of, 38; Henry Holden, influence of, 64; individual rights, acceptance of, 48; infallibility, view of, 55; James II, interpretation of, 50; Jansenist ideas, acceptance of, 58; medieval tradition, departure from, 66; Milner's objections to, 52, 72; miracles, view of, 63; name, 13; natural rights philosophy, acceptance of, 36; not schismatical, 59; political philosophy of, 26; private judgment, understanding of, 44; Protestant views of Scripture and tradition, influenced by,

82; reason and faith, understanding of, 61–62, 66; religious liberty, support of, 42; religious pluralism, response to, 70; second generation of, 135, 163, 187; spirituality of, 175–187; toleration, definition of, 37–39
Cisalpinism, and Catholic Enlightenment, 185; demise, reasons for, 128; 187; essence, 133; negative apologetic, 174; social strengths and weaknesses, 157
Clairvaux, Bernard of, 185
Clermont, Council of, 51
Clifford, Hugh C., 69
Cloud of Unknowing, 186
Cognet, Louis, 184
Colville, John, 81
Communion of saints, 159
Comparative View of the Grounds of the Catholic, and Protestant Churches (J. Fletcher), 106
Concanen, Luke, 69
Conference avec M. Claude (J. B. Bossuet), 86, 88, 106
Confessions of Faith (C. Butler), 71, 95
Congar, Yves, 93
Constable, Charles Stanley, 37
Constance, Council of, 90
Constitutionalism, 50, 57, 168
Corbishley, J., 73
Counter Reformation, 76–77, 159
Cranmer, Thomas, 102, 124
Curr, Joseph, 140
Cyprian, Saint, 93

Daniel, John, 10
Davenport, Christopher, 81
De Statu Ecclesiae (Johann von Hontheim), 6
Defensio Declarationis Conventus Cleri Gallicani (J. B. Bossuet), 34, 83, 93, 96
Demangeot, Jean-Baptiste, 48
Devotions, 168–175
Digby, Kenelm, 134

Dissenters, 13, 15, 28, 38, 42, 106
Divine Right of Episcopacy (J. Milner), 52
Dolman, Charles, 163
Dominis, M. Antonio de, 52
Douglass, John, 17, 45, 144
Dublin Review, 146, 151, 163

Ecclesiology, 14, 42, 43–60, 86–98, 168
Ecumenism, 4, 16, 42, 86–87, 92, 98–106, 168, 171–173
Edinburgh Review, 38
Egbert, 101
Elizabeth I, 35, 55, 128
Emancipation, 15, 18, 32–33, 38, 47, 54, 70, 134, 146, 165
English Catholic Board, 42
English Catholics, 11–12, 138; a minority, 68–69; and acceptance of veto, 29; and denial of pope's temporal power, 35; and ultramontanism, 18; cooperate with Dissenters, 28; cooperate with Friends of Religious Liberty, 39; governed by *Apolosticum Ministerium*, 47
English College, Douai and Rome, 6–7
Enlightenment, The, 36–38, 62, 97, 114, 126, 128, 138, 157, 168, 175, 183, 186
Errington, George, 160
Essay towards a Proposal for Catholick Communion (anon.), 35, 68, 86, 102, 105
Eucharist, 99–103
Eustace, John Chetwode, 37, 39, 120, 137
Evangelicals, 62
Exposition of the Doctrine of the Catholic Church (J. B. Bossuet) 33–34, 68, 81, 93, 95–96
Eyre, Thomas, 9

Faith of Catholics (J. Berington

and J. Kirk), 53, 71, 78, 80, 83, 103
Febronianism, 32, 37, 59
Feijoo, Benito, 3
Fell, Charles, 171
Fénelon, François, 181, 183, 185
Fléchier, Esprit, 80
Fletcher, John, 37, 119, 134, 139, 144, 170, 174, 179, 185, 188; and congregational participation, 168; and theological anthropology, 10; birth, 6; Church and state, view of, 35, 37; civil liberty and private judgment, distinguished between, 39; education, 11; emancipation, struggle for, 14; humanism and mysticism, combines, 185; interior life, view of, 181–182; moderate political views, 11; natural rights philosophy, acceptance of, 36; publishes Bossuet's *Exposition*, 96; residence, 11; response to social changes, 157; student of history, 108
Fleury, Claude, 3, 34–35, 58, 109–111, 133
Florence, Council of, 90
Fox, Charles James, 38
Francis de Sales, 185
French Revolution, 128

Gallicanism, 33–34, 38, 55, 58, 77, 83, 92, 95, 109, 131, 133, 146, 157, 164, 174, 188
Garden of the Soul (R. Challoner), 142, 145, 166, 168, 186
Geddes, Alexander, 120
General Board of British Catholics, 41
Gentili, Luigi, 146, 172, 180
George III, 15
Gerson, Jean, 34, 93
Gibbon, Edward, 109, 113–114
Gibson, Matthew, 9, 45
Gibson, William, 27, 45, 103, 134
Gillow, John, 9
Goldsmith, Oliver, 119

Görres, Joseph von, 146
Gordon Riots, 70, 111
Gother, John, 68, 81, 167, 186
Gothic Revival, 166
Gradwell, Robert, 119, 124, 129, 133–134
Grattan, Henry, 21
Gregori, Domenico, 131–132
Gregory VII, 170
Gregory XVI, 133
Grenada, Luis de, 4
Griffiths, John, 9, 155
Groethuysen, Bernard, 157
Grotius, Hugo, 49, 153
Guéranger, Prosper, 133

Hallam, Henry, 114
Hawarden, Edward, 8, 65–67, 102
Henriques, Ursula, 43
Henry VIII, 128
Henry, Robert, 111
Heylin, Peter, 111
Hilton, Walter, 186
Historical Memoirs of the English, Irish, and Scottish Catholics (C. Butler), 122, 126
History of England (J. Lingard), 110, 112–116, 119–120, 122–128, 130–134, 164, 188
History of the Variations (J. B. Bossuet), 81, 83
Holden, Henry, 34–35, 64–66, 81, 84–85, 102
Hontheim, Johann Nikolaus von, 6, 59
Hornyold, Charles, 69
Hume, David, 49, 111, 113, 119, 127
Husenbeth, Frederick Charles, 135, 137–138, 140, 144, 154, 162–163, 170, 187, 214n

Imitation of Christ (Thomas à Kempis), 181, 185–186
Indulgences, 5, 160, 172
Infallibility, 55, 90, 96
Innocent III, 90, 127, 132

Inquisition, 11
Irish Remonstrance (Peter Walsh), 35

Jacobinism, 58
James II, 50
Jansenism, 3, 5, 10, 57, 83, 97, 111
Jansenists, 184, 186
Januarius, Saint, 137
Jeffrey, Francis, 38
Jesuits, 54, 58, 186
Jones, John, 165–166
Joseph II, 4, 30, 32
Josephinism, 59
Jurieu, Pierre, 49

Keble, John, 164
Kellison, Matthew, 81
Kendal, George, 9
Kirk, John, 6, 11, 14, 36, 45, 69, 71, 80, 95, 108, 112, 119, 122–123, 134, 136, 144, 168, 170, 173–174, 188

Lamartine, Alphonse de, 147
Lamennais, Félicité de, 147, 163
Lami, Giovanni, 4
Lanfranc, 102
Latitudinarianism, 120, 132
Le Chevalier de Roujoux, 127
Lee, John, 74
Leibniz, Gottfried Wilhelm, 73, 105
Leon, Luis de, 4
Letter Addressed to the Catholic Clergy of England on the Appointment of Bishops, A, A. Second (J. Throckmorton), 51, 107
Libellus de Ecclesiastica et Politica Potestate (E. Richer), 87
Liberal Catholicism, 187
Liberalism, 133
Life of the Rev. Robert Richmond (F. C. Husenbeth), 187
Liguori, Alfonsus, 185
Lingard, John, and Henry Hallam, 115; and reform of religious practice, 164–175; answers report of the House of Commons, 30–32; as "Amicus Justitiae" 119; as "Candidus, 119; as "Philorthodoxos," 119; at Ushaw College, 11; authority, understanding of, 43, 49, 63; authority, criticism of his view of, 122; Berington, compared with, 115; Berington, subdued approval of, 53–54; Berington and Butler, compared with 111–112, 116; biblical study, view of, 149–150; birth, 6; Bossuet, influenced by, 92; breviary, advocates reform of, 170; Cartesianism, rejection of, 7; catechism, view of, 142, 154–164; Catholic prayers and services, criticism of, 139–140; Christocentricity of, 179; Church and state, view of, 20, 22, 33–36; Cisalpine principles manifest in his works, 126; common law tradition, refers to, 81; communion of saints, views on, 159; compares his own works, 119; comparison with Augustine Thierry, 127; comparison with Hume, 113; complete synthesis, 186; consistency of opinions, 29; controversy with Shute Barrington, 16, 18–20; crusades, comments on, 115; defends *History of England*, 121; devotion, view of, 143; devotional life, ecumenical dimension of, 171–172; devotional life, reform of, 168–173; Dissenters, supports cooperation with, 39; doctrinal development, rejection of, 82–84; ecclesiology of, 60, 86–93, 161; education, 11, 108; emancipation, struggles for, 14, 18, 32–33; English Catholic Enlightenment, last representative of, 188; Enlightenment historical tradition, relationship to, 113;

eucharist, understanding of, 99–102; evaluated by Tierney, 117; external devotions, opposed to, 172–174, 179–180; *Faith of Catholics*, opinion of, 206n; Fletcher's spirituality, acknowledges force of, 182; Gallican tradition, relation to, 8, 33–34; historical mentality, roots of, 116; *History*, compared with Milner's, 123; *History*, contemporary evaluations of, 114; *History*, defense of, 123–124; *History*, French reactions to, 127–128; *History*, Italian reaction to, 129–132; *History*, motivation for writing, 113; history, definition of, 113 influence of Catholic tradition on his historical mentality, 115; influenced by Bollandists and Maurists, 109; influenced by Parisian school, 92; indulgences, view of, 160; interprets Church's power to absolve, 104–105; interprets Thirty-third Article, 103–104; Irish Gallicanism, relation to, 34; lives in Hornby, 11–12; *Lives of the English Saints*, attitude towards, 170–171; litanies, view of, 141, 166, 169–170; Middle Ages, attitude towards, 113; Milner, relationship to, 48–49; miracles, view of, 120, 137–138, 145; natural rights philosophy, acceptance of, 36, 48, 54; Nestorian terminology employed, 162; papal authority, attitude towards, 57, 92, 121, 132; piety of, 120; plagued by criticism, 118; prayer, definition of, 169; prayer books, view of, 142; prayers compared with Challoner's, 166; private judgment, view of, 62; Protestants, openness towards, 69–70, 119, 160, 163; purpose of his writings, 16; nationalism of his thought, 97, 174; reform party after 1829, center of, 144; reform, view of, 147–148; response to Tory polemics, 19; rule of faith, view of, 78, 80; scholasticism, rejection of, 8; sacraments, view of, 159–162; "sacrifice," definition of, 162–163; Scripture and tradition, views on, 79–80, 82, 85; Second Spring, defensive attitude towards, 164; Second Spring, evaluates course of, 135; Second Spring, views during, 154, 163, 170; social changes, response to, 155–157; spirituality, sources for, 185–186; spirituality, view of, 126, 176–180; supports elective process in the Church, 54–55; theological anthropology, his, 10; theology of, 157–164; toleration, definition of, 16, 24, 26, 39; treatment of Thomas of Canterbury, 120; vernacular liturgy, view of, 166–167; veto, his position on, 27, 32, 37, 196n; Wiseman, conflict with, 187

Litany of Loreto, 139–141, 169, 179

Liturgical reform, 5, 165–168, 220n

Lives of the English Saints, 170

Locke, John, 7, 36–38, 43, 47, 49, 57, 75, 133, 189

Mabillon, Jean, 4, 80, 109–110, 133

McDonnell, Thomas Michael, 135–136

Magalotti, Lorenzo, 3

Mahieu, L., 7

Mair, Jean, 34

Maistre, Joseph de, 132–133

Massillon, Jean Baptiste, 80

Manual of Devout Prayers and Exercises, 186

Manual of Prayers on Sundays and during Mass (J. Lingard), 165–166, 179

Manzoni, Alessandro, 147

Marca, Pierre de, 35

Martène, Jean, 109–110
Martimort, Aimé-Georges, 93
Martyn, Francis, 154
Maurists, 109
Memoirs of Gregorio Panzani (J. Berington), 53, 126
Mémorial Catholique, 127–128, 132
Metaphrastes, 110
Methodists, 62
Milner, John, 49, 57, 69, 115, 120, 122, 133–134, 138, 170, 188; accuses Cisalpines of heresy, 97; accuses Lingard of heresy, 103, 118, 170; and "Bibliomanists," 148; and denial of pope's temporal power, 35; and Douai treatise on grace, 9; and indulgences, 160; *Antiquities of the Anglo-Saxon Church,* reaction to, 48–49; appeals to Propaganda, 124; authority, view of, 48; compared with Lingard, 117; criticizes Charles Butler, 125; criticizes Lingard's *History,* 119–121; doctrinal development, idea of, 84; ecclesiology of, 202n; equates "Beringtonianism" and Jansenism, 58; inconsistency of, 56; links Cisalpines together, 125; Locke's political theory, rejection of, 36; miracles, view of, 144; opposition to accommodation, 72; papal infallibility, view of, 55; religious freedom, opposition to, 38; Scripture and tradition, understanding of, 81; Throckmorton, reaction to, 51–52; veto, initial support of, 195n; veto, rejection of, 21–22, 27; views equated with orthodoxy, 144; views of relationship between reason and faith, 61
Miracles, 120, 137–139
Mirari Vos (Gregory XVI), 133, 145
Molinism, 10

Montesquieu, 6, 113
Muratori, Ludovico Antonio, 4, 58

Napoleon, 20
Natural rights, 25, 36, 43–48, 57
Needham, Turberville, 7
New Version of the Four Gospels (J. Lingard), 149–153, 155, 157, 164
Newcastle-upon-Tyne, 41
Newman, John Henry, 102, 164, 171
Newsham, Charles, 158–159, 162
Newtonianism, 5, 7
Nice, Council of, 51
Nicolas, James, 9
Nicole, Pierre, 34, 83
Novalis, 146

Oaths (1778 and 1791), 21
O'Conor, Charles, 96, 199n
Orthodox Journal, 41, 58, 67–68, 119, 121
Osservazioni sulla storia d'Inghilterra ("Bastia"), 128
Oxford Movement, 187
Oxford theologians, 154, 160

Palmer, R. R., 184
Papal authority, 89–92, 96–97
Papenbroeck, Daniel van, 109
Paul V, 55
Peel, Robert, 133
Penswick, Thomas, 155, 165
Percy, John, 84
Perpétuité de la foy de l'eglise (Pierre Nicole), 83
Phelan, William, 9
Phillipps, Ambrose, 134
Philosophes, 127–128, 130
Pilling, William, 7
Pistoia, Synod of, 5–6, 57, 59, 160
Pitt, William, 13
Pius IV, 76
Pius V, 35, 55
Pius VI, 59

Pius VII, 68–69
Pius VIII, 131
Pithou, Pierre, 34
Plongeron, Bernard, 4, 38, 48, 60, 145
Plowden, Charles, 35, 48–49, 51, 53, 55–57, 134, 202n
Plowden, Francis, 35, 58, 72
Plowden, Robert, 73
Pluralism, 66–69, 146
Pombal, Marquis de, 4, 32
Ponsonby, George, 21, 195n
Pope, supremacy of, 45–46; temporal power of, 18, 24, 56–57
Poynter, William, 27, 29–30, 39, 69, 95–96, 103, 124, 148
"Practice of Living in Union with Jesus Christ" (J. Lingard), 176–179
Pragmatic Sanction, 90
Presbyterians, 104
Price, Edward, 135
Price, Richard, 38
Priestley, Joseph, 38, 49, 62, 80, 82
Primer; or, Office of the Blessed Virgin Marie, 186
Private judgment, 42–43, 63
Prospectus of a New Translation of the Holy Bible (A. Geddes), 148
Protestant Apology for the Roman Catholic Church (W. Talbot, "Introduction," J. Lingard), 22, 71, 82–83, 85–86, 100, 105
Pugin, Augustus Welby, 166
Pusey, Edward Bouverie, 164
Puseyites, 155, 163, 171

Quesnel, Pasquier, 58, 83
Quietist controversy, 183

Rapin, Paul, 112
Rationalism, 38, 66, 70, 97, 114, 133, 171, 183
Ratramnus of Corbie, 101, 103
Reason and faith, 42, 61–67, 98, 184

Reflections Addressed to Hawkins (J. Berington), 87, 94, 186
Reflections on the Principles and Institutions of Popery (J. Sturges), 95
Reflections on the Spirit of Religious Controversy (J. Fletcher), 37, 39
Reform Bill, 165
Religious Liberty, 28–30, 32, 41, 67, 145
Revelation, 80–81
Ribadaeira, 110
Ricci, Scipio, 5, 59
Richer, Edmond, 52, 58, 87
Ridley, Nicholas, 102, 124
Rigby, John, 96
Rigby, Thomas, 148
Robertson, William, 113
Robinson, Robert, 38
Rock, Daniel, 135
Rodríquez, Alfonso, 185
Rohrbacher, René-François, 133
Rokewode, R. Gage, 69
Rolle, Richard, 186
Roman Catholic Principles in Reference to God and Country (J. Berington), 18, 50, 125
Roman Catholic Principles in Reference to God and King (anon.), 35
Romanticism, 114, 134, 136, 144, 151, 175, 185, 187
Rule of Catholic Faith (F. Veron), 63–64, 100
Rule of Faith Truly Stated (E. Hawarden), 63

Sacraments, 158–160
Scripture, 148–154
Scripture and tradition, 77–86
Scupoli, Lorenzo, 185
Second Catholic Committee, 13
Second Catholic Relief Act, 13
Second Spring, 133, 136, 146–147, 164, 169–170, 215n

Separatists, 62
Sermons on Various Religious and Moral Subjects (J. Fletcher), 181–182
Sharratt, Michael, 7
Sharrock, William, 69
Shrewsbury, Earl of, 146
Silvertop, George, 27, 39, 41, 69, 149, 154
Smith, Sydney, 38
Smith, Thomas, 27, 29, 39, 54, 124, 165
Smollett, Tobias, 111, 119
Society for the Protection of Religious Liberty, 38
Socinianism, 42, 62
Solari, Benedetto, 5
Southey, Robert, 114–115
Southworth, Richard, 9, 118
Staffordshire clergy, 46–47
Standish, Charles, 69
Stapleton, Thomas, 76
State and Behaviour of English Catholics (J. Berington), 13, 50, 107, 122, 126
Stillingfleet, Edward, 65, 111
Stourton, Lady, 171
Strickland, Joseph, 35, 51
Sturges, John, 53
Surin, Jean Joseph, 185

Talbot, John, 122, 133
Talbot, Thomas, 45
Talbot, William, 119–120
Tamburini, Fortunato, 4
Tamburini, Pietro, 38
Tate, Robert, 139, 155, 160, 163, 165, 171, 179
Tauler, Johann, 185
Tavard, George H., 81
Taveneaux, René, 184
Teresa of Ávila, 4, 185
Tertullian, 93
Thierry, Augustine, 127
Thirty-nine Articles, 100–105

Thomas à Kempis, 181, 185
Thompson, Richard, 118, 163
Throckmorton, John, 35, 37, 51, 55, 57, 69, 107, 134
Tierney, Mark Aloysius, 117, 135, 144, 154, 163
Tillotson, John, 104
Toleration, 13, 41, 134; and John Locke, 37–38, 49; and freedom of conscience, 20; Catholics and Dissenters cooperating on, 15; compatibility with Catholic belief, 39; definition of, 33; different conceptions of, 16; Lingard argues for, 24; Lingard's definition of, 26; Protestant definition of, 24
Tractarians, 170
Transubstantiation, 99–102
Traditionalism, 133
Trent, Council of, 10, 12, 76, 82, 100, 102, 158–159
True Church of Christ (E. Hawarden), 86
Turner, Sharon, 114–115

Ultramontanism, 18, 50, 77, 84, 87, 131–132, 135, 163, 174
Unigenitus (Clement XI), 4, 9
Unitarians, 38
United States, 31–32
Ushaw College, 49, 154, 180
Ussher, James, 86
Utrecht, Church of, 52, 57, 59

Van Espen, Zeger Bernard, 31, 35, 58–59
Ventura, Giacoma, 129, 132
Vernacular liturgy, 167
Veron, Francis, 34, 63–64, 66, 77–78, 82, 84, 86, 99, 102, 160
Veto, 21–22, 26–27, 29, 37, 53, 195n
Vincent de Paul, 181
Vincent of Lérins, 84
Voltaire, 113–114, 127

Walker, John, 135, 144, 154–156, 160, 163, 167, 170, 173, 179–180
Walmesley, Charles, 45–46
Walsh, Peter, 34–35
Weedall, Henry, 137, 139
Weld, Humphrey, 69
Wheeler, James, 37, 39
White, Thomas (1593–1676), 81
White, Thomas (1764–1826), 125, 175, 221n
Wilkes, Joseph, 46–47
Wilkinson, William, 7
Wiseman, Nicholas, 133–134, 141, 146–147, 151–154, 160, 163–164, 187
Woods, John, 143

This book was composed in Janson, a type face that originated in Leipzig around 1670. It is a letter of fine ancestry that has been remodeled to suit current taste. The display type is Libra, a modern type created by S. H. DeRoos of Amsterdam. The typographic design by Howard N. King, the book was composed by the York Composition Company, and bound by The Maple Press Company, both of York, Pennsylvania. The paper is 60 lb. Glatfelter Natural B-32; the cover is Arrestox B-grade pyroxylin and with Laurel endpapers. We are indebted to The Colophon *and the late William Dwiggins for the lovely vignettes used throughout the book. This edition was first published in April, 1980.*